THE PERFECT MASTER
VOLUME 1

THE WAY OF THE

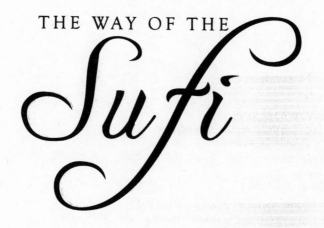
Sufi

by Osho

FULL
CIRCLE

THE WAY OF THE SUFI

© 1980, 2007 OSHO International Foundation

This New Edition, 2007
First Reprint, 2009
Second Reprint, 2010
ISBN 978-81-216-1249-4

Published by **FULL CIRCLE** *PUBLISHING*
J-40, Jorbagh Lane, New Delhi-110003
Tel: 24620063, 24621011 Fax: 24645795
E-mail: contact@fullcirclebooks.in • *website:* www.fullcirclebooks.in

For more information: www.osho.com

The material in this book is a transcript of a series of original OSHO Talks, *The Perfect Master, Volume 1,* given to a live audience. All of Osho's talks have been published in full as books, and are also available as original audio recordings. Audio recordings and the complete text archive can be found via the online OSHO Library at www.osho.com

Typesetting: SCANSET
J-40, Jorbagh Lane, New Delhi-110003

Printed at Nutech Photolithographers, New Delhi-110020

PRINTED IN INDIA
07/10/03/08/20/SCANSET/NP/NP/NP/OP250/NP250

CONTENTS

INTRODUCTION

Every few thousand years an individual appears who irrevocably changes the world around them in ways that are never immediately apparent, except to the most perceptive.

Osho is one such individual: his spoken words will resonate for centuries to come.

All those words have been recorded and transcribed into books like this one, written words that can carry a transforming message to the reader.

For Osho, all change is individual. There is no "society" to change — it can only happen to each one of us, one at a time.

So, no matter what the subject matter of the book, the thread that runs through all Osho's words is like a love song that we can suddenly, mysteriously, hear at just the right moment. And strangely, no matter what the words seem to be referring to, they are really only referring to us.

And this is no ordinary love song, more an invitation to open our hearts to hear something beyond the words, beyond the heart...a silence beyond all understanding. Where we all belong.

PREFACE

The way of the Sufi is the way of the drunkard, the dancer, who becomes almost intoxicated in his dancing, who is transported through his dance. He is inebriated; his dance is psychedelic.

It is said that Mohammed once said to Ali, "You are of me, and I am of you." When he heard this, Ali became ecstatic and involuntarily started dancing. What else can you do, when a man like Mohammed says to you, "You are of me, and I am of you"? How to receive this? Ali did well.

And remember, it is not anything that he did. It was involuntary. He started dancing; out of ecstasy the dance started flowing.

Another time, Mohammed said to Jafar, "You are like me in both looks and character." Here again, in wajd, Jafar started dancing. What else to do? When Mohammed must have looked into the eyes of Jafar, wajd, samadhi, was created, the transfer beyond the scriptures happened. How to receive this? How not to dance? It would have been impossible not to dance. Jafar danced.

It is said: "The enrapturing of the Sufi by the divine, or rather the pull of the divine, keeps the Sufi continually in spiritual, inner dance and movement...." It is not that the Sufi dances — godliness keeps dancing in him. What can he do?

Whenever a wave of such divine rapture strikes the heart of the Sufi, it creates great waves in the lake of his inner being... He is just a receptacle. To say that the Sufi is dancing is not right. The Sufi is being danced. He cannot help it, he is helpless. Something is pouring into him and it is too much; it starts overflowing in his dancing and singing.

This, in turn, causes his body to move. Upon seeing such movement non-Sufis have often supposed that the Sufi is dancing. In reality, however, it is the waves of the ocean of God that are tossing and turning the anchorless vessel that is the heart of the Sufi.

On the surface, from the outside, the Sufi seems to be dancing. But he is not dancing, because there is no dancer. It is pure dance. Existence has taken possession of him. The Sufi is drunk, intoxicated. His state is that of non-being. He is anchorless. The waves of the ocean toss and turn. First his inner being is stirred, great joy arises there; and then it starts spreading towards his body.

That's what you are doing; that's what is happening. You are participating in something immensely beautiful in Sufi dancing. Remember it: forget the dancer and be the dance.

The way of the Sufi is the way of dance, song, celebration.

Osho
The Secret

CHAPTER 1

WHEN THE DISCIPLE IS READY

A certain man decided that he would seek the Perfect Master.

He read many books, visited sage after sage, listened, discussed and practiced, but he always found himself doubting or unsure.

After twenty years he met a man whose every word and action corresponded with his idea of the totally realized man.

The traveler lost no time. "You," he said, "seem to me to be the Perfect Master. If you are, my journey is at an end."

"I am, indeed, described by that name," said the master.

"Then, I beg of you, accept me as a disciple."

"That," said the master, "I cannot do; for while you may desire the Perfect Master, he, in turn, requires only the Perfect Pupil."

The master appears only when the disciple is ready. Never otherwise. In no other way. At no other point in life's journey. The disciple has to be ready and ripe; only at that moment does the master become visible. The disciple has to earn eyes, to earn ears, to create a heart, to feel. How can the sun appear if you are blind? The sun may appear but you will go on missing it.

Unless you have eyes, there is no beauty in the world. The flowers will bloom, but not for you. And stars will fill the sky with immense beauty, but not for you. Unless you have eyes, there is no beauty in the world.

If you don't have love in the heart, you will not find the beloved. The basic requirement has to be fulfilled. Only love finds the beloved. Eyes find beauty. And the ears find music and melodies.

But there are people, and they are many — the majority consists of those — who go on searching and seeking something out there without creating a corresponding receptivity in themselves. I have come across many seekers who are searching or a master — not at all aware that the disciple is completely absent. The disciple is not there at all. How can you find a master?

The master is not just an objective phenomenon there. First he has to be something interior in you. That's what disciple hood is: a preparation, a thirst, a passionate desire, a great passion for truth. That is lacking. And then people go on searching. And if they don't find, it is not surprising. They are not going to find! They may come across many masters, but they will go on missing.

How can you see the master if you are not vulnerable to him? How can you see the master if you don't know even what it is to be a disciple? The beginning of the finding of a master starts by being a disciple. The real seeker does not worry about the master, where he is. His whole concern is how to create the disciple in himself, how to be a learner, open to reality; how to function from innocence, and how not to function from the state of knowledge.

If you function from the state of knowledge, you will find many teachers but never a master. If you already know something, and you think that you know, then you will find other knowers, claimers, who are ahead of you. You will meet only the people whom you can meet. You will meet people like you. A person who functions from the state of knowing that he has gathered will find many teachers and will learn many things — but will never find a master.

To find a master you have to be a child. To find a master you have to be utterly innocent, not knowing anything, the mind empty — full of passion for truth, but without any conclusions about it. This is the state of real learning. And then you need not even go anywhere: the master will come to you.

There are many sannyasins here who have not come to me because of their search but because I have found them. They have come because of me, not because of themselves. That is the real coming. When you come because of yourself, you don't come at all. You remain there, stubbornly, too much of you, full of you — there is no space for me to enter into you.

This is one of the basic requirements for a seeker: that he should be a learner. What I mean by "learning" is that one should always function from the state of innocence. One should not carry conclusions inside oneself — because those conclusions won't allow you to learn. If something goes against them, you are bound to reject it. And if something does not go against them, then you are not learning anything — only your old prejudice is strengthened more.

If something agrees with you, there is no learning. It has simply strengthened the old mind. And the master cannot do it — he has to destroy the old for the new to be; he has to take away all that you have been carrying all along. He has to create space in you. If you cling to conclusions, prejudices, ideas, philosophies, you will not be able to meet a master — because his whole work consists in destroying all kinds of philosophies. He is interested in the real thing. He is not interested in speculation about things.

Just the other day I was reading a statement of Burke:

"Most people will grant that potatoes are important. Discourse about potatoes, however, does not enjoy the same popularity as do potatoes. When the chips are down, talk about potatoes is just no substitute for the original thing. So it is with religion."

I like the statement. The master is interested in the real potatoes — not philosophies about the potatoes. And if you come with conclusions, you can't come. Those conclusions stand like great barriers between you and the master. One has to come open, available. One has to come not knowing. This should be obvious: if you know already, then you are not available. Your very knowledge obstructs the way.

Become a disciple. Don't be worried about the master. When you are ready, the master appears.

The master appears in strange ways sometimes, but it always happens. Whenever someone is ripe, God starts coming in many forms to him. The master is the last form of God that comes to the disciple. After the master there is formlessness. He is the last experience of form; Beyond him there is formlessness — then there is God with no form.

The master is the last who looks like you, who lives like you, whom you can touch, with whom you can have a dialogue, who speaks like you. Beyond the master is silence — utter, absolute, virgin. Beyond the master is bodilessness. The master is just exactly in between the world and God.

If you are really tired of the world and the rut and the routine of it, don't start searching for a master — rather, search how to become a disciple. Start unburdening yourself from prejudices, dogmas. Forget all that you know....

Ramana Maharishi used to say to hug disciples: If you want to be with me you will have to unlearn. If you don't unlearn, then I have nothing to give you. You are already too full.

You know the famous Zen story?

A professor of philosophy went to see a great master, and he asked about God, and he asked about karma, and he asked about the theory of reincarnation, and he asked many things...questions and questions and questions. And the master said, "You are tired, the journey has been long, and I can see you are perspiring, coming uphill on such a hot summer afternoon. It must have been tiring. You wait; there is no hurry. These questions can wait a little. Let me prepare a cup of tea for you. And who knows? — while drinking the tea you may get the answer."

Now the professor was a little puzzled and became a little suspicious whether it was right to come to this madman. "How can the questions be answered just by drinking tea?" But now there was no way of going; he had to rest a little. "And the tea is not going to hurt in any way, so why not drink it and then escape from here?"

The master brought the tea, started pouring from his kettle into the cup, and went on pouring. The cup was full, and the tea started overflowing into the saucer, and the saucer was full. Then the professor said, "Stop! What are you doing? The tea will start overflowing on the floor. Now the cup has not even space for a single drop more. Are you mad or something?"

The master had a hearty laugh, and he said, "So, you are intelligent! You can understand. If there is no space in the cup then we cannot pour any more tea into it. Is there space in your head? I would like to pour all that I am, but is there space in your head? Is it not overfull, too much stuffed?

"This is my answer," the master said. "Come again. First empty your head. Come in a state of not knowing. You are too knowledgeable. I can hear all the noise that is going on inside you. Come a little more in silence. And you have not come to learn – you have come to argue."

Knowledge always hankers to argue. It is not interested in learning. In learning it feels humiliated. That's why it becomes more and more difficult: the more grown up you are, the less is the possibility of your learning anything. Children can learn because they don't have any ego, and they learn fast, and they learn very easily. If you have to learn the same thing when you are thirty-five or forty or fifty, it is very difficult, almost impossible sometimes. What happens to your intelligence?

After fifty years of experience your intelligence should be more than it was before, but it is not. You have gathered much junk on the way. The functioning of the intellect is no longer free; it is too much burdened – and burdened with crap! And you feel humiliated in learning anything. You cannot bow down. You cannot say, "I do not know." And the disciple is no who can say, "I do not know – teach me. I am ready to learn. I have not come with any conclusions to you. I have not brought any knowledge. I come empty! Fill me!"

The real search is how to become a disciple, how to empty the cup of your being, so when you come across a being who is overflowing with God you can be filled – filled to your heart's content. But people search for a master; they don't search for disciple hood – that's where they go on missing. Then you will come across many many people, and you will always feel unsatisfied. And the reason for dissatisfaction is not outside you: it comes from your own inner mind. You have brought conclusions with you.

I was reading the other day about a very beautiful Hassid mystic, Levi-Yitzhak. He was so full of God and the song of God and the dance of God that when he worshipped or prayed he would go wild. It is said about him that he simply radiated the divine dance in its total wildness. He worshipped with such abandon that the frightened faithful instinctively moved away. If he was worshipping in the temple, people would escape to their homes, because his worship was very wild. He gesticulated, howled and danced, jumping from one corner to the other, pushing and overturning whatever was in his way. People ceased to exist for him. When he prayed, he himself ceased to exist.

Now, if you have come with some conclusions already about how a master should be, you will think his a madman. If you think a master should be just sitting like a Buddha under a Bo Tree, and this madman, turning things upside down and running all over the place, and he has scared the worshippers, they have all run out because nobody knows what he is going to do.... But this man was a perfect master.

God descends in many forms – sometimes as Buddha and sometimes as Krishna and sometimes as Mahavira and sometimes as Mohammed. And God comes always in new forms, and your conclusions are always from the old. If you are born in a Buddhist family, how can you think that this mad Hassid mystic can be a Buddha? Impossible!

If you go with a conclusion, you will be in difficulty. If – and there were many disciples of this mad Hassid – if they come across Buddha they will deny, they will not be satisfied with Buddha. They will say, "Where is his dance? Why is he not howling? Just sitting silently under the Bodhi Tree — what kind of master is he?" But we go on carrying deep-rooted prejudices in us.

And remember: those prejudices may look very rational to you. Just the other day, Adi asked a question: "Osho, now I cannot trust you any more. "What has happened to Adi? Why can't he trust me any more? A simple thing. I said that the same tree exists in Bodhgaya under which Buddha became enlightened, and the same tree still vibrates with something of the quality of the Buddha, of that beautiful morning when Buddha disappeared and God appeared in him. Now he quotes a history book and says it is written in the history books that the tree was cut and destroyed by a Hindu king, and the temple was converted into a Hindu shrine. So how can the same tree exist? If the history books are right, I am wrong. And how can Adi trust me when I go against the history books?

Don't be so short of trust, and don't be in such a hurry. If I say something, wait, search, and you will find the way. Just reading a history book and your trust is destroyed! I still say it is the same tree, and the history books are right. The shrine was converted into a Hindu shrine and the tree was destroyed...but before the tree was destroyed, Ashoka sent a part of the tree, a branch of the tree, to Ceylon to be planted there. So the tree continued in Ceylon. Then when the shrine was converted again into a Buddhist temple, a branch of the tree from Ceylon was brought back and replanted.

It is the same continuum. It is the same tree. And according to Buddha, even the same tree is never the same for two consecutive moments — it changes. It is continuously changing. Your body changes continuously. In seven years' time, your body is completely new; the old disappears and the new has taken place. Not even a single cell remains of the old. But it is a continuity: the same in the sense of the continuity. It is the same tree in the Buddhist, in the scientific sense.

But don't be in a hurry. If you lose trust so fast and so soon and so easily, it is not worth much. It is not trust really. You go on keeping your prejudices in the background, and you go on watching for when you can find something that you can mistrust. You are more interested in mistrust than in trust. You are trusting in spite of yourself. Your natural tendency is to mistrust and doubt. You will feel very good if you can doubt. If you cannot find anything to doubt, you may start feeling suffocated — because with the doubt your ego is back on the throne. With trust, the ego has to commit suicide.

This is a beautiful parable, and Sufis are past masters in parables. Sufis know how to say in parables things which cannot be said. They have created the best parables in the world. Go slowly into this parable. It is small but of immense significance.

A parable is a way of saying things in an indirect way. Truth cannot be asserted directly. That is too violent, too aggressive, too male. Truth can only be said in a very indirect way. It can be hinted at, indicated. You cannot be convinced of the truth: you can only be persuaded.

And the master is one who is not going to convince you of the truth but who is going to seduce you into truth. Parables are very seductive. Even those who were not searching for any truth may be suddenly struck by a parable: something may become suddenly available to them.

And people like stories. And the stories have a tendency to hang around your consciousness. It is difficult to forget them; it is very easy to remember them. They have a way of reaching to the deepest core of your being. Hence, Sufis have been using parables. It is a totally different world from Zen, Tao, Yoga, Tantra.

I welcome you into the world of Sufis today.... It is more artistic, more poetic, more aesthetic, and its ways are very subtle.

A certain man decided that he would seek the Perfect Master.

Now, to decide is wrong, because the decision will come out of your past experiences. One cannot decide to seek a perfect master. One can only become available in a passive way. Seeking, decision, are active ways. One has to be more feminine; one should not be in such a hurry. One should be more watchful, more alert about what one is trying to do.

Have you known any master before? Have you any experience of a master? Whatsoever you have heard is borrowed. You are not certain, you cannot be certain of its truth. How are you going to decide? And how will you seek a master? What will be the criterion of judgment? How will you weigh that this is really the perfect master? Are you capable of weighing, judging a perfect master? Then you are higher, you are already higher than the perfect master. You are sitting in the seat of a judge. You are not a humble, passive disciple. And the master happens only in your passivity, in your humbleness, in your simplicity.

A certain man decided that he would seek the Perfect Master.

And why the perfect master? The ego always seeks perfection. If you are after money, the ego wants you to be the richest man in the world, the most perfect man in the world. If you are after morality, you want to become the most perfect saint. The ego has a very deep desire to be perfect. All egoists are perfectionists, and all perfectionists are neurotic. The idea of perfection drives people mad.

A humble person know imperfections, and a humble person accepts his imperfections. And a humble person does not ask for the impossible. It is the ego that always asks for the impossible and fails. And feels frustrated, betrayed, cheated. But again it starts asking the same thing.

Why do you need a perfect master? You have taken one thing for granted: that you are such a great man that less than that will not be worth your while, will not be satisfying; less than that will be below you. You are such a perfect man, you need a perfect master. Ordinary masters won't do — something extraordinary it has to be. You can only be interested in the extraordinary.

And the paradox is that the extraordinary exists in a very ordinary way. The extraordinary never exists as the extraordinary, because all those pretensions of being extraordinary are foolish and stupid.

A real man, an authentic man, has no idea of being superior in any way to anybody else. He lives in a world where comparison does not exist. Now, the very idea of seeking a perfect master is based in comparison.

A certain man decided that he would seek the Perfect Master.

He read many books...

But how can you find a master by reading many books? You will become more and more stuffed with knowledge, and that will be the barrier. But that's what happens. Somebody starts thinking of God, or truth, or beauty – he starts reading books. He thinks that is a way to find it.

I am reminded of a great Indian poet, Rabindranath Tagore. He was continuously thinking about beauty, what it is. A poet, naturally, is interested in beauty. His mind was meditating on what beauty is. One full-moon night, he was in his boat and the night was just majestic: the full moon in the sky and the silence of the river and the forest around. And he was alone in the boat. Just once in a while a bird might call – that was all – and then the silence would become deeper than before.

But Tagore was pondering over the question: What is beauty? And he was looking into an ancient scripture. He had only a small candle burning in the cabin. Tired, in the middle of the night, frustrated, because even in that old scripture he could not find something real about beauty, just words and words and words...he blew the candle out and he could not believe his eyes.

Suddenly, as he blew the candle out, from the windows, from the door, the moonlight immediately came in. He was transplanted into another world! He rushed out. He looked at the moon, at the silence of the night, and the moon reflected in the river, and the whole river silvery, and the deep dense forest on the bank...and this was beauty!

But he had been looking into the book – and beauty was waiting for him, just waiting by the door. But that small yellow candle-light was preventing the splendor of the night. And he had become so much engaged and occupied with the thoughts of the scripture that he had forgotten completely that this was a full moon night.

He threw the scripture into the river, and that was the last day he ever thought about beauty. He said: Thinking won't help. Beauty is there — we have to be available to it. He said: We have to blow out the candle, the small candle of the ego, then God comes in, in many ways, and the beauty penetrates you.

But that's what happens. If you start thinking of finding a perfect master, you will go into books to know who is a perfect master. Now, books will confuse you, because every book will tell a different story. If you read a Jain book, it simply describes Mahavira, and says these are the characteristics of a perfect master. They are not! They are the characteristics of a particular perfect master, Mahavira. If you read a Buddhist book, they also describe the characteristics of a perfect master — they are not either, but only those of one manifestation of the perfect master, Buddha. And so on and so forth.

And once you get caught into some conclusions from the books, you start searching, but your search is doomed to fail from the very beginning. You already have an a priori prejudice. Now you are looking for Buddha and Buddha is never repeated. Now you are looking for Zarathustra and Zarathustra is only once and never again. Now you are looking for Lao Tzu, and Lao Tzu never comes again. Once is all. Nothing is ever repeated. God's creativity is infinite. He is not repetitive.

And if you read a Buddhist, a Confucian, a Taoist, then you will be more confused — because they describe different things. And you may be a very clever person, an intelligent person, intellectual, and you may join all those characteristics together. Now you will never find the perfect master. Now you have an idea which is absolutely absurd. It is like taking one part from the bullock cart, taking another part from a Rolls Royce, and putting them together — and parts from cycles and parts from engines.... You will have something strange and it won't work. Even a bullock cart is better than that, howsoever slow, but you can go along, you can reach somewhere, you can use it. This will be utterly useless, this monster that you have created. And that's what happens.

People who read many scriptures and many books, they slowly

slowly create an idea of who the perfect master is. And this idea is just a combination of many characteristics taken, collected, from different sources. It is not possible. Such a man has never existed, and such a man is never going to exist. Now you are searching for a mirage — you will never find it. And you may come across many masters! But because of your idea you will go on rejecting them, because something or other will be lacking in him. It is because of your idea that you are missing, not that masters are not there — they are always.

The world is full of masters always, and God is not a miser, remember. Jews say that there are only thirty-six masters in the world at a time — just thirty-six? Is God such a miser? And why thirty-six? But still Jews are generous if you think of other religions. Joins say that there are only twenty-four perfect masters in the whole of creation, from the beginning to the end. One creation, from the beginning to the end, that means millions and millions of ages...only twenty-four? So for millions of years there is not a single master available.

Hindus are even a little more miserly: they say only ten. Christians even more: they say God has only one son, Jesus Christ. Only Jesus Christ is the perfect master, nobody else. Then how can you find a perfect master?

I say to you: God is generous. There is no limitation, there is no fixed number. Masters go on happening. Just people are blind, people are deaf. This hurts! To know that you are blind and deaf, this hurts. That's why these theories have appeal. Twenty four only, ten only, one only: that is a great consolation to you, remember. That means if you have not found the perfect master, what can you do? It is not your responsibility. Only once in a while the perfect master happens, and this time he is not here. It is not your fault that you have not found him. If anybody is at fault it is God, not you. You are relieved.

I say to you: perfect masters are always available — just as roses are always available and lotuses are always available. And the sun rises every morning, and there are millions of stars always available. You just have to open your eyes, you have not to be blind.

But our situation is really in bad shape. I was reading a story — this is the story of you:

A woman had just had a child but had not yet seen it. She asked the doctor that it be brought to her, but he did not comply:

"I am afraid it would not be a good idea for you to see him right now."

But as she insisted passionately, he began to justify his refusal:

"You see, Madam, through a most unfortunate accident of fate, your child was born abnormally, and I feel it would be good for you to recover fully from the delivery before seeing your child."

"Tell me doctor!! I must know what has happened!!! I must see my child."

The doctor, wishing to spare her the sight of her child, ventured to explain to her the nature of the deformity: "I will be blunt, Madam. Your child has no legs!"

She gasped, but recovering from the blow, she composed herself and asked to see the child.

"Madam, wishing to spare you the naked truth, I have omitted to tell you the whole situation...your child has neither legs nor arms."

"Doctor," she cried, "bring me my child. He will have my legs and my arms. I must see him."

"I see," he replied, "I must be even more cruel – your child has no torso either."

"No legs! No arms! No torso!!" ,she sobbed. "Bring him to me. He needs me all the more."

The doctor finally conceded and brought her the baby. She started as she saw it. Wrapped in a towel was a foot long ear.

She took the ear and rocked it comfortingly: "It will be all right, dear, we will make it somehow...."

The doctor interrupted her: "Madam, you are wasting your breath. The child is deaf."

That's the situation man is in. You are blind, you are deaf, you have no heart...but to see it hurts. It is painful to realize it, to recognize it. So we go on finding explanations to avoid the truth about ourselves.

The disciple is not ready — that's why he cannot see the master. But he goes on saying there is no master.

I was a student in a university, and it was Buddha's enlightenment day — it was celebrated in the university. And the vice chancellor said, with great passion and with great emotion, "If I had been in Buddha's time, I would have renounced the world, sat at his feet, followed him like a shadow."

And I knew the man! I could not conceive of him ever following a Buddha. I had to stand up. And I said, "You please take your words back, because I know you perfectly well: you are the last man who would have followed Buddha. And do you think Buddhas are not available now? Did you ever go to Ramana Maharishi?"

He had to say, "No."

I said, "But he was alive. Just a few years ago he was alive. He was your contemporary."

This incident happened somewhere near 1955, and Ramana died in '51, just four years before. And the vice chancellor was an old man of seventy. I said, "He was your contemporary. Arunachal is not very far away. In Buddha's time it may have taken you years to journey to Buddha — it was only one hour's flight. Did you go there? Have you been to J. Krishnamurti ever? He is still alive. And you are talking with such emotion and passion. Whom are you trying to be fool?"

But he was a good man. He understood the point. Tears cam to his eyes; he took his words back. Later on he called me and he said, "Listen, if you have to say something to me you can come in private."

"Why private? You made the statement in public: I had to refute it in public. And never make such a statement again, because I will still be here for two, three years. Think it over. You were in Buddha's time too," I told him.

He was startled. He said, "How do you know?"

I said, "I know! You just look into my eyes: you were in Buddha's time too, but you never went. And now you are talking with such emotion. You are deceiving others, but that is not the big thing: you are deceiving yourself."

People go on thinking that masters used to happen only in the past, now they don't happen, now they are no more there. And the same was the case in Buddha's time. There are stories: people would come and ask Buddha, "Are you the perfect master?" There were people who would go to Jesus and would ask, "Are you the Messiah we were waiting for?"

The Messiah is there standing in front of their eyes, in front of them, and they are asking, "Are you the Messiah?" If he says no, they will be happy. If he says yes, they will be offended.

Jesus said yes, that's why they were offended. "So this pretender thinks he is the Messiah? This son of a carpenter, Joseph? And we know him from his childhood. He has been playing in the streets of the town, and now suddenly he has become the Messiah?"

They have always been asking. In Buddha's time they were saying, "In the past there used to be perfect masters, in the days of the Upanishads, in the days of the Vedas, there used to be perfect masters. But now, in these ugly days, they have all disappeared."

And they go on saying the same thing now! And they will go on saying the same thing forever. They really don't want to see.

A certain man decided that he would seek the Perfect Master.

He read many books, visited sage after sage, listened, discussed, practiced, but he always found himself doubting or unsure.

You can read, you can argue, you can become very logical about it, but nothing is going to help, the doubt will persist – unless you experience. Only experience kills doubt. But how to experience a master? You have to be a disciple first; you have to fulfill that requirement. And what is the requirement of a disciple? Prayerfulness is the requirement of disciplehood. Capacity to wait. Capacity to be empty. Capacity to surrender. Capacity to be available. That's what prayer is! And if you know how to pray, you will know all that is needed to know. Not only will you come across a perfect master – you are going to come across God himself.

Meditate over these words of Rainer Maria Rilke:

"Pray: to whom? I cannot tell you. Prayer is a radiation of our beings suddenly set afire; it is an infinite and purposeless direction, a brutal accompaniment of our hopes, which travel the universe without reaching any destination. Oh, but I knew this morning how far I am from those greedy ones who, before praying, ask whether God exists. If he no longer or does not yet exist, what difference does it make? My prayer, that will bring him into being, for it is entirely a creative thing as it lifts towards the heavens. And if the God that it projects out of itself does not persist at all, so much the better: we will do it over and it will be less shabby in eternity."

Prayer creates God. Prayer creates the perfect master. Prayer is creative. Prayer reveals — it is revelatory. It prepares you for the revelation.

One should not go in search of a master: one should learn how to pray...and the master comes. And the master comes of his own accord. Or he calls you forth wherever you are, but then the journey is totally different — when you are called forth. The quality is different, the intensity is different. You don't feel you are going: you feel you are being called. You know that there is no possibility to resist it. It is irresistible. You are pulled as if a great magnet is pulling you. You are helpless, but you are thrilled because you have been chosen. You come dancing. You are fortunate you have been chosen.

Just prepare wherever you are. Don't ask: If there is no perfect master, what is the point of preparing for disciplehood? Don't be worried. The masters always exist. That is the meaning of these beautiful words of Rilke:

"Prayer is a radiation of our beings suddenly set afire; it is an infinite and purposeless direction..."

In the beginning you don't know where your prayer is going; it cannot have any address, it cannot have any direction.

How can you pray to God? You don't know God — that's why you are praying. You would like to know what God is, but you don't know. That's why you are pouring your heart out. It is waiting for the unknown to take possession of you. This is faith, this is trust.

The skeptical mind wants first to be certain whether there is a God: "Then I will pray." Rilke is right:

"Oh, but I knew this morning how far I am from those greedy ones who, before praying, ask whether God exists."

"We will pray only if God exists" — then you will never pray, because you will never know without praying that God exists. You have made an impossible condition for praying. It is not to be fulfilled. You have to pray. Don't ask the question whether God exists or not. God is irrelevant at this point. At this point, make prayer possible.

Prayer is a song of the heart addressed to the unknown. Maybe he is, maybe he is not, but that is not the point. One is joyous in pouring one's heart out. It is a joy unto itself. Whether God exists or not is secondary. Prayer is primary. And when prayer is primary, it reveals God, it opens your eyes. It creates God. Suddenly the world becomes afire when you are afire. When your heart is aflame, suddenly you see the whole world aflame with the divine, with the unknown, with the mysterious.

"If he no longer or does not yet exist, what difference does it make?"

This is beautiful. This is how a really religious person thinks.

"My prayer, that will bring him into being..."

Prayer will become the womb. I will give birth to God through my prayer. This is the Sufi approach. Rilke is almost reflecting the very heart of Sufism. But this is how lovers have always felt, and the poets and the mystics.

"If he no longer or does not yet exist, what difference does it make? My prayer, that will bring him into being, for it is entirely a creative thing as it lifts towards the heavens. And if the God that it projects out of itself does not persist at all, so much the better: we will do it over and it will be less shabby in eternity."

We will go on doing it, we will go on creating God. In fact, it is not creation: it is revelation. But for the person who prays, and for whom God is revealed for the first time, it looks like creation — as if the prayer has created it. It reveals. It takes a thick layer of darkness from your eyes. Your heart starts pulsating as it should. You fall in rhythm with the whole. Suddenly God is there.

But before God appears, appears the master. The master is a link between you and the God. First the prayer reveals the master. That is one step, and half the journey. And the second step and the journey is complete.

Prayer is naive: it is waiting for someone who never comes...asking for something or someone who is not there, not at least now.

"If there be a God who loves man, let him speak. Now."

This is what the poet Seneca says in his tragedy *Thyestes*. The prayerful heart is saying, "I am speaking to you, I am provoking you — are you there? Just give me a little hint, a small word, a gesture, and that will do. Are you there?" And a thousand and one times you shout to the skies and there is no response. Your prayer disappears into nothingness. But even though the prayer disappears into nothingness, and there is no response from the other side, from the other shore, still the prayer goes on changing you.

The effects are very visible. It may not change the reality outside you, but it goes on changing you. You become softer and softer, more feminine and more feminine, and one day when you have really melted, when you are no more hard and solid, when you are a flow, the response comes — and not from the other shore but from the innermost core of your being. Really, that is the other shore.

But before that happens, you will come to the link between this shore and the other, between this and that — that link is the master. And in fact to ask for a perfect master is foolish, because to be a master is to be perfect; it is a repetition of words. There are not such categories: imperfect masters and perfect masters. A master is perfect! If he does not look perfect to you, then you have a certain idea of perfection that he is not fulfilling. He never fulfills anybody's idea. He lives his own life, but he lives in perfection.

Remember, when I use the word "perfection" I always use it in the sense of completion. I never use it in the sense you use it. This is a constant problem. When I say "perfection," you start thinking that "He will be like this, he will be like that...that he will never be angry." But there have been masters who have been angry, and when they are angry they are perfectly angry.

Even Ramana Maharishi, such a silent sage, used to become angry sometimes. And then he was really angry. He was anger, pure anger. One day it happened: a scholar came and started asking stupid questions. Ramana listened. His questions were very long and he quoted scriptures to support his question. And Ramana said again and again, "You please meditate. The only thing for you to do is to ask the question: Who am I? No other question is relevant."

But the man wouldn't listen, and he went on and on and on. Suddenly, the disciples could not believe it, Ramana took his staff, rushed after the man and the man became so afraid that he escaped outside the room, and Ramana followed him to the very boundary of the ashram. And then he came back laughing. The disciples could not believe it, and they said, "But you, and angry?"

And he said, "Look at the perfection of it."

If you have the idea that a master is never angry, should not be angry, then there will be difficulties. If you have the idea that a master should not look worried, you will have difficulties. Krishnamurti sometimes looks very worried. He has no worry of his own, but he becomes worried about you. He goes on saying one thing and people don't understand, and they go on persisting in their ignorance and he becomes very angry, almost on the verge of beating himself.

One man came to me and he said, "I used to think that Krishnamurti must be like a Buddha, but today I saw him in his discourse — he became so angry. And for no reason at all!"

I said, "You just tell me the whole story."

He said, "He was talking about the fact that no method is needed, no meditation is needed. You have to drop all methods, all meditations, all paths. And then an old woman, a very old woman stood up and asked, 'How to do it?' And he became very angry."

I said. "I know that old woman, because she comes to me too.

And I can understand; I feel all sympathy with Krishnamurti. And that woman has been listening to Krishnamurti for almost fifty years. She is one of the constant audience, and she is always sitting in that corner, for fifty years. Whenever Krishnamurti comes to Bombay, she is there. Krishnamurti must be getting tired of her also. And she always asks the "how?" And he is telling continuously that there is no "how" — a method means how. When we say that there is no method, we are saying there is no how. Either be enlightened right now, or remain unenlightened — that is your decision — but there is no how. Decide to be or not to be, but don't ask how. There is no how! Either open your eyes and see, otherwise keep your eyes closed and dream, but don't ask how.

And for fifty years he has been saying the same thing, and the woman persists. And she always stands and asks, "How? How to do it?" It is natural. He is not really angry in the sense you become angry: it is his response, it is his compassion really. It has a different quality. He is compassionate! He loves! He wants to help! But when he sees you go on and on in the same rut, to shake you up he becomes absolute anger.

"The idea of perfection in your mind is that he should be like this, he should be like that, he should be like.... He is not like ;anybody else. He is just like himself. Only one thing is true, that he is always total. Whatsoever he is doing he is total in it. He is never partial, never fragmentary. If he is angry, then he is totally angry. If he is loving, he is totally loving. That totality is the only quality. That's what I mean by 'perfection'."

All masters are perfect, so there is no question of searching for a perfect master. Become more and more of a disciple. That is where you have to start the journey.

He read many books, visited sage after sage, listened, discussed and practiced, but he always found himself doubting or unsure.

After twenty years he met a man whose every word and action corresponded with his idea of the totally realized man.

Now he was carrying a certain idea for twenty years. He was looking for a carbon copy. He had already decided what a perfect master is; now all that was needed was somebody to fit with his idea. And remember, it is his idea that somebody else has to fit. This is ego, pure ego. This is not humbleness. This is not the way of a disciple. This is not the way of a humble man. This is not the way of a real seeker.

He is functioning through a conclusion. He has already decided that his conclusion is right. How can your conclusions be right? If your conclusions are right, you yourself are a perfect master and there is no need for any master.

After twenty years he met a man whose every word and action corresponded with his idea of the totally realized man.

Must have been a coincidence.

The traveler lost no time. "You," he said, "seem to me to be the Perfect Master. If you are, my journey is at an end."

But see, still the "if" persists. Because he has a certain conclusion already arrived at in his ignorance, how can he trust it? If he cannot find somebody to correspond with his idea, he is not a master. If he finds somebody who corresponds, just by coincidence, now the great doubt arises: maybe his idea is right, maybe his idea is wrong. Hence the "if." So he says:

"You seem to me to be the Perfect Master. If you are, my journey is at an end."
"I am, indeed, described by that name," said the master.

Because for a master all these are just names. Call him a Buddha, call him an enlightened person, a Christ, a Messiah, a perfect master — these are just names. They don't describe his reality. These are just labels. Maybe people need them, but the master does not need them. He has come home, where all words have become meaningless. He has come to that silence where words don't exist, to that wordless silence.

So the master says:

"I am, indeed, described by that name."

He does not say "I am" or "I am not." He simply says, "Yes, people describe me by that name."

"Then, I beg of you, accept me as a disciple."

But this man has not prepared himself as a disciple at all. And now suddenly he wants to be accepted.

"That," said the master, "I cannot do; for while you may desire the Perfect Master, he, in turn, requires only the Perfect Pupil."

Twenty years' search wasted. Twenty years' search gone down the drain. And the master is right. He says, "What do you think? If you want a perfect master, then the perfect master wants a perfect disciple. Go, become perfect! Go, become a disciple first!"

People think disciplehood is nothing to be attained. It needs great discipline to become a disciple. Both words, "discipline" and "disciple", mean the same. The original root means the capacity to learn. This man is incapable of learning. Twenty years he has been moving with his set conclusions. He has not learnt a thing. In twenty years he has come across many sages, but he has valued his own ideas more than those sages. He has not looked at the reality of those beings that he has come across. He has remained tethered to his ego.

And now he says, "Because you correspond to my ideas, I think you are the perfect master. Not that you are the perfect master, but only because you correspond to my ideas." Now, who are you? And how can your ideas decide? How can they be decisive? From where have you gathered? From books? From discussions? From arguments? They are all borrowed. And in your ignorance you have gathered all kinds of nonsense.

In fact, when you read a book, you don't understand what is written there — you understand only that which your ignorance can understand. How can you understand the Koran? To understand the Koran you will need the heart of a Mohammed. How can you understand the Gita? To understand the Gita you will need Krishna-consciousness.

Listen to a few stories:

"Mummy," said little Jimmy, "I want to live with Carol next door."

"But you're both only six years old," smiled his mother. "Where will you live?"

"In her bedroom."

"What will you live off? You don't have any money — and what will you do if babies come along?"

"Well," said Jimmy seriously, "we've been all right so far...and if she lays any eggs then I'll tread on them!"

The man in ignorance is almost like a child, like this child, Jimmy. What ideas can you have of perfection? Of a master? Of God? Your ideas will be childish. And you will go on understanding that which you can understand. And words are always vague. They don't really carry meaning. The meaning has to be projected by you into the words. The word is just empty. You have to fill it with your meaning.

Two hippies are slipping and sliding through the Louisiana marshlands. As one hippie stepped up onto dry land, the other hippie said, "Hey man, an alligator just bit off my leg."

"Which one?" , the first hippie said.

"I don't know, man. I can't tell one alligator from another."

Words don't have meaning. It depends on you what meaning you are going to give to them.

A doctor was called to see a lady who led a very gay life. When asked to explain how she felt she remarked, "I haven't slept much lately. Last night we dined at the Carlton after the theatre and then had drinks. I really feel that my stomach is out of order."

"I'm quite sure of it," he said. "You'll have to diet."

"Oh, doctor, how lovely!", she said. "What color?"

Or:

An Irishman visiting America remarked about the strange American customs. "You take a glass of ginger ale," he said, "and add whiskey to make it strong and then water to make it weak; lemon to make it sour and sugar to make it sweet. You raise the glass and say, 'Here's to you,' and then you drink it down yourself!"

When you see something, you read something, you give meaning to it. It is always your meaning. It can't be otherwise. So you can go on reading as many books as possible and you will gather much rubbish — but the meaning will be yours. You can quote the Bible, but you will simply be quoting yourself.

And that has happened down the ages. When one scripture is translated into another language, much changes in it. It has happened to the Bible, because Jesus spoke in Aramaic, then it was translated into Hebrew, then into Greek, then from Greek into English. It has been translated so many times that its original fragrance is completely lost. It is no more the same. It can't be. So many interpreters, so many translators, stand in between. They have given their own meaning to it.

In John 8: 24 we read: "Except ye believe that I am he, ye shall die in your sins..." But here the word "he" is not found in the original manuscript at all. The early translators were puzzled by the absence of an object, and thus they simply assumed that a word was missing. They changed the statement: "Except ye believe that 'I am'" — this is the original statement — "Except ye believe that I am." They had to change it; it looked incomplete: "Who are you, just saying 'I am'? It looks incomplete." So they made it read: "Except ye believe that I am he — I am God."

Thus the beauty and the immense significance of the original was lost. It is still that way in the Bible: "I am he." Jesus is simply saying: "I am!" That I amness is the very quality of existence. He is not saying "I am God" — because if you say "I am God," you have already accepted the duality of "I" and "God" Then the "am" is only a bridge between the duality.

When Jesus says "I am" he is simply saying that you can call it God or you can call it 1. It is the same thing — two ways of expressing the same thing.

This is far better, far superior to the Upanishadic statement that says: "Thou art that." It has accepted the duality. To deny, it has accepted. It denies; it says "Thou art that," but the duality is accepted. Jesus is far superior in his statement when he says "I am".

Moses asked God when he met him on the mountaintop, "People will ask me about you. How am I to say anything about you?"

And he said, "Just go and tell them that God says: I am that I am".

Strange words, but of great significance.

When Jesus speaks, he speaks from his consciousness; he pours his consciousness into it. But when it reaches you, only the empty word roaches. His spirit is lost on the way. Then you fill that empty word with your own spirit, and you say that you have read it in the Bible or you have read it in the Koran or in the Veda, but you are reading only yourself.

All scriptures function as mirrors — you see only your face. And remember: if a monkey looks into a mirror, he is not going to find an angel there.

This man read, listened, discussed, practiced, but the doubt remained. Twenty years searching, he came across many sages but could not feel contented with any. He would not have felt contented

even if God had been encountered! And maybe, who knows, he may
have encountered God too – because God comes in so many sizes
and shapes....

There is a story about a great mystic:

The mystic was Mohammedan and he lived in a mosque, but he
had a Hindu follower. The Hindu was a Brahmin and the Hindu
would cook food for him and would bring it to the mosque, and
he used to live five miles away from the mosque. And unless the
master ate, he would sit there and wait – and the master was a crazy
man. Sometimes he would eat in the morning, sometimes in the
afternoon, sometimes in the evening, sometimes in the night, and
the disciple would wait and he would not eat till the master had
eaten. So sometimes he had to remain hungry the whole day. And
by the time he reached home he was so tired that he would think,
"Tomorrow, now who wants to prepare food again?" He would fall
asleep hungry.

One day the master said, "Listen, you need not come so far. I
can come there myself, so tomorrow you prepare the food and I will
come. It is too hot to come, and then sometimes you have to wait
the whole day – change it now. You are ready: I will come."

The next day he prepared delicious food for the master, because
he was to come for the first time. He was thrilled. This was grace:
his master is coming to his home! He decorated the house, he threw
flowers on the path...but nobody turned up, only a dog. He chased
the dog out because the dog wanted to eat, and he chased and the
dog would come back and would try to snatch food. He had seen
many dogs, but this dog was strange. He beat the dog but he still
came. He really gave him a good beating, then he saw tears coming
out of the dog's eyes. And then he disappeared.

Till evening he waited, and then he thought, "This man is crazy
– he may have forgotten." So he took the food, went to the mosque
– and he saw tears in the eyes of the master. The same kind of tears!
He was puzzled and he said, "Why are you crying?"

And he said, "Why shouldn't I? You have beaten me so
much!"

And the disciple said, "What are you talking about? I, and I can beat you? And you never came and you had promised!"

And the master said, "I came – and not only once. At least twelve times!"

Then the disciple remembered the dog – exactly twelve times the dog had tried to enter.

And the master said, "You have to be capable of seeing the formless now. Don't be too much attached to the form. Why should I be thought of only in this form, in this body? Why can't you find me in other forms?"

So I say maybe this great seeker had come across God...in fact how can you avoid God? Whomsoever you come across, you always come across God. But he had great ideas, and even God could not fulfill those ideas. He remained empty, doubtful, untrusting, and the search continued.

And one day when he comes to a man who fulfills his ideas, he creates another problem. Then the master says:

"That I cannot do" – *I cannot accept you as a disciple –*

"For while you may desire the Perfect Master, he, in turn, requires only the Perfect Pupil."

The master is saying, "Had you prepared yourself these twenty years to be a disciple, you would have found me much earlier. You cam across me many times, but you missed. And this time also you have to miss."

This is the Sufi approach for having contact and communion with a master: Become a disciple. Don't search for the master: search for disciplehood. And let me repeat: the master appears when the disciple is ready.

Enough for today.

CHAPTER 2

THERE IS COMMUNION

The first question:

Osho,
Yesterday you mentioned that to be a disciple one needs to be in
prayer – but what exactly is prayer?

Prayer is an experience of resurrection, A rebirth, the birth of a
new vision, a new dimension, a new way of looking at things,
and a new way of being. Prayer is not something that you do: prayer
is something that you become. It is a state of being. It has nothing to
do with the words that you utter in the temples, mosques, churches.
It is a silent dialogue with existence. It is to be in tune with the total,
with the whole. To fall in harmony with the whole is prayer.

The experience is so enormous that it is impossible to be exact
about it. It is indefinable. All definitions fall short. Each definition
says something about it, but only something. Much remains
unsaid.

And prayer is such a vast experience that it contains contradictions.
So one can say: Prayer is silence – and he is right, absolutely right.

And another can say: Prayer is a dialogue — and he is right too, because prayer is a dialogue in silence. Now, dialogue and silence seem to be contradictory. In dialogue you speak, in silence you hear. In dialogue you communicate, in silence you are simply there — there is nothing to say.

What can be said to God? He knows all that you can say in the first place. You can bow down. You can celebrate. But still your bowing down, your celebration, your festivity, your thankfulness, your gratitude, they are still ways of speaking. You are trying to say something without words, because words are very small and the heart really wants to say something.

So it is a dialogue, although silent. It is a communication in a sense, because you are there and the whole existence becomes your beloved, the whole existence becomes a "thou." And yet there is no "I" and there is no "thou" — both disappear. Both meet and merge into one unity, one organic whole. Just as the dewdrop disappears in the ocean, you disappear. There is no separation between you and existence, so how can there be a dialogue?

Both the definitions are true. Those who say prayer is a dialogue — Christians say that, Jews say that, Hindus say that — they are right. But they are talking only about one fragment of the enormous experience called prayer. Buddhists say: There is no dialogue. Jainism says: There is no dialogue — because there is no "I" and no "thou." There is absolute silence. They are also right, but then it is very difficult to be exact about prayer.

It has to remain vague. It has to remain incomprehensible. You can have only glimpses of it, fleeting glimpses, but you cannot have the whole of prayer in your hands. It can't be reduced to a simple definition.

Just as science gives definitions, religion cannot give them. You ask science: science is exact. You ask "What is water?" and it says "H_2O." So simple! Nothing is left behind H_2O — all is said, because water is an object. It can be analyzed.

Prayer is subjectivity. It is not an object that can be analyzed. In fact, you cannot show your prayer to anybody. And if somebody insists that "I don't see any prayer in you," you cannot prove it either. It is like love — less like water, more like love. That's why Jesus says: God is love. Love is also indefinable.

Always remember one thing: there are things below you and there are things above you. Things that are below you, you can be exact about them. Things that are above you, you cannot be exact about them. They are bigger than you. When prayer exists, it is not that prayer exists in you — on the contrary, you exist in prayer. Prayer is higher than you. You just vibrate in that enormous dimension, that plenitude.

But we have been taught, particularly in this century, to be exact about everything. That has destroyed many beautiful values in life, that constant desire to be exact. And if you cannot be exact about something, then the mind tries to deny it.

You cannot be exact about God, so the mind says, "Then God cannot be." You cannot be exact about love; then the mind says, "Love is just dreaming and nothing else." You cannot be exact about beauty; then the mind says, "Beauty is just fantasy. It is not a truth." But then what is left? Then the world is no more beautiful, no more loving, no more good — because there is no more God. Then the world is empty of meaning. Not that the world is empty of meaning, but your mad desire to be exact about everything has made it empty of meaning.

Meaning is a delicate phenomenon. It is like the fragrance of a flower. You cannot catch hold of it in your hands — but it is there, still it is there, whether you can catch hold of it or not, whether you can keep it in a safe deposit or not. It is still there!

How can you define music? If you go to define it, you will destroy it. Then it is just an arrangement of sounds, nothing more. It is noise arranged in such a way that it no more looks noisy. Just a soothing kind of noise. Is that all that there is to music? Music is more than the notes, more than the sum total of notes.

If you go on asking this question again and again...then what is poetry? Just a certain arrangement of words? It is not. It is something that happens in a certain arrangement of words, but it is more than the certain arrangement of words itself. It is not grammar, it is not language – it is something transcendental. It is provoked by the words. The words are used as an occasion for the poetry to happen.

And exactly that is what music is. The instruments are used, notes are used, sounds are used, for that silence that is music to happen. Between two sounds is music, and between two words is poetry, and between two lines is all that is significant. It is never in the lines but always between the lines. And one has to learn to read the intervals, the gaps.

Still, a few things can be said about prayer – but they will not be exact, so I cannot fulfill your desire. The very nature of prayer prohibits it. And to try to do something against its nature is sacrilege.

So the first thing that I can say about prayer is: a feeling of immense gratitude, a thankfulness. You are here, in this beautiful world, with these trees and rivers, mountains and stars. In this tremendous beauty you are pulsating, you are alive. This opportunity you have not earned. It is a gift. Prayer is a thankfulness for this gift of life. Just to breathe is such a joy, just to open your eyes and see the greenery. Just to listen to the chirping of the birds, or the sound of running water, or the silence of the night and the velvety darkness. Or the dawn and the sun rising...we have not earned it! It has been given to us, and we have not even thanked.

Whether there is a God or not is irrelevant – thankfulness is a must. People think that "If there is a God, then we will thank him." I tell you just the opposite: "If you start thanking, you will find him." There is no other way. If you start feeling grateful, you will find him because he happens only in that dimension of gratitude.

Just as you cannot see from the ears and you cannot hear from the eyes – eyes can only see, ears can only hear – exactly like that, only gratitude can find God, can feel God. Gratitude is your sensitivity for God. Prayer is that sensitivity.

Second thing: prayer is a way of living. It is not just something that you do early in the morning like a ritual. If it is a ritual, it is meaningless. If it is a ritual, it will not make you religious – it will make you a Hindu, it will make you a Mohammedan, but not religious. Prayer has to be something absolutely informal, of the heart, not a ritual. Not something that you finish somehow in the morning because you have to do it and you have been taught to do it — it has become a duty. If you don't do it, you feel a little guilty; otherwise, doing it, you don't feel any joy out of it. When you don't do it, only guilt arises. To avoid that guilt, you go on doing it. This is not prayer.

Prayer is a way of living. What do I mean? A man of prayer remains in prayer twenty-four hours a day. He sleeps in prayer; his sleep is a kind of prayer. He relaxes into sleep as if he is relaxing into the lap of God. When he is going to sleep, he sleeps in God. When he wakes up, he wakes up in God. He opens his eyes and the first thing that comes to his heart and to his being is gratefulness, utter gratefulness. He eats God, he drinks God. He walks in God. He breathes in God, he breathes God. His twenty-four hours are a continuum of prayer. It goes on running like background music. Whatsoever he is doing, that does not make any difference — the prayer continues.

And I am not saying that you should start repeating "Rama, Rama, Rama," or "Allah, Allah, Allah." It is not a question of repetition. If you start repeating, "Ram and Ram and Ram," then it will be an interference in your life. Then you will not be able to drive rightly on the road, because your mind will be divided. Then you will not be able to do any work totally.

So I am not saying to repeat anything. It is not a question of verbal repetition. It is just a feeling, presence. Just as the mother sleeps in the night and her child is there by the side of her...and it may be the rainy season, with clouds and thunder in the sky, but she will not be awakened by the clouds and the thunder. But if the child just becomes a little uneasy, starts crying, she will be awakened immediately. Thunder was not enough to wake her, but her child.... Even in her sleep a part of her being remembers the child. That's how prayer is.

You live in the marketplace, you work, but deep down at the very core of your being, you go on bowing to God — prayer continues, gratitude continues. Sometimes it surfaces when you have a silent moment; otherwise, it continues underground.

Prayer is a way of living, not having, but a way of asking. It is not compelling, not wanting to live from power and possession, but imploring to be allowed to be. Asking is the opposite of demanding. Asking is risky. It is entrusting yourself to the silence and the uncertainty of existence.

Prayer never demands. There is no possibility of any demanding in prayer, because we cannot claim anything. But we can ask, just like a small child asks his mother. There is no demand in him; he is helpless, he is dependent. He simply asks. When he is hungry, he cries — that's what prayer is. It is childlike helplessness.

We are so small and existence is so infinite...we are only for a few moments here, and existence has been always here and will be always here. We are just small waves in this infinite ocean. We can ask, but we cannot demand. We can ask because we are not strangers to existence, we are not outsiders. We belong to it. We are part of it. Existence has peopled us. It is existence's desire that we are. We can ask. But in asking, there is no demanding. If it is fulfilled we are thankful. If it is not fulfilled, we are thankful. Remember that. That is the beauty of prayer.

If it is fulfilled, we are thankful, obviously. If it is not fulfilled, still we are thankful. Why are we thankful even when it is not fulfilled? Because then the man who knows what prayer is, who lives prayer, also knows that sometimes we ask for a thing which is not good for us. Existence knows better. If it is needed it will be fulfilled. If it is not needed it will not be fulfilled.

I have heard:

A young child's doll was broken. As she cried over the tiny pieces, she said to her brother, "I'm going to pray to God to put the pieces together."

"Do you expect God to answer your prayer?" he asked.

"You will see that God will answer," she predicted.

Two hours later when the brother returned he demanded of the little girl. "Well, has God answered?"

"Yes," she replies, pointing to the pieces. "He said, 'No.'"

This is prayer. You can ask, but you cannot demand. If he says no, then it is perfectly okay. Finally, the decision is with him. Demanding means the decision has already been taken. Demanding means you want God to follow your will. Asking simply means, "I am putting my desire before you, but follow your will — thy will be done, thy kingdom come." These last words of Jesus on the ass — this is prayer!

A great poet, Huub Oosterhuis, says:

No one can pray without words, because no one exists outside language and everything is a dialogue.

Now, you see? Buddha says: Prayer is silence. And both are right. Oosterhuis is also right. From a certain standpoint it is true: no one can pray without words — because no one exists outside language. Language is for us almost like the ocean is for the fish. Language is our ocean.

So Oosterhuis is right. And because he is a poet, he understands the significance of language. Only a poet understands the significance of language — not a linguist, not a grammarian. The grammarian knows only the body of the language, the poet knows its heart, its soul, its spirit, its invisible dimension.

He is right: no one exists outside language and everything is a dialogue.

Yes, prayer is a dialogue. The part is talking to the whole. The part is addressing the whole. And you will have to learn this dialogue. Has not the desire sometimes arisen in you to talk to the trees? knowing perfectly well that they will not answer. Have you not sometimes said hello to a rose flower on the bush? You may not have said it because it looks so absurd, but has not the desire arisen in you? Have you not sometimes felt to talk to the stars? If you have not felt, then you have lost the capacity to feel. Have you not sometimes touched a rock with great love and passion? the texture of it! Have you not felt sometimes to say something to all the invisible that surrounds you? That is prayer, that is dialogue.

And one has to gather courage. Yes, one has to be so courageous — only then can prayer happen. It is very easy to go into a church and pray, because people accept that. Nobody will call you mad. In fact, people will think you are greatly religious, a good man, a good Christian, Catholic or Hindu. People will respect you for it. But if you start talking to a tree.... Just see: you can talk to a cross in the church, which is dead wood — you cannot talk to a tree which is alive. And if you cannot talk to a tree, how can you talk to the cross?

Start talking with existence, with nature. Be a little mad. Sometimes get out of your prison of so-called sanity. It is driving you insane, this so-called sanity. Thousands of people go insane every day. Thousands of people commit suicide around the earth every day. And millions go on living a dull and drab life, for no other reason — just for one single reason: they have not prayed. They have not been able to talk to existence. They have not been able to pour their hearts out. Do you know why psychoanalysis has become so important in the modern world? Because people have forgotten how to pray.

The priest is being replaced by the psychoanalyst for one single reason: because people used to pour their hearts into nature; now they don't find any way to pour their hearts out. They go to the psychoanalyst, they pay for it. The psychoanalyst listens — they pour their hearts out. This is absolutely meaningless. You can do the same sitting in your garden. And the trees are better psychoanalysts because they listen so attentively, so intensely. Talk to the rocks! and you can say anything and they will not be offended. You can pour your heart out and your burdens will disappear and your tensions will disappear.

In the past man always lived such an unburdened, tensionless life. The only reason was: everybody was capable of going into prayer. It was natural. People would go and talk to the mountains or to the rivers or to the sun or to the moon...these are all faces of God! manifestations of him. Alive, throbbing, pulsating, right now.

And when I say start talking with nature, I am giving you the first lesson of prayer. Churches are man-made. And whatsoever is man-made, avoid it — because the man-made thing carries all kinds of neuroses that man has in him. Why not go to something that is God-made? If you want to feel God, go to something that is made by him, where you can find his signature.

Churches are man-made, so are temples, so are gurudwaras. There you will find only man and his politics. There you will find man and all his stupidities. Trees are less stupid, stars are not stupid. You go to them, you open your heart – start a dialogue with nature. And the miracle happens one day, when suddenly you see that the tree has responded – then you will know what prayer is, then you will understand Oosterhuis who says prayer is a dialogue. Yes, the tree answers one day, you just have to wait long enough. You Just have to convince the tree that you are really talking to her, that's all. It takes a little time.

And man has been so destructive to the trees that they have become closed. Let the tree feel that you are not a madman, that you are not violent, aggressive, that you have come with love, great love, that you want to feel God. And the creator can be felt only in his creation – that is the beginning of the journey.

So prayer first has to be a dialogue – a dialogue with whom? I say a dialogue with nature. So even an atheist can go into it. I don't bring God in yet. First move into dialogue with nature – that is the ABC of prayer. And then, slowly slowly, start moving into silence with nature. Sit by the side of a rosebush and move into tremendous silence, no words between you and the rosebush, just silence pulsating...waves of silence.

Through dialogue you will know God as he is manifest in nature, and through silence you will know God as he is unmanifest. Through dialogue you will know God as creation, and through silence you will know God as creator.

So Buddha is also right; he is talking about the ultimate in prayer. But the ultimate is possible only if you do the immediate. The ultimate is only through the immediate.

The ancient Jews had a word; that word is *maranatha* – it means "Come, Lord, come!" That is prayer. "I am ready. My heart is open for you! I am waiting. Come, Lord, come!"

A great awaiting, with all the doors open and all the windows open, for his breeze to blow through you. And his sun to come to your deepest core and fill you with light: "Come, Lord, come!"

Jews had another word; that is Hosanna — that means "Come and deliver us! Come and deliver us from our ignorance! Come and deliver us from our finitude. Come and deliver us from our limitations, from this imprisonment that we have created around ourselves. Come, and give us freedom! Come and deliver — come and liberate us!"

And the name of Christ, Jesus, means one who liberates. The original is "Jehoshuah" or Jesus. It means one who has come to liberate "Hosanna" and "Jehoshuah" — two words from the same Hebrew root, related to each other like question and answer, hope and fulfillment, prayer and the answer to the prayer.

If you really go into intense passion with God, it is answered. Jesus is an answer to many people's prayers. Buddha is an answer to many people's prayers, so is Mahavira, so is Mohammed, so is Nanak. These are the answers! Think of them as the answers to people who had prayed.

Just the other day I told you: When the disciple is ready, the master appears — and in no other way. When the disciple has really prepared his heart, has opened himself up, is vulnerable, has dropped his armour, the master immediately appears. The disciple is the question: the master is the answer.

Prayer is the bridge between the question and the answer between the disciple and the master, between the seeker and the sought, between the immediate and the ultimate, between the desire and the fulfillment.

Prayer is born out of our experience of love, the way we address each other. Have you not felt sometimes the difference? We use the same words, but the quality changes. When you say "you" to somebody to whom you are indifferent, the word is the same, but there is no prayer in it. And when you say "you" to the woman you love or the man you love, the word is the same but the quality is different. When you say "you" to a woman you love, there is prayer, there is love. The word is pulsating, alive, streaming. When you say "you" to somebody in the marketplace, the word is dead.

Prayer has arisen, slowly slowly, out of the experience of love.

When a person falls in love with one person, such great joy arises that, slowly slowly, it became apparent to people who were intelligent enough, aware enough, that "If so much joy comes by falling in love with one person, how much joy will come if I fall in love with the whole!" Love paved the way to prayer.

People pray to each other when they are in love. See the eyes of lovers when they look at each other. That look is sacred. It may be momentary, it may be lost, but for a moment the flame is there. For a moment, the guest has arrived from the beyond. People pray to each other when they are in love. The way one man says "you" to another, respectfully, intimately, desperately. The way someone says "you" to you — hopefully, expectantly, intensely, his voice seeking or caressing.

It may be that prayer to God grew out of this way that people have of speaking with each other when they are in love. Yes, that's how it has slowly slowly dawned into the consciousness of man — that if we can say "thou" to existence with great love, expectant, desperate, seeking, imploring, asking, with tears in the eyes, with hope, with helplessness; if we can say "thou" to existence, that is prayer, the beginning of prayer. A point comes when "I" and "thou" also disappear — that is the end of prayer, the crescendo.

In the old days prayer was so much a matter of fact that not in a single scripture has the question been raised: What is prayer? The Vedas don't ask the question: What is prayer? The Koran does not ask the question: What is prayer? Prayer was taken so much as a matter of fact, it was so obvious to the people...when a thing is obvious, nobody asks a question. Now people are asking: What is prayer? What is love? These things have disappeared from life; they have become questions.

If you go far back into the beginnings of human consciousness, nobody asks: What is God? Who is God? Does God exist or not? It was almost as if God was walking with people on the earth, he was living with people on the earth. He was so visible, nobody asked the question. Just think — has anybody asked the question: What is the sun? What is light? Nobody has asked.

But if one day suddenly the whole of humanity goes blind, and once in a while a man with eyes arrives, then people will ask him: What is sun? What is light? The question simply shows into what impoverishment we have fallen.

In the Bible, there is no word for prayer. It was such a diffused experience that even a word was not needed for it — so much so that in the Hebrew language it is difficult to translate the word "pray", "prayer". Praying was calling, rejoicing, laughing, crying, reviling, imploring, according to how one felt. But there was no single word for it.

Man has lost many capacities, and one of the most important has been the capacity to pray — because it is only through prayer that we make a bridge between our tiny self and the infinite and the absolute.

You say: *"What exactly is prayer?"*

I cannot define it exactly — I can only indicate. I can hint. A few directions I can give to you. You will have to know it by your own experience.

They say that man can be divided into three groups: those who make things happen, those who watch things happen, and those who wonder what happened. Please be of the first category. Move into prayer — that is the only way to know what it is. Love if you want to know what love is; have a taste of it. How can you explain to somebody who has never tasted wine what it is and what happens through it? He has never been drunk. There is no way to explain. All that you can do is to invite him, let him drink. Let him feel lost. Let him forget the world. Let him disappear in the world of intoxication...and he will know. That is the only way to know.

Prayer is an intoxication. Prayer makes one drunk with God. But only drunkards know it, what exactly it is. And even those who know it cannot put it into words. Let it become an experience Let us not only discuss it — let us go into it. This very moment! If you feel grateful, a great silence will surround you, a great benediction will start surrounding you. This very moment! right now! you can be thankful for all that the whole has done for you.

If you are a religious person, you can think of the whole in terms of God; if you are not, there is no need to use the word "God". Forget all about it. Words don't matter. Call it "the whole" Just feel what it has done to you, how much it has given to you and how much it goes on pouring into you. And you have never thanked it; you are so ungrateful. And still it goes on pouring! Its sharing, its giving, is unconditional.

And the moment thankfulness arises in you — this can arise this very moment — there is prayer. Nothing stirs in you, all is still. But suddenly one feels like bowing down to some unknown force, to some mysterious force. That bowing down is prayer.

The second question:

Osho,
Every time I sit down to write you a question, the answer always comes before I am finished writing. Yet this desire to write to you and be answered remains. What is this desire?
P.S. I know the answer.

Anahata, no answer is going to help — that's why the desire remains. A question arises, and if you silently wait it is bound to happen that the answer will arise. In fact, the answer is there, that's why the question has arisen. The answer is there before the question has arisen in you.

The answer is hiding in the question itself. If you go deeply into the question you will find the answer. The question is nothing but a hard shell around the answer. You will always find the answer if you wait long enough. And if you wait silently. But still, no answer is going to help — that's why the desire to ask remains.

One has to go beyond questions And beyond answers — because

each answer will create new questions in its own turn. So if one question is answered, the answer will create ten questions in its turn...and so on and so forth. And you can go on and on. And you can go on chasing and chasing, and you will never arrive.

When all questions disappear — and not only questions but all answers too — then the desire to ask will disappear. Never before it.

I am reminded by your postscript of a very famous Sufi story:

A Sufi mystic was going to Mecca on Haj — for his pilgrimage. He came into a town, a small town, and even before he reached the town the message had reached that a great mystic was coming into the town, so the whole town gathered. The mystic was a very silent one, and the townspeople asked him, implored him to deliver a discourse to them. "We have been waiting for months, and now that you have come we can't let you go unless we have heard something from you."

The master was reluctant. He said, "But I have nothing to say." But they wouldn't listen. They persisted. The master said, "And that which I know cannot be said!" But they wouldn't listen. The more reluctant the master was, the more interested they became, naturally.

And they said, "We will sit here, we will fast and we will not eat till you give us a message — because rarely has such an enlightened person passed through this village. We cannot allow you to go."

So the master agreed. They went to the mosque. The whole town gathered, with great expectation about what the master was going to say. And they knew it perfectly well, that never before had he spoken in any other village. He had been traveling, coming from a thousand miles, and everybody had been asking him, but he kept silent. They were very happy — it was a privilege! that the master had agreed to speak to them.

The master came. He faced the audience and asked one question: "Do you know what I am going to say to you?"

They all said, "Of course, how can we know? We don't know." They all said, "We don't know what you are going to say."

The master said, "Then I cannot speak to such ignorant people who don't even know what I am going to speak about!"

The people were very much puzzled and the master went away. Their desire became more aflame. They thought their answer was not right. "Yes, the master is right: how can he speak to such ignorant people?" They rushed, brought the master back and they said, "You ask again. Our answer was wrong, but you come — give us one more chance."

The master came and he said, "Do you know what I am going to speak about?"

They said, "Yes! We all know what you are going to speak about."

And the master said, "Then finished! If you already know, then what is the need for me to tell you? Such an enlightened town!"

Now the people were even more puzzled. And the master left them again. They talked around amongst themselves; the whole town was agog with only one thing: "What to do? And tomorrow morning he is going to leave! Some way has to be found."

They talked and they discussed and they found a way and they went in the middle of the night and they woke up the master and they said, "We have come — our answer was wrong, we are sorry. You ask again!"

The master went back to the mosque and again he asked, "Do you know what I am going to say to you?" And half of the people said, "Yes," and half of the people said, "No." That was the only way. Now how can he escape?

And the master said, "Ha, ha, ha! So those who know should tell those who don't know. How am I needed? Just tell the people, talk between yourselves. I am absolutely unnecessary."

In fact, if you go deep into your own questions you need not ask anybody. All asking is unnecessary, because whatsoever answer I give to you is really there inside you. I only make it apparent. I help it to surface in you. I have no ready-made answer for you. I have no catechism. It is not that my answer is fixed forever.

You ask the question. I look into your question.

I try to do what you should have done yourself, and then find the answer there, and I make it clear to you. The work of a master is to make your own answers clear to you. He brings clarity, he does not give you any answers. A master is not a scholar, he is not a professor. He does not give you answers. He simply brings clarity, vision, capacity to see.

So if you are here...as Anahata is here, and he has been listening to me, and the clarity is growing, and the transparency is growing. So whenever a question arises in him, suddenly the answer is there. This is beautiful. This is how it should be — to everybody. Then I will be spared the trouble.

But remember: it is not a question of questions being answered. Something more is needed. Only that "something more" will be the manna that will satisfy you, fulfill you, quench your thirst. That transmission — that transmission of energy from a master to the disciple, like the flame jumping from the lit candle to the unlit candle. It is not a question of answer or question. It is not verbal, it is not intellectual. It is existential.

It is needed that a flame jumps from me to you, so you also become aflame, afire, so that your inner being is no more in darkness. In darkness all kinds of questions arise. If you become a little more intelligent, clear, alert, aware, you will find the answers.

But each answer will bring many more questions. It is an infinite process, ad nausea. You can go on and on.... That is not going to transform you. That's why, Anahata, the desire to ask still remains.

The third question:

Osho,

My becoming a sannyasin has created a great stir in my community. They think that I have gone crazy, although I have never been so happy and blissful as I am now. Osho, would you say something about it?

They are right! You have gone crazy. They have a certain idea of what sanity is. Because of that idea, they cannot say that you are sane. If you are sane, then they are insane. That idea can allow sanity to only one: either to them or to you. And who is willing to lose his own sanity?

They said the same thing to Jesus, "You are mad." They said the same thing to Socrates, "You are mad." They say the same thing to me, that I am mad. They will say the same thing to you, that you are mad. They are not really saying anything about you; they are simply saying that your presence creates a disturbance in them. Your very presence makes them suspicious of their sanity.

And, naturally, the suspicion becomes very strong because you are joyful and you are happy and you are celebrating and they are miserable. Sanity should give people joy. It has not given them joy. They become suspicious, doubtful. Whenever they come across a person who is really joyous, they become suspicious of their whole life-style: "Is there something wrong in it?" And, naturally, to defend their life-style they have to say to you that you are wrong. That is their defense measure. Don't be angry at them, just understand their problem.

Their problem is that their whole way of life is at stake because of your presence. They will call you mad. And if it becomes too difficult for them to tolerate your presence, they will murder you. They did that to Jesus. They have been doing that to thousands of mystics down the ages. And I am trying my best to transform you into a mystic.

This sannyas is no ordinary phenomenon. It is a quantum leap into the mysteries of life. And, of course, I am giving you a totally different vision. They are bound to react. And they will be hard with you.

I remember an old story of a college professor named A^2:

A^2 lived in Flat Land. Everything in Flat Land had just two dimensions, height and breadth. Nothing had depth. If a friend turned sideways, you couldn't see him. People lived in flat houses, ate flat meals, drank flat cokes, thought flat thoughts, and lived flat lives.

A^2 taught higher mathematics at the university. One night, he threw a party for some of his friends. Upstairs his precocious little son, Pentagon, tried to sleep. As he tossed on his bed, he began to dream. He dreamt a dream no one had dreamt before. Suddenly, Pentagon dreamt that everything had not only height and breadth, but depth! Houses and trees and especially girls looked so different. He felt different. Life took on a whole new scope. This new dimension affected the way people thought and acted. Then, as unexpectedly as it had started, the dream ended.

Pentagon couldn't keep a dream like that locked up inside himself. His bare feet hit the floor and carried him downstairs right into the middle of his father's party. There he stood in his rumpled pyjamas pouring out a dream of an unheard-of dimension of life. Pentagon tried to explain what depth looked like and felt like. People didn't have to go on living flat little lives and thinking flat little thoughts. They could sink their roots down into a whole new dimension of depth.

A^2 couldn't hide his embarrassment. Nor could he shut Pentagon up. The party ended in a shambles. Far into the night A^2 tried to reason with his son, but Pentagon stamped his foot and kept saying that another dimension of life existed.

The next morning, Pentagon talked to anybody who would listen. People thought the poor boy had lost touch with reality. So for the sake of his sanity and theirs, they locked him up.

People are living in a flat land. They have lost the dimension of depth. And that dimension is God! I am teaching you depth here. And once you start living in depth, you will be constantly in trouble — trouble from the people. You will be utterly happy inside yourself, immensely happy, as you have never been before. Your life will become richer and richer every moment. You will know things as you have never known them. The whole existence will turn psychedelic. Trees will be greener and roses will be rosier, and for the first time you will sing the songs of the birds. And for the first time you will see in what a wonderland you have always been living with closed eyes. Your life will become a dance, a song will explode in your being.

But from the outside, from the herd, from the crowd, there will be shouts. They will say that you have gone mad, that you are crazy. This is not the way to be! To dance, to sing, with such abandon? To love, to live, with such abandon? This is not allowed. This is against the rules of the game. One has to be serious and sad, and one has to be a long face. At least saints are not expected to dance, or sing, or be joyous, Saints have to be dead men.

By becoming a sannyasin you have entered into a new vision. That vision will be constantly in a world which is not supporting it, which cannot support it. You will not be supported by the people. You will be colliding with them. So you have to learn one thing: when you are with people, don't be too joyous. Keep it in. And don't try to talk about the dimension of depth — unless somebody is willing to hear it. Act as if you are sad. Act as if you are a long face. Act that you are a dead saint. Avoid people. When you want to dance, dance alone.

And this is not a new teaching I am giving to you. Sufis have always said it, that when you pray, pray when you are alone. Nobody should hear it, nobody should know about it. Not even your wife! In the middle of the night, wake up and bow down in immense joy, delight. Don't let the woman know, because she will talk to the neighbors tomorrow and the thing will go around, exaggerated in many ways. And you will be in trouble.

These people are living a very sad life, neurotic, not healthy at all, pathological. So when somebody turns to being healthy, he has to be very alert.

One of my friends became mad once. He was caught by the police — the story is old, before India was divided — and he was kept in a prison in Lahore. He was imprisoned there for nine months. After six months, just an accident...but he became sane. He was mad and he found a tin of phenyl, so he drank it. The tin must have come for the bathrooms. He found it in the bathroom and he was mad so he drank it.

It gave him great nausea, naturally. For fifteen days he had diarrhoea, vomiting, but that diarrhoea and vomiting cured him of his madness. Maybe it was a good catharsis; all the poisons in the body were thrown out. And after fifteen days, when he became healthy again and the nausea disappeared and the diarrhoea disappeared, he was perfectly sane. Then the trouble started.

For six months he had lived amongst twelve hundred mad people, and there was no problem because he was also mad. Now he was sane, and twelve hundred mad people...think of him! Somebody is pulling his leg, somebody is trying to sit on his head — and he is sane! They were doing this for six months, but then he was insane himself, so there was no problem in it. It was accepted. It was exactly as things should be.

He went to the superintendent and he said, "Now it is difficult — I am sane now." But the superintendent wouldn't listen because he said, "They all say that they are sane — all mad people say that they are being tortured unnecessarily. They are sane?!" Each mad person thinks that he is the sanest person in the world. In fact, psychologists say: The day an insane person thinks he is insane, he is already sane — because insane people never think that they are insane. So nobody would listen to him.

Those three months, he was telling me, were such a hell that he started praying to God "Make me mad again!"

To live with these mad people, even for three months, one needs to be mad.

You are living with a certain kind of world, a flat world, joyless, depthless, superficial. People's lives are just trivial. They live for money or for power, prestige — which are all meaningless. In the ultimate reckoning they carry no weight. Death comes and all money and all power and all prestige disappear — and you are thrown to the dustbin. Nobody ever remembers you again. You may have been a prime minister or a president of a country — nobody cares a bit. You may have been the richest man in the world, but death is very communistic. Whether you are a beggar or a rich man, death treats everyone equally. It comes and destroys all, without any exception.

People are living in a flat world. So when you start moving into the dimension of depth, you have to be a little alert — otherwise you will be in trouble from the outside. The inner joy will grow, and as it grows, the outer conflict will grow proportionately. So unless you enjoy that conflict, act as if nothing has happened to you. Only share your joy with those who understand.

That's why satsang is immensely valuable. You can share your joy with other orange people. They will understand. They will be happy. They will be joyous through your joy. They will see what has happened to you. But don't go on sharing it with those who don't understand — unless you enjoy it. If you enjoy it, then it is perfectly okay.

A saint once heard about the evil city of Sodom. Being a saint, he went to the city with love and concern for its people. When he saw wickedness all about him, he began to preach and plead and protest daily.

After many years of this, a friend asked, "Why all the bother? You have not changed them a bit!"

The saint replied, "In this city of madness and sin, I must go out to shout, to preach and plead and protest — not that they should become like me, but that I should not become like them."

All that you can do, and all that is needed is: don't become like them. Do everything, take every precaution. If you feel a very strong desire to share with people who don't understand, then move into that knowing perfectly well that they will treat you the same as they have always treated others. Go knowingly into it; then if they start throwing stones at you, don't complain. This is your choice. If they crucify you, don't complain. This is what you have chosen of your own accord.

A farmer was driving his wagon past an insane asylum. One inmate cried out to him, "What have you got there in the wagon?"

"A load of horse manure," was the farmer's reply.

"What do you do with the horse manure?" asked the inmate. "Spread it on strawberries," answered the farmer.

"That's really wild," the inmate called out. "You should be in here. We put sugar and cream on ours."

Always remember with whom you are talking...otherwise you will create trouble for yourself.

The last question:

Osho,

My wife is very much against reason. She calls all reasoning "rationalization." What is reasoning? And what is rationalization?

I can understand your trouble. Reason is male, emotion is female – hence the difficulty of communication between a man and a woman, between husband and wife. They are always shouting at coach other, but the message never reaches to the other – because their way of understanding things are totally different.

In fact, because the ways are different, that's why they are interested in each other, they are attracted to each other. They are polar opposites like positive and negative in electricity. They are pulled together. But because they are opposite, communication is very difficult, almost impossible.

The man always talks from the head, and the woman always talks from the heart. Now these are two different languages: as if you talk Chinese and I talk German. And there is no communication. You can ask Hari Das: Hari Das talks German and Geeta, his girlfriend, talks Japanese. But this is so with everybody! With all Hari Dasas and all Geetas. Languages are different.

They were having a quarrel and the husband said, "Let's not quarrel, my dear, let's discuss the thing sensibly."

"No," said the angry wife, "Every time we discuss something sensibly, I lose!"

If the woman is ready to lose, only then can she talk rationally, sensibly. And every woman knows that, that is not the way to win. She will be defeated! because the male mind is an expert in reasoning. So rather than being logical, she starts crying — now you are defeated. You love the woman and she is crying. Now what is the point of arguing with her? You say, "Okay, you are right." And she has learnt the way, that tears work far better. So it is not a question of what is right: it is a question of who wins.

If you really want to communicate with your woman or a woman wants to communicate with her man, the only way is that both should disappear from reason and emotion, both should become more meditative. Meditation is neither reason nor emotion — it is going beyond, it is going beyond the polarity. It is transcendental. Meditation takes you beyond reasoning and beyond emotions; it is neither of the head nor of the heart. And the only possibility of any communion, of any communication, between man and woman is meditation. Otherwise, there is no possibility.

The woman will call your reason rationalization. And what do you call it when your woman starts being emotional? You call it sentimentality. These are condemnatory words. Rationalization is a condemnatory word. When you call the woman's emotion "sentimentality," that is a condemnatory word. And you feel right in yourself, and the woman feels right in herself. Different ways of thinking. No one is right and no one is wrong — because all ways of thinking are wrong. A state of no thought is right. A state of no emotion is right.

So when you love a woman and the woman loves you deeply, there is communion, because in that love there is meditation.

But that love comes and goes. You are not yet capable enough of containing it forever, so the honeymoon disappears soon. When you fall in love with a woman, everything goes well. You both agree with each other. Never is there any argument. So understanding of each other, so compassionate towards each other, so sympathetic. But after the honeymoon is over, then small things...so small that when you want to talk about them you feel embarrassed. It happens every day to me:

A couple comes. They have been fighting, on the verge of separation. And I ask, "What is the matter?" And the man says to the woman, "You say it," and she says, "You say it." The fact is that both are embarrassed because the matter is nothing, trivial. Just a small thing. Maybe the quarrel has started...the woman wanted to wear one sari and the man didn't like the color, and he said, "I am not going with you to the party in this sari!"

How stupid — stupid of both, but it can lead to, it can trigger, a great argument. And then they start bringing great things into it, and all their differences immediately surface. They are at daggers drawn. They have made a mountain out of a molehill. And they go on condemning each other: "You are wrong — all your reasoning is just a rationalization." And I am not saying that all your reasoning is reasoning — ninety-nine percent it is rationalization. And I am not saying that all the emotions of the women are emotions — ninety-nine percent they are sentimentalities.

Mind is very tricky — both, male or female. Mind is very cunning.

A man of fifty married a woman of thirty. The marriage caused quite a bit of talk in their circles. Once, when someone asked the newly married man about the great difference in age, he replied, "It's not bad at all. When she looks at me she feels ten years older and when I look at her I feel ten years younger. So what's wrong? We're both forty!"

This is a rationalization. A rationalization is a way of hiding things. It is a clever way, very clever. You can rationalize about everything possible, and you can pretend that it is reasoning. It is not. Reasoning has to be objective, without any prejudice on your part.

Once a man came to me. He has written many books, and he is the head of a department in a university for paranormal or parapsychological research work. He came to me and he said, "I am trying to prove that reincarnation is a scientific truth."

I asked him, "Unless you have proved it, don't say it – because that shows a prejudice. You have already accepted the idea that it is a scientific truth, now all that is needed is to prove it. This is not being objective or scientific. This is not being rational. Deep down you are a Hindu and you accept the theory. If you were a Mohammedan, you would be trying to prove that 'There is no reincarnation and I am going to prove it scientifically.'"

Neither is a scientist. The Mohammedan does not believe, so he tries to prove his belief with the help of science. You are trying to prove your belief with the help of science. This is rationalization.

A man of pure reason has no belief, no prejudice, no a priori idea. He simply goes into inquiry with no judgment, no conclusion. The inquiry will decide what the conclusion is. It will be decided by the inquiry itself. If you have even a lurking desire to prove something, you will prove it, but you have destroyed its scientificness. It is no longer reason. It is rational.

And so is emotion. Emotion is a purity; sentimentality is a trick. You have learnt a trick. The woman knows that if she cries, she is the winner. Now, sometimes the crying is not coming at all, because crying is not so easily manipulated. But she tries to bring it, she acts, she pretends. Those tears are false. Even if they are flowing through the eyes, they are false – because they are not coming, they are being brought.

Sentimentality is emotion created, manipulated, cunningly. Rationality is one thing; rationalization is a manipulation of reason just as sentimentality is a manipulation of emotion. If you are rational, really rational, you will become a scientist. If you are really emotional, you will become a poet. These are beautiful things. But still, dialogue will not be possible – it will be easier. With rationalization and sentimentality it is very difficult, but with reason and emotion it is not so difficult — still there will be difficulties, but there will be compassion, an effort to understand each other. The rational man will try to understand the woman's viewpoint rationally; and the woman will try to understand the man's viewpoint — emotionally, of course, but compassion will be there.

First step is: drop all rationalizations and all sentimentalities. And the second step is: drop reason and emotion too. And then in that state of ecstasy, of meditation, there is communion. And that communion is prayer. In that communion when you say "thou," there is no woman, there is God; there is no man, there is God.

Enough for today.

CHAPTER 3

A ROLLING STONE

A wandering seeker saw a dervish in a rest-house and said to him, "I have been in a hundred climes and have heard the teachings of a multitude of mentors. I have learnt how to decide when a teacher is not a spiritual man. I cannot tell a genuine Guide, or how to find one, but half the work completed is better than nothing."

The dervish rent his garments and said, "Miserable man! Becoming an expert on the useless is like being able to detect rotten apples without learning the characteristics of the sound ones.

"But there is a still worse possibility before you. Beware that you do not become like the doctor in the story.

"In order to test a physician's knowledge, a certain king sent several healthy people to be examined by him. To each the doctor gave medicine. When the king summoned him and charged him with this deceit, the leech answered, 'Great king! I had for so long seen nobody but the ailing that I had begun to imagine that everyone was ill and mistook the bright eyes of good health for the signs of fever!'"

Existence is a dialectics. It depends on polar opposites: man/woman, yin/yang, life/death, day/night. But the basic polarity in all the polarities is that of positive and negative. Only positive cannot exist, neither can the negative exist alone. They depend on each other. They are opposites and yet not opposites.

If you understand this, you have a great key in your hands: they are opposites and yet complementaries, because they cannot exist without the other. The other feeds them — negates them and feeds them. And the whole existence progresses, moves, flows, because of these two polar banks. No river can flow without these two banks.

Everything is divided into these polar opposites. They attract each other, they repel each other. Just like man and woman: they are attracted to each other and they are repelled by each other; they want to come close and they resist; they love and they hate — and it is all together. You cannot separate them. You cannot separate love and hate because you cannot separate the positive and the negative. At the most, you can emphasize one more than the other — that's all.

Just the other day, Yoga Chinmaya has asked a question: "Why does man have two eyes, two ears, two lungs, two kidneys, two hands, two feet — why two?" Because of the polarity. Your one kidney is male, your other kidney is female. Your one hemisphere of the mind is male, your other hemisphere is female. You cannot exist without this polarity. Your body will disappear. There is a constant opposition between the poles, and attraction.

One of the greatest discoveries of modern psychology is that no man is just man alone, and no woman is woman alone either. Every man has a woman within him, and every woman has a man within her.

This polarity is a must.

The mind is also divided in two parts: the left hemisphere of the mind is male, the right hemisphere of the mind is female. I am saying this so that I can explain to you why there is such a phenomenon as Zen-and-Sufism — they are polar opposites. Zen is the path of via negativa; it is basically male-oriented. It is the path of intelligence, meditation, awareness. Sufism is the path of via positiva; it is feminine. It is the path of love, affirmation.

The Buddhist moves by negating: This is not the truth, that is not the truth — neti, neti — neither this nor that, says Sosan. Go on negating, eliminating. When you have eliminated all, that which remains and cannot be eliminated any more is the truth.

Sufism is based on positivity: Don't negate, don't use no, say yes. And don't search in a negative way; move in an absolutely positive way. Don't think of the wrong, think of the right. Don't think of illness, think of health. Don't think of thorns, think of flowers. Don't think of ugliness, misery, think of beauty and joy.

Both are there. And you cannot use both together — you will go mad if you use both together. That's really what happens when a man goes mad. He starts using both his polarities and both those polarities go on negating each other. That's why he becomes paralyzed in his intelligence. One has to use one; the other will be there but as a shadow, just complementary to it.

In Zen you use no, and, slowly slowly, all that is meaningless is cut from the very roots. But the meaning remains, because meaning cannot be cut. The significance remains; that is impossible to destroy, it is indestructible. So there is no problem! People who follow Zen reach. They reach to health by eliminating diseases. That is their way.

The Sufi way is just the opposite: it moves through the positive, through health, through yes-saying. And, slowly slowly, it arrives at the same goal. And, in a way, the path of the Sufi is more full of joy, more full of songs, because it flows through the valleys and mountains of love.

Zen flows through a desert land. The desert also has its own beauty — the silence of it, the vastness of it, the purity of its air — the desert has its own beauty! If you are a lover of the desert, don't be worried about it. People have reached through the desert to the ultimate. But if you are not, then there is no need to torture yourself in the desert. There are green valleys too.

Sufism moves through green valleys. Now this too is very strange, but this is how the mind functions: Sufism was born in a desert; Zen was born in a green valley. Maybe that's why it happened so. The people who live in a desert can't choose the path of Zen. They are already in a desert, tired of the desert. Outside is the expanse of desert and desert alone. They would not like to choose the inner desert too; otherwise, the polarity will be lost. Outside is desert, inside they have to create a green valley of love, of positivity. That will make things balanced. That will help the dialectical process.

Sufis talk about love, of paradise, of the garden of paradise. They think of God as the Beloved. They talk about wine; wine is their symbol. They talk about drunkenness; they are drunkards, drunkards of the divine. They abandon themselves in dance and song. They feast, they celebrate. That seems absolutely logical. Enough of the desert – they have to balance it by an inner garden.

Buddhism was born on the banks of the Ganges, one of the most fertile lands in the world, one of the most beautiful, in the shadows of the Himalayas. All was beautiful outside, all was green outside. Now to think of greenery inside too will be monotonous. To think of beautiful valleys and rivers will be boring. Buddha thinks of inner emptiness, nothingness, the inner desert, the silence of the desert, the utter purity of the desert – no dance, no song. You cannot imagine Buddha dancing.

You cannot imagine Rumi not dancing. If Rumi is anything at all, he is nothing but a dance. He attained to his first samadhi by dancing continuously for thirty-six hours. He danced and danced... and his ecstasy was such that hundreds of people started dancing. He created such a field of ecstasy that whosoever came to watch what had happened to him started dancing. By the time he reached his ultimate samadhi, thousands of people were dancing around him. That's how he attained. He fell on the ground for hours in utter drunkenness – just like a drunkard! When he opened his eyes, he had seen the other world, he had brought the beyond with him.

Buddha attained to his ultimate samadhi sitting silently doing nothing – so utterly silent that you could have thought that there was no man but just a marble statue. It is not just a coincidence that Buddha's statues were the first to be made, it started with Buddha's statues. His statues were the first, then others' statues followed. He was so statue-like. In his silence, sitting under the Bodhi Tree, he must have looked like a piece of marble: cool, white, still. The white marble became a metaphor for Buddha.

But you cannot make a statue of Rumi, because he is never for two consecutive moments in the same posture. If you want to make a statue of Rumi, you will have to make a statue of a fountain, or a willow in a strong wind. Impossible to make a statue of Rumi.

Buddha lived, was born, in Nepal under the shadows of the eternal Himalayas and its eternal beauty. This is again a polarity. Outside is the beauty of the Himalayas, and Buddha searches for an inner desert of absolute negation. Rumi lived in a desert; outside is the infinite desert, inside he creates a small garden, a paradise, a walled garden. That is the meaning of the word "paradise," firdaus – a walled garden, an oasis.

Sufism's emphasis is on the positive. And I am talking about both Zen and Sufi. You have to choose. The choice should not be from the head; the choice should be from your totality. Feel both. Feel Sufi dancing, and feel Vipassana. And whatsoever fits with you...and when something fits, you will know. There will be no need to ask anybody, because it fits so absolutely – that it is meant for you and you are meant for it – suddenly everything falls in tune, a great harmony arises.

Don't decide from the head, because then you can move in a wrong direction. Allow it to be decided by your total being. Feel all the possibilities – that's why I am making all that is possible available to you, so everybody can find what suits him. Then that is your path.

And never impose your path on anybody else, never, because that may not be the path for the other. Share your joy, but never try to convert anybody to your principle. Share your experience, but never become a missionary. The word "missionary" is dirty. Make your heart available – if somebody wants to choose, let him choose, but don't in any way, not even indirectly, try to convert him to your doctrine.

Your experience, your sharing of the experience, is beautiful – it is your love, it is your compassion. But your principle, your doctrine, your path, is dangerous. It may not be the other's path. And when

I am saying "the other," I don't mean the stranger — it may be your child, it may be your wife, it may be your husband, it may be your brother. "The other" includes all others — even your child whom you have carried in your womb for nine months, who is your bone and your blood and your marrow, who has pulsated with you for nine months, but still he will have to live his own life. He comes through you, but he is not you. He has his own individuality. He has to bloom in his own way. Make available all that you have experienced, all that is good and all that is bad; make your whole life open to the child, but never indoctrinate him. Never try to make him a Christian or a Hindu or a Mohammedan. Help him to move according to his nature. And nobody knows what is going to bloom in him. Just help him so he grows, becomes stronger. That is love.

When you start indoctrinating, that is not love, that is hate. You are afraid, you are possessive, you are ambitious, you are egoistic

You want to dominate the other through your doctrine. You want to kill the spirit of the other. You may think that you are helping, but you are not helping — you are hindering the growth. You are only crippling the other. He will never be able to forgive you.

That's why children are never able to forgive their parents — they have been indoctrinated, something has been forced on them. It is a kind of rape, and the worst kind: you have raped their consciousness. You have violated one of the most fundamental laws of life. You have interfered with their freedom. And the greatest freedom is the freedom to grow towards God, and everybody has to grow in his own way.

The rose has to offer its fragrance, and so does the marigold. The marigold need not become a rose, it cannot. The marigold has to bloom in its own way; it has to offer itself. That offering will be accepted — only that offering is accepted which comes from your innermost core, which has roots in you.

So Zen or Sufi, you have to feel. And there is no hurry. Go on feeling. One day, suddenly, everything falls in tune, everything comes together, and the vision opens.

The story:

> A wandering seeker saw a dervish in a rest house and said to him,
> "I have been in a hundred climes and heard the teachings of a
> multitude of mentors. I have learnt how to decide when a teacher
> is not a spiritual man. I cannot tell a genuine Guide, or how to
> find one, but half the work completed is better than nothing."

The man must have been deeply rooted in negativity, in negation. He could have easily become a follower of Buddha, but not a Sufi. He had a philosophic bent of mind. Doubt was his style, skepticism was his system of thought. That is not the way of the Sufi.

Each word of the story has to be understood, because these are not just stories but parables. You cannot change a single word. If you do you will change the whole texture, the whole flavor, the whole meaning of the story.

Sufis use these stories in such a way that they have many meanings. They can be understood on many levels.

A wandering seeker...

A seeker is always a wanderer. Those who really want to seek remain with a master, they don't wander. The one who goes on wandering is curious, greedy. He wants to know as much as he can. Hence, he cannot stay with one master. And these things are such that unless you stay with one master, in deep intimacy, with great love, you will not grow roots. You will be a rolling stone which gathers no moss. You can go on rolling and rolling forever, but you will not be enriched by your wanderings. In fact, the more you wander, the more impoverished you will become because life is wasted, time is wasted.

This is not the way of satsang. Sufism depends very much on the intimacy with the master. If you go on transplanting a tree from one place to another place continuously, you will kill the tree. When will it grow its roots? You have to leave it in one soil for a long enough time. If it is a seasonal flower, it's okay; it comes within weeks, and then it is gone within weeks. But if it is a Cedar of Lebanon which has to live for thousands of years and which has to rise high in the sky and whisper with the clouds, then transplanting it again and again is harmful, is killing it. It is murderous.

And the soul is a Cedar of Lebanon. It is not a seasonal flower. A master is a soil. You have to become grounded in the master. You have to spread your roots into his being, only then will you be nourished. That's what satsang is.

If you go on wandering, you may gather much information, you may become very knowledgeable, obviously, but you will remain as ignorant as ever. Maybe more so, because now you will become egoistic too. You will think "I know" – and you don't know! You have gathered unnecessary baggage. You will become more and more burdened, stuffed. But this is not real growth. Real growth is totally different. It needs time, waiting, patience, love, intimacy, trust.

Satsang is approaching a new birth. Being silenced. Hearing silence. Listening behind the words and forgetting them. Doing nothing, and being interior. Deeper than all expression. That is satsang. And Sufism depends on satsang. It depends on the intimacy with the master. One sits with the master, deep in the night, in the silence of the night. The master may not speak at all, or may speak one word or two. One simply sits with the master, feeling his presence, absorbing his presence, becoming part of his energy field. Breathing with him, pulsating with him, slowly slowly, the ego dissolves. One never comes to know when it dissolved. No overt effort is made to dissolve it. It dissolves of its own accord, just as the sun rises and the snow starts melting.

If you come to the master, the sun has started rising. You need not do much; you are not required to do much. The magic of the presence of the master will do. All that is needed on the part of the disciple is great trust, surrender.

A wandering seeker...

...must have been a curious man, a superfluous seeker. Goes on wandering, goes on knocking from one door to another, is a beggar. Never gathers enough courage and patience to stick to one place, hence remains rootless.

A wandering seeker saw a dervish in a rest-house...

A dervish is one who is drunk with God. You can see from his eyes: they are red with the wine of God. You can see from the way he walks. You can see in a thousand and one ways that he is not just in the body — in the body, of course, but somewhere else too. He is not only the body, but more than the body, more than the sum total of his body and mind. You can feel the presence of the beyond very alive in him, almost tangible, visible to those who have eyes to see. You can see the dancing energy around him! He has bloomed — you can smell the fragrance, his delicateness, and the sweetness of his milieu. His vibe is that of wine.

You will never find that with a Zen master. The vise is totally different, because the Zen master has achieved through the negative. He cannot be drunk. He is fully alert and aware. You will find a very sharp sword in a Zen master, ready to cut you in one blow. A Zen master is sharp! sharp because of his awareness.

A Sufi master is drunk, soft, a shower of love. You will find with a Zen master great compassion, but not love. Compassion because of his awareness, because of his enlightenment. But the Sufi is full of love. His God is love. For the Zen master there is no God — there is only utter nothingness. For the Sufi there is nothing else but God — he breathes God, he eats God, he drinks God, he lives in God like a fish lives in the ocean. How can he remain undrunk? You can see in the way he walks, the way he sits, that he is completely drunk.

It is not accidental that wine became one of the most significant metaphors of Sufism. Oman Khayyam is a Sufi master — totally misunderstood by the West, because the translators, particularly Fitzgerald, took every word of Omar Khayyam literally. And they are metaphors! they are not literal. When Omar Khayyam talks about "the woman" he is talking about the God, because Sufis think of God as woman, not as man.

Hindus also think of God as woman sometimes, but always as "the Mother." Sufis think of the woman as the beloved. When the woman is your mother, the relationship is of respect, not really of love. When the woman is your mother, you are full of reverence, but not full of love. When the woman is your beloved, it is a totally different relationship. Sufis are the only people on the earth who have been daring enough to call God "the Beloved."

And when Sufis talk about wine, they are talking of the love of God that flows into you if you allow, if you are ready to receive the gift. If you are in a let-go, it comes — it comes absolutely, it comes certainly. If it is not coming, that only shows that your doors are closed.

One learns, living with a master, how to open one's doors. It is not a question of learning knowledge: it is a question of learning a different kind of being — an open being, not a closed being.

A wandering seeker saw a dervish in a rest-house...

This word rest-house is also significant, because one who is drunk with God is at home, he is at rest. He knows what rest is; nobody else knows.

In 1905, Albert Einstein declared that there is no absolute rest, and since then there has been none. Albert Einstein is right: as far as the outer world is concerned, there is no absolute rest. Things are always moving, even things which seem to be static are moving. Even the wall of your house is in a constant turmoil, in a chaos. All is change! Nothing abides and remains the same, not even the Himalayas. They are also changing, continuously changing. Maybe our lives are very short and we cannot see the change. Scientists say: If we can condense the whole history of the Himalayas into twenty-four hours, then you will see the Himalayas are nothing but like changing waves in the ocean. The change is slow compared to our life span, but the change is there. There was a time when the Himalayas didn't exist.

You may be surprised to know that the Himalayas are the youngest mountains in the world, adolescent, and still growing, still becoming higher every year — by inches only, but change is continuous.

Either a thing goes on growing upwards or it starts falling downwards, but change is the only thing that never changes. And Albert Einstein is true about the outside world, but he does not know anything about the inner. If he had known anything of the inner, he could not have said this, that there is no absolute rest — there is!

It is not there outside: it is in the heart, in the deepest core of your being. I know it! I am in it. You can also know it. And the man is only fulfilled when he comes to know about the absolute rest in himself. Call it soul, call it God, call it Nirvana, or what you will, but there is a point, at the deepest, at the ultimate core of your being — that point is the center of the cyclone. There is rest.

These Sufi stories are metaphorical. The dervish is at the rest-house and the seeker is a wandering seeker. The seeker is searching, the dervish has arrived. He is a siddha — he has arrived. There is nowhere to go. He has come home! He is at home.

A wandering seeker saw a dervish in a rest-house and said to him, "I have been in a hundred climes and heard the teachings of a multitude of mentors."

Remember, one master is enough, and one thousand and one mentors are not enough. Mentors are teachers, tutors they are. A master is not a teacher, he is not a mentor, he is not a tutor. The function of the master is that of creating an infection — it is not a teaching, it is an infection. He does not teach you a certain thing. He simply creates an energy field around you, surrounds you, and in that surrounding energy something starts responding from within you. That is intuition. The teacher depends on tuition, he teaches you. The master depends on intuition.

He creates a situation. In that situation, something that was not functioning before in you starts functioning, that's all. But he does not give you anything. He is a catalytic agent. He gives you only that which you had already, and from the very beginning, but you had

become unaware of it, you had forgotten about it. He reminds you.
He provokes something in you which is asleep. He digs a well in you
– but the water is yours! He breaks, blasts, rocks within you, but
that which comes welling up is yours, authentically yours. He gives
you your own being.

The seeker said to the dervish:

> "I have been in a hundred climes and heard the teachings of a
> multitude of mentors."

He has been moving from one door to another, he has been like a
beggar with a begging bowl, asking for truth, searching for truth.
He has learnt much. He knows many doctrines, scriptures. He has
become very very efficient in philosophizing. He says:

> "I heard the teachings of a multitude of mentors. I have learnt
> how to decide when a teacher is not a spiritual man."

And all that he has learnt is doubt. All that he has learnt is a negative
kind of mentality. All that he has learnt is worthless as far as Sufism
is concerned. He has learnt how to know that a certain man is not a
really spiritual man. He has learnt to detect the illness. He has learnt
criticism. He has become critical.

That's what happens to a knowledgeable man: he becomes
critical. And that is not the way to reach God. One has to become
loving. To be critical is basically rooted in hatred, in antagonism. To
be critical is part of your destructiveness.

Now, this man has moved, wandered, listened, learnt many
things, and the total result is that he has only become capable of
deciding when a certain master is not really spiritual. What kind of
richness is this? How are you going to be enriched by it? But this is
what happens.

Unless you live with a master long enough, you will learn the
negative. The negative is on the surface. The positive is at the core.

The negative can be on the surface because it has no value. The positive is a treasure. If you go to a master and only listen to what he says and not to what he is, you will not know the positivity of it.

That's what happened to this man. This calamity happens to many.

"I have been in a hundred climes and heard the teachings of a multitude of mentors. I have learnt how to decide when a teacher is not a spiritual man. I cannot tell a genuine Guide, or how to find one, but half the work completed is better than nothing."

He is consoling himself. There is a famous statement of Friedrich Nietzsche. He was a madman, but sometimes mad people say beautiful things: sometimes they have glimpses of truth. He says: It is better not to know at all than to know in a half-hearted way — better to know not at all than to know in part. Better to know not at all than half know. Why? The ordinary logic will say: It is better to know at least something than not to know at all. That is not so.

To know the useless will create great sadness in you, hopelessness in you, meaninglessness in you. To know the negative will dry you of all life and life's juices. You will start freezing. You will become cold. You will become unloving. You will start losing all hope. You will be in despair, in anguish. And that's what has happened to many people.

For example, Sigmund Freud — he knew only the negative. He knew what is wrong with the mind of man, but he was never aware about anything that can be right. He depended on the negative side. He became very expert on all kinds of illnesses of the mind — abnormalities, perversions, diseases, neuroses, psychoses, and all that. But he completely forgot that there have been Buddhas too. In fact, slowly slowly, the more he became accustomed to the abnormal, the perverted, the ill, the unhealthy, the more he started suspecting whether Buddhas can even exist. He started suspecting Jesus. Not only that: psychoanalysts have written books, treatises, proving that Jesus is neurotic. They have not worked so hard on Buddha, but if they work, the same will be the case with Buddha. Maybe they will

use some other word for him — "repressed". If they think about
Ramakrishna, they will say "hysterical". And the same they will say
about Mohammed — "neurotic", "crazy".

Why is Jesus neurotic? Because he talks with God. He is neurotic
because he hears voices in the sky. He is neurotic because he feels
something which we cannot see, only he can see. We cannot trust
him, because whatsoever he feels, he cannot prove objectively. He
must be mad.

Just think of the implications of what Freud is saying. Health is
impossible, health is suspect. A healthy, whole, holy man is suspect.
Not only suspect — condemned. Then what is left? Then the whole
of humanity has to live in despair, without hope.

And that's what Freud says, that there is no hope for man, that
at the most man can endure but cannot enjoy. In fact, he himself
never enjoyed — he endured life. He himself was neurotic in many
ways. He was very much afraid of death; he had many phobias. He
was a very angry person, so much so that when he would get into a
rage he would fall on the floor in a swoon. He was so afraid of death
that even a mention of death was enough to make him tremble. And
he was so ambitious and so political that he was continuously afraid
of others conspiring against him. He was a paranoid. He destroyed
many of his disciples because of suspicion, because he was not able
to tolerate anybody coming closer to him — closer in the sense of
intelligence, understanding. He wanted only slaves. And whenever
there was an intelligent disciple — and there were people like Jung,
Adler and others — the only way for them was to escape from the
master. His presence was not nourishing but poisoning. And this man
goes on giving judgments on Buddha and Lao Tzu and Zarathustra
and Jesus and Mohammed. And these are the few people who were
really healthy.

Just think of one thing: if illness exists, that is proof enough that
health is also possible — at least possible. If darkness is there, light
is possible. And if death is there, life is possible. In fact, how can
death be if there is no life? How will you decide that somebody is ill
if there is no health? If there is no Buddha in the world, how will you
decide who is mad? Then everybody is mad! Maybe different kinds
of madness, but everybody is mad.

Freud became very skillful about the negative, an expert about illness and disease. Naturally, his experience was such that he had to deny — he never came across a Buddha. That is not the way you come across a Buddha. Buddha will not come to Freud for psychoanalysis. For forty years he was only analyzing ill people suffering from a thousand and one kinds of mind projections, phobias. Naturally, forty years watching, listening to people's dreams and phobias and fears and split people and schizophrenic and hysterical — naturally, after forty years if he decides that "I have never seen a single healthy person" in a way it is right. He has never seen a single healthy person. And forty years is enough time: he has watched thousands of people. But he has forgotten one thing: that a Buddha is not going to come and lie down on his couch and talk about his dreams, because in fact he has no dreams!

It happened once:

A man was brought to me who is a well-known psychic. His capacity to read people's thoughts is immense. Just sitting in front of you for a few moments, he will become silent and concentrate and he will start saying what thoughts are moving in your mind.

Somebody brought him to me and he wanted to read my mind. I said, "Okay, you read." Half an hour passed and then he opened his eyes and he said, "But there is nothing! — what can I do?" "You read nothing...?"

A Buddha has no dreams. A Buddha has no thoughts. A Buddha does not exist as an ego, so how can he be afraid? Even of death he is not afraid. There is no question of death. He has already died — died as an ego, and now there is only the immortality, the eternity, the timelessness.

For what will Buddha go to Vienna? There seems to be no reason. In fact, sooner or later, one day Freud will have to come to a Buddha. You will find many psychoanalysts here. They have to come — because they are losing all perspective.

Listening to people's miseries day in, day out, they are losing all hope. A Buddha can give them hope again. A Buddha can help them to be ecstatic again. They have lived with agony too much. Do you know that psychoanalysts commit suicide more than any other profession, almost double? And psychoanalysts go mad more than any other profession, almost double. This should not be so! A psychoanalyst should not commit suicide and should not go mad. But they go mad more and they commit suicide more.

But I understand. I have all compassion for them. Their whole life's work is such — agony and agony and agony — seeing people's wounds in the soul and the pus oozing day in, day out, they live in a kind of hell.

I have heard:

One psychoanalyst died. He had a ticket for heaven, but he went to hell. The Devil was surprised. He said, "But you have a ticket for heaven — why have you come here?"

He said, "I am a psychoanalyst. I have to get accustomed slowly slowly. Heaven will be too much right now. I will not be able to believe in it. First let me live in hell for a few days, let me get accustomed to better things."

A psychoanalyst lives in a far worse state than hell. Naturally, he becomes blind to the healthy side. But there are good signs on the horizon: new ways of psychology are evolving. What Freud has done, Assagioli is undoing. What Freudian psychoanalysis has done, holistic psychology, humanistic psychological trends, are undoing. Good signs!

But it happens if you go on collecting knowledge without becoming more and more rooted in the being, you will become despair itself, you will be anguish itself.

The man said:

"I have learnt how to decide when a teacher is not a spiritual man. I cannot tell a genuine Guide, or how to find one, but half the work completed is better than nothing."

That is not so. Just to become skillful in the negative, skillful in doubting, skillful about the wrong side of things, skillful and expert about thorns, is not going to help in any way to know about flowers. You can know as much as you want about thorns, but that will not help you to know anything about the flowers. In fact, if you know too much you will start disbelieving flowers. Even if they bloom, you will think they are imaginary. That's what Freud says: Buddha is imagining that he has attained — because there is no attainment! Krishna is imagining that he has arrived, and Jesus is just hallucinating, talking to God and angels.

I can understand why it happens. And if you also understand, it will help you tremendously.

Lulu Zezas, the Wyoming oil and cattle queen, tells about a ranch owner who was always complaining that his boots were too tight.

"Why don't you have them stretched?" suggested Lulu.

"Nothin' doin'," replied the rancher. "These boots are too tight and that's the way they're going to stay. Every morning I gotta get up and round up all the cattle that busted out during the night, and mend the fences they tear down, and watch my ranch blowing away in the dust, and then spend the evening listening to my wife nag me about moving to the city. When I get ready for bed and pull these tight boots off, that's the only real pleasure I get all day."

The negative person becomes enclosed in a prison, and the only pleasure he gets sometimes is to forget all about it. He goes and drinks too much — and the boots are off, those tight boots. Or in sex — somewhere where he can lose himself and his tightness. That is his only pleasure in life: whenever he can forget himself.

Now, this is stupid, because there are ways you can forget yourself forever. Sufism is one of the ways — you can drown yourself forever. There is no need to search for drugs. Sufism gives you the ultimate drug: God himself. Once the ego is gone forever, there is no pain, no agony, no suffering, no hell.

This is the way Ramana Maharishi experienced the sudden opening into ultimate consciousness, in which his individual identity was almost entirely lost. A family relation had died, and young Ramana decided to explore directly the experience of death. His motive stemmed more from curiosity than any feeling of bereavement. Ramana removed all his clothes, lay on the floor of his room, and with tremendous intensity, imagined his body dead. He closed his eyes, simulating the state of deep sleep. Suddenly there flashed into view, timeless and complete, the primal awareness that lies at the source of our being, the ultimate consciousness that is the source of being itself. And when he opened his eyes, he was totally a different man.

What happened? Somebody had died, a relation. Ramana was only seventeen. He was not a very extraordinary student or anything — nothing special about him, except one thing and that was his deep sleep. So deep was his sleep that it was almost impossible to wake him up. The family was tired. You could go on shouting, pulling him from the bed.... And sometimes the sleep used to come any time of the day — he might fall asleep in the school, and the children had to carry him back to his home. That was his only specialty. Other children would be playing and he would fall asleep on the ground, and they would poke, and they would pummel and they would beat him, and he would not be there at all. And they would have to carry him home.

That was his only speciality, but of great significance, because deep sleep is very close to samadhi, just the threshold of samadhi. That has been my speciality too.

It was almost a problem in my college in university — because I would fall asleep. My teachers were very angry, because who wants somebody falling asleep? And I was a student of philosophy, and there were not many people because very few people go to study philosophy. In my MA class we were only three students, so I would be sleeping just in front of the teacher. And he would come and shake me up.

Sometimes it would happen that I would be the only person, the other two had not come. And just looking at me he would say, "Finished! You go home. And I will go home, I can sleep myself. What is the point?"

Deep sleep is the threshold. That's why this incident was possible. Somebody died; Ramana was only seventeen and he thought, "What is death? Let me experience it." He threw his clothes, simulated death, fell on the floor. He had seen the relative lying on the floor, so just the same way he fell on the floor, closed his eyes, and started thinking, "I am dying, I am dying, I am dying."

And he died! The ego disappeared. And here the ego disappeared and there God appeared — the primal awareness. And when he opened his eyes he was no more the same person. He left the home, immediately, without saying anything to anybody. It was not a renunciation. He simply left the home because there was no point. It was not that he was against the world or anything. There was no point any more. He went out and never came back. The mother searched for him for years; finally, after ten years, she found him in Arunachal in a mountain cave. But he was a totally different man. And the mother asked him, "Why didn't you inform me?"

And he said, "But the thought never came to me. In fact, thoughts have stopped coming to me. I sit and sit and days pass, and there are no thoughts coming. Good that you have come! Live with me...."

This primal awareness is God, thoughtless awareness is God. This is the wine Sufis talk about, and once you have drunk of this wine, nothing else is needed for you to forget yourself — because you are no more, there is no need to forget.

The dervish rent his garments and said, "Miserable man! Becoming an expert on the useless is like being able to detect rotten apples without learning the characteristics of the sound ones."

Rending the garments is a Sufi expression. In fact, Sufis do that. They are so passionately in love with humanity that when they see that you are trapped in a kind of misery unnecessarily they become so concerned, they become so anxious for you, yes, they rend their garments.

The dervish rent his garments and said, "Miserable man!"

And this is how misery is created. It is doubt, it is negativity, that creates misery. It is entrust that creates misery. The root cause of all misery is there.

"Becoming an expert on the useless is like being able to detect rotten apples without learning the characteristics of the sound ones."

Just the other night I was reading about a philosopher. He writes:

"I used to wonder why a rotten apple placed in a barrel of sound apples would make the sound apples rotten, while a sound apple placed in a barrel of rotten apples would not make all the rotten apples sound. I also wondered why a man infected with smallpox, when turned loose in a gathering of sound people, would by his mere presence make many of the sound people sick, while a sound man walking through a hospital of sick people would not by his mere presence make the sick people well.

In other words, I wondered why God, if he were a good God, had made a universe in which soundness and health seemed futile, and rottenness and sickness seemed contagious.

But one day I stopped wondering and examined the so-called sound apple, and I found it was not sound. Oh, I knew the grocer would contradict me, he would see no defect. He might even sue me for slander if I persisted in spreading the report that he was selling apples that were not perfect. But if he pressed me for proof, I could prove it. I would ask him to look beyond the apple to the stem. There, in the most vital, the most crucial spot of all, he would find the mortal wound that I refer to. He would find that the apple had been torn away from its parent vine, it had been hopelessly separated from its source of life.

When I discovered this, I learnt one of the truest facts of life: that nothing, whether it be fruit or vegetable or man, when separated from its source of life is sound!"

All are ill – because all are separated from the source of life. And unless you join yourself with the source of life again, you will not be healthy. Only in God is health and wholeness and holiness. Only the presence of God heals. But we have forgotten completely about God. We have started living on our own, as if a tree has forgotten about its roots and has started living in the branches — it is going to die, it will become ill.

That's why the whole of humanity is ill. And Freud and company are right about ninety-nine point nine percent of people: people are ill! They are no more connected with the source of life. But that point one percent is the hope. There are people who are connected with life.

And I would like to say to this philosopher: there are people whose health is contagious. When a Buddha moves, his very movement heals people.

That is the meaning of the miracles of Jesus — the miracles that he heals blind people and suddenly eyes are there, and he heals the deaf and dumb and they start listening and taking, and he heals the crippled and they are no more crippled. These are parables. It is not about the physical crippledness: it is something about the spiritual crippledness. And whenever a man of God moves, or people who are fortunate come and live in the company of a man of God, they are healed, spiritually healed. Their spiritual wounds start disappearing, they again start growing roots. And soon the roots find the sources of life, the waters of life, and all is green again, and all is blooming again. And the spring has come, and the celebration.

That celebration is Sufism.

The dervish said:

> "But there is a still worse possibility before you. Beware that you
> do not become like the doctor in the story.
>
> "In order to test a physician's knowledge, a certain king sent
> several healthy people to be examined by him. To each the doctor
> gave medicine. When the king summoned him and charged him
> with this deceit, the leech answered, 'Great king! I had for so

*long seen nobody but the ailing that I had begun to imagine that
everyone was ill and mistook the bright eyes of good health for
the signs of fever!'"*

Ramakrishna falling unconscious is a sign of great health, but the
psychologist will say he has fallen into a kind of hysterical fit.
And the hysterical fit and Ramakrishna's going into unconsciousness
look alike from the outside. From the inside they are not alike.

Ramakrishna has moved from the small tiny consciousness to the
primal consciousness. He is no more there as an "I", as an individual.
He is there as the source, as the goal. He is there as existence itself.
He is one with the whole. When somebody falls into a fit, into a
hysterical fit, he loses the consciousness that he has but he does not
attain any other consciousness. From the outside it is the same.

If you see Buddha asleep and somebody else asleep, from the
outside what difference are you going to see? They will look alike. But
they are not. The other person who is asleep by the side of Buddha
is deep in dreams, and Buddha's awareness burns bright as ever. As
it is in the day, so it is in the night. There is no change. But from
the outside it is the same.

When somebody dies and Buddha dies, what is the difference?
Difference is from the inside; it is an inside story. Unless you are a
Buddha you will never know it, because how can you know the inside
of a Buddha without becoming a Buddha yourself? That is the only
way to be an insider.

When Buddha dies, nothing dies. There is no clinging to life,
there is no problem. Buddha simply slips out of the body – just as
you change your clothes, exactly like that. Do you think each time
you change your clothes that you are dying? Exactly like that Buddha
slips out of the old clothes, slips out of the cage, and his soul is free
and the whole sky is available. He is utterly thrilled. He is blissful in
his death, because his death is not an end but really a new birth. He
is moving into a far greater life than there was before it. It is from
life to more life.

When you die you are moving from life to no life. From the
outside it is all the same. From the inside it is not.

This story is beautiful:

"In order to test a physician's knowledge, a certain king sent several healthy people to be examined by him."

Strange this king must have been. But this is the way, this is the Eastern way to judge. The real doctor is not one who knows what disease is: the real doctor is one who knows what health is. Disease even quacks can know. Disease is not such a great phenomenon; it is on the surface. Anybody can learn about it. But health is very deep; it is not easily available. Only a wise physician knows what health is about.

Do you know? In ancient China this was a rule: that the physician was paid not for curing illness but for keeping people healthy. People had their own private physicians, just as they have now. But the physician was paid if his client did not fall ill. Each year the client would pay the physician because he had not been ill. Now we pay the physician when we are ill and he cures us. This is a totally different thing. The Chinese idea was far superior.

And our idea is dangerous too, because to pay the physician when you are ill and he cures you makes him interested in your illness, his investment becomes in your illness. He wants you to be ill so that he can cure you. The Chinese idea is far superior. His investment should be in your health, not in your disease, so he remains concerned that you should not fall ill — because if a person falls ill he will not pay. The physician has to cure him without any fee; that is his responsibility. It is his fault! What was he doing the whole year?

And the Chinese have remained one of the healthiest races in the world, particularly in the past. Sooner or later this is going to be the case again. In Soviet Russia they are thinking about it, to make it a rule: the physician has to be paid only when you remain healthy — for the health.

"In order to test a physician's knowledge, a certain king sent several healthy people to be examined by him."

As if a Buddha is sent to Sigmund Freud. Sigmund Freud will prescribe whatsoever he has been prescribing to others. He will talk about repression and he will talk about paranoia and he will talk about this and that – then he has failed. Then he is not yet aware of what he is doing. Only confronting a Buddha can be the test for Sigmund Freud. If he can declare Buddha healthy, then he knows something about health. But how can you recognize a Buddha if you are not a Buddha yourself?

> "To each the doctor gave medicine."

When you go to the doctor, he has to find something or other wrong. Try it: when you are feeling perfectly healthy, go to a doctor and he will make you feel very unhealthy. He will find a thousand and one things wrong with you. His investment is there. But this is cheating.

> "To each the doctor gave medicine. When the king summoned him and charged him with this deceit, the leech answered, 'Great king! I had for so long seen nobody but the ailing that I had begun to imagine that everyone was ill and mistook the bright eyes of good health for the signs of fever!'"

This happens every day. When you are dancing here and an outsider comes and watches you dancing, he thinks, "These people have gone mad. What is happening?"

That's why it is very difficult to find a sympathetic journalist, very difficult – because he comes for one or two days and he looks around and he sees all kinds of things which he has never seen anywhere. He becomes worried. He has his prejudices that these are the things only mad people do. How can sane people do these things? So this is a mad place. When he sees you so happy, he cannot believe it, because happiness is impossible. Then you must be hypnotized; somebody has hypnotized you. That's why you are feeling happy – this is a hallucination. You have fallen into an illusion.

These are logical conclusions for him, because he comes with a prejudice. And people have prejudices and prejudices, layers upon layers of prejudices. That's why it is very difficult to make them understand. They have always been misunderstanding people like me and their work. And the reason is what the doctor says:

> "Great king! I had for so long seen nobody but the ailing that I had begun to imagine that everyone was ill and mistook the bright eyes of good health for the signs of fever!"

The dervish said to the seeker, "You have fallen into the first trap of being negative. Now there is a worse possibility for you — don't become like this doctor! You say, 'I can know who is not spiritual.' This is the first step. The second step will be a logical conclusion. Slowly slowly, seeing everybody as not spiritual, the natural conclusion will arise that there is nobody who is spiritual — all are fake, all are pseudo, deceivers, hypocrites, charlatans.

"If that decision is taken you are doomed, because then there is no hope. Because when you say nobody is spiritual, you have denied your own possibility of becoming spiritual. When you say, 'No Buddha has ever existed,' you have cut your whole future. If you say there has never been any flowering in the world, then, of course, how can you allow yourself to flower? That is a worse possibility."

The dervish is right. Remember these two things from this story. One: look positively — rather than finding who is not spiritual try to find who is spiritual. Rather than looking for thorns, look for roses. And rather than looking for the darkness, look for the stars; rather than looking for diseases, look for health. Always move positively. Then there is a possibility that out of a hundred you may be able to find that one, that oasis in the desert. And with that oasis your life will be transformed. That is your master. Being with him you will also become an oasis.

Sufism is the path of via positiva. Zen transcends mind through the negative; Sufism transcends mind through the positive. Both transcend mind, both go beyond it, so both reach to the same goal.

But, let me repeat, Zen moves through a desert land; Sufism moves into dark, shadowy, but green flowering valleys. You choose! but not from the head. Feel...pulsate with both. And wherever you feel that your inner music starts flowing, then that is it. You have found your key.

Enough for today.

CHAPTER 4

VIA CONFUSIVA

The first question:

Osho,
Whatever you say seems to be right from the point of view of what
you are saying at that moment. But it may be contradictory. You
draw the listeners in one direction confirming a particular point,
and at the same time you go via the backdoor to the opposite
point. It is a spiral – the listener hardly realizes what may be
happening. Is this not fooling the listener – unless he realizes that
the real answer lies beyond your spoken words?

All statements are of the moment. No statement can contain
eternity. And those who claim that their statements are eternal
are simply lying. They don't know what they are saying.

The moment can contain only the moment. So whatsoever I say
at the moment belongs to the moment. It is a flower of that moment.
If it is raining, I say it is raining. Later on it may not be raining. The
clouds may disperse. It may become sunny.

Yes, my statement is contradicted by another moment — but it is contradicted only if it was claiming that it has to be true forever.

I am not giving you dogmas. A dogma is a statement with the claim that it is true forever. I give you only momentary flowers. I am not giving you a system that will remain forever and forever true. That is what has happened in the past, and man has suffered enough because of it.

What Buddha said was his response to his moment. What Mohammed said was his response to the life that he encountered. It can't be true forever. And if it has to be true forever, then life will never change, then life will become stagnant. That's why people who believe in dogmas become stagnant. Their life is no more a flow, they are not riverlike. They become frozen. Christians, Hindus, Mohammedans, Buddhists, they are frozen people. They have lost track of all that goes on constantly changing.

Except change, nothing is eternal.

If I was creating a dogma here, then I would never contradict myself. You would be happy with that! because you would have something to cling to. You have not come here to become enlightened, you have come here to become knowledgeable. My effort is not to impart knowledge to you: my effort is to awaken you. I can't allow you to cling to any statement — hence I contradict. I am always in a hurry to contradict, so you don't have any time to cling to anything. I want to take all knowledge away from you. I want you to be left alone, in utter emptiness and its purity, and its virginity.

That's why my moment is for the moment. It does not claim anything beyond it. Each statement that I make is only for this moment. Enjoy it! Just enjoy the rose that has bloomed this morning — be full of its fragrance, sing it, dance with it, celebrate it. You are fortunate you have been able to see this flower. But don't hope that you can keep it forever. Unless it is a plastic flower it can't be eternal. Only false things can be eternal, artificial things can be eternal.

The reality is changing, it is flux, it is a river. Tomorrow I don't know what I will say. I don't remember what I said yesterday. I am in no way concerned with my past, and not concerned with my future either. This moment is all for me. Nothing else exists beyond it. I am utterly disconnected from the past...and have no plans for the future. When the tomorrow comes we will see. And what I am saying to you now is not going to become an obligation for me to go on saying it forever. I have no obligation to confirm my past again and again. Yesterday is gone, so are the statements that were made yesterday.

But I understand your problem. Your problem is: Then in what to believe? How to believe? But who is telling you to believe in anything? Rejoice! Don't believe. Can't you see the difference? The emphasis is different. I am not telling you to believe in anything.

Of course, if I am telling you to believe in something, then I have to persist again and again with the same thing; I have to say it again and again. That will be a kind of hypnosis. When something is repeated constantly, you become hypnotized by it. I am not here to hypnotize you. I am here for just the opposite thing: to dehypnotize you — not only of the statements that I have made in the past but of the statements of all the enlightened people that have ever existed.

I have to destroy your knowledge, your belief. I have to destroy anything that you can cling to. Only nothing has to be left there....

One sannyasin has done well. He has called my path via confusiva — that's right. That's perfectly right. It is neither via negativa nor via positiva — it is via confusiva.

If you can be so much confused that you drop all belief, out of that confusion will come clarity. When do you feel confused? When exactly? Whenever one of your beliefs is attacked — you become suspicious: Now what to believe in? Whenever a doubt arises...but how is a doubt possible if there is no belief?

The man of no-belief cannot doubt either. There is nothing to doubt. By destroying your belief I am destroying the very possibility of doubt. Can you see the point? Doubt is a shadow of belief. It looks like the opposite — it is not. Only believers can doubt. If you believe in God, doubt can arise. But if you don't believe in God, from where can doubt arise? How can doubt arise? A man without any kind of belief will be without any kind of doubt too. That is clarity.

When I say something and it goes against your belief, doubt arises: Now what to choose? You have put so much at stake with your belief, you have lived with it for so long, and now suddenly doubt arises! It shakes you up. It makes you frightened.

And if I go on saying contradictory things every day, great courage is needed to listen to me, a great heart to contain, great love to understand me, and an intense desire to know, a passionate desire to know: "Whatsoever the cost, I am going to know. If all beliefs are to be destroyed and all systems have to be dropped and all religions to be thrown into the fire, I am ready. But I am going to know."

When this passionate desire is there, you will meet with me. Then you will understand my contradictions. It is a device. It is creating a situation. I will not allow my people any possibility to believe in anything, not even in me. When all belief has gone, what is left? You are just like a mirror reflecting all the moods of life, reflecting all the climates. Summer comes and you are summer...and winter comes and you are winter...and day comes and you are day...and the night comes and you are night.

This I call totality. And to live in totality is to live in God.

All that I am saying is not a kind of doctrinizing – it is not at all. Its purpose is totally different. But the purpose is so different, that's why such questions arise. When you go to listen to somebody else, he is there to propound a philosophy; he is explaining his philosophy to you. I am not explaining because I have no philosophy. I am utterly anti-philosophic.

When you go to a priest he is there to explain to you a certain dogma that he believes in; he is there to convert you. I am not here to convert you: I am here just to destroy you.

So remember: all statements are of the moment, just as all flowers are of the moment. Spring comes...and there are so many flowers. And then the spring is gone, and you never go to nature and say, "You look very contradictory. Where are the flowers? And how can you go on contradicting yourself in this way?"

Tao is contradictory. It has to be. That is the dialectics of life. But you never go to nature! If a cuckoo is calling and then suddenly it stops for no reason at all, you don't go to the cuckoo and say "Why have you stopped? This is so contradictory! Calling so beautifully, and then falling into silence? Either be silent or go on calling – be consistent!" But you don't say that.

In the rains the trees are green. In the summer the leaves will disappear and branches will be standing bare, naked, dry, against the sky. But you don't go to the trees saying "How dare you be so contradictory!"

I am part of this Tao. I am not a philosopher. So all my statements are of the moment, for the moment. Remember it. There is no need to believe in them. Enjoy them! Relish them! While the flower is there, drink its beauty. It will be gone soon. Before it is gone, celebrate its being.

Celebrate me! Rather than believing in me, celebrate me. That is the difference – the difference of emphasis. Let my presence be a feast to you. It should not become a prison. It should not become a definition of your mind. It should not fill you with ideas but with dance and song.

If you want to remember me, never remember me as a philosopher, as a priest – no, never. Those are dirty words for me. Remember me as a poet. You never go to the poet and say to him, "You are contradictory," because you understand. A poet has no obligation to be consistent. He can sing a thousand songs of different moods. When he is sad, he sings a sad song; and when he is happy, he sings a happy song. You don't go to him....

My being is more that of a poet. And if you really want to feel my presence, you will also have to learn the way of poetry. Art to me is the greatest religion – the religion of the future. Aesthetics to me is prayer.

And second: there is no opposite for me. It looks contradictory to you; for me it is not. For me there are no contradictions at all, because each contradiction is nothing but a complement. There is no way to really contradict. The night does not contradict the day. It only gives rest to the day energy to be revived again in the morning. If there was no night, there would be no day again. It is through the night that the day lives, regains vitality. And it is through the day that the night is born. It is through life that death arrives, and it is through death that life comes back again and again. They are not enemies: they are friends, partners in the same game, complementaries.

So if you understand me with great love, you will see that those contradictions look like contradictions to you because your understanding is small. When your understanding is a little greater, when you have moved to a little higher stage of consciousness, those contradictions won't look like contradictions – they will be complementaries. They will make whatsoever I am saying very rich. It makes them rich.

If you talk only of Zen, it has a kind of richness. If you talk only about Sufis, it has another kind of richness. But when you talk about both Sufis and Zen, your richness is immense. It is more than the sum total of Zen and Sufism. It is not only Zen plus Sufism: it is Zen multiplied by Sufism – it is multi dimensional.

Hence I go on speaking through different windows. Sometimes I stand at the window that opens to the east and I talk about the east and the sun that rises and the morning. And sometimes I stand at the window that opens to the west and I talk about the evening and the sunset and the beauty of it. And I go on changing because there are many doors to the divine.

Jesus says: There are many mansions in my God's palace. There are millions of possibilities. That is the infinity of God, that you cannot exhaust him. But to take note of all possibilities certainly makes you infinitely richer.

So there are no opposites for me, but only complementaries.

And third: there is no answer, real or unreal. I am not giving you any answer as such. What I am giving you is an insight into the mystery of life, not an answer but an insight into the mystery of life. If my answer provokes the mysterious in you, I have succeeded. If my answer becomes an answer to you, I have failed.

Don't take my answers as answers. I am not a schoolteacher. I have no answers to give you. That which I have to give you is the sense for the mysterious and the miraculous.

But I understand. It is difficult – I speak one language, you speak another language. When I say "language" I don't mean English,

German or French. I mean...my language comes from my being,
your language comes from your being. We may be speaking the same
language on the surface, but deep down it is almost untranslatable,
what I am saying to you. It is impossible to translate it into your
language. Then why am I saying it at all?

I am just crazy. I cannot resist. It is overflowing. There is no way
to prevent it. I have to say it — just like a cloud is burdened with
rainwater and it has to rain! Whether you are able to soak it in or
not, that is not the point. Rocks may not be able to soak it in. Or,
some soil may be able to soak it in and will be full of greenery and
beauty will arise. But that is all undecided. It is an open thing. It may
happen, it may not happen. It depends how you let me in.

I have heard a beautiful story:

A few years ago in France, an extraordinary meeting took place.
Some leading philosophers from England and America had been
invited to meet with their continental counterparts. They were to
exchange ideas, share experiences, and discover the extent of possible
"communication" among them. In a very congenial atmosphere,
meetings were held, discussions took place, and speeches were made.
Many friendships must have been established and no little quantity
of wine consumed, but apparently no philosophic communication
took place.

For instance, Gabriel Marcel was trying to explain his ideas about
God, grace and transcendence. He continually met resistance from
the audience, from other philosophers: "But what do you mean by
that? But surely you don't mean this? How is it possible that...? Isn't
it true that...? etc, etc...."

After a while Marcel became exasperated, and the audience as a
whole restless. Finally, someone in the audience asked Marcel why
he did not simply say what he meant. Since he had been trying to do
just this for some time, he merely replied, "Perhaps I can't explain
this to you, but if I had a piano here I could play it."

And because there was no piano, no communication was
possible.

But I am suspicious: even with a piano it may not have happened — because the other may not understand the language of music either.

Yes, exactly that's what is happening here. What I am trying to say to you is a kind of music that I have heard. It has not been heard verbally. It is in the sound of the running water. It is in the wind passing through the pine trees. It is in the songs of the birds. It is in the silence of darkness. It is in the dancing rays of the sun. It is all over the place! But it is a music. And unless you are capable of understanding this music, you will not be able to understand me. You will go on misunderstanding me.

You say: *Is this not fooling the listener?*

You must have come here to gather some belief — and then certainly you will feel fooled, because you cannot gather any belief. On the contrary, whatsoever you had will start slipping out of your hands. If you have come to gather a little more knowledge, you will feel cheated. When you go, you will not have more, you will have less. In spite of yourself you will have less. You will have lost something here. We rob people of their knowledge.

So you may feel that there is some kind of befooling going on. When I say something, it looks so clearly, so absolutely right — and the next moment I contradict it. Then whatsoever I say to contradict it looks again right. But again I will contradict it!

Just think of the people — you are here only for a few days — just think of the people who have been listening to me year in, year out. They have almost stopped listening, but a new kind of communication, a communion rather, has started. They are no more worried about my words. That is no more a concern. They have lost that enthusiasm for words. I have destroyed it.

I have contradicted myself so much that now they are aware of it — there is no need to cling, tomorrow I will take it away. So what is the point? Wait for tomorrow. Slowly slowly, they have learnt the beauty of non-clinging. Slowly slowly, they have learnt how not to let my words interfere, and a direct communication, a communion...their energies start flowing with me. They can flow only when the word is no more important. Then something far superior takes place.

That's why I have been speaking so much. It is not to communicate with you through words: it is to destroy the meaning of the word itself. You will be surprised. The reason why I speak so much is that I want to destroy all meaning in the word. Listening to me, slowly slowly it disappears. And with the disappearance of the meaning of the word an existential connection arises. That is real initiation — when you start hearing my music, when you become attuned to my presence, when you breathe with me. It happens...it has happened to somebody.

Vasumati has written this:

> Today and for the last few days in discourse, as soon as you begin to speak, my body lies down on the floor. And something starts to happen. Your voice caresses me, unwinds my muscles strand by strand, gently lulls me and pulls me into your silence until I am like a piece of seaweed in the waves of your infinite ocean. Oh, Osho, my heart dies with you, rises and falls with you, breathes with you. Can it be that I am in love with you, gone with you, with your vibrant, warm and scented presence? When I am near you, all questions simply dissolve and there is nothing but my heartbeat, the rain and your voice.

Yes, Vasumati, this is it. When words start disappearing, something far deeper, profounder takes place. Communion. The meeting of the master and the disciple, not as two minds but as two presences, merging into each other, melting into each other, losing into each other.

Soon that moment happens when the disciple is no more separate, the master is no more separate. They have become one. That unity is the goal of all disciplehood. When that unity has happened, you have known the master, you have drunk out of him, you have absorbed him. You have come home.

The second question:

Osho,

Sometimes when you speak, I get the vision of living a kind of Zorba the Greek life – eat, drink and be merry – lusty and passionate, and I think this is the way. Other times I feel you are saying that the way is to sit silently, watchful and unmoving, like a monk. So who are we to be – Zorbas or monks – and how can a blend of them be possible? I sense that you have managed to integrate the contradictions, but can we be both Zorbas, moved by passion and desire, and Buddhas, dispassionate, cool and calm?

That is the ultimate synthesis – when Zorba becomes a Buddha. I am trying to create here not Zorba the Greek but Zorba the Buddha.

Zorba is beautiful, but something is missing. The earth is his, but the heaven is missing. He is earthly, rooted, like a giant cedar, but he has no wings. He cannot fly into the sky. He has roots but no wings.

Eat, drink and be merry is perfectly good in itself: nothing is wrong in it. But it is not enough. Soon you will get tired of it. One cannot just go on eating, drinking and merrying. Soon the merry-go-round turns into a sorry-go-round – because it is repetitive. Only a very mediocre mind can go on being happy with it. If you have a little intelligence, sooner or later you will find the utter futility of it all. How long can you go on eating, drinking and merrying? Sooner or later the question is bound to arise – what is the point of it all? Why? It is impossible to avoid the question for long. And if you are very intelligent, it is always there, persistently there, hammering on your heart for the answer: Give me the answer! – why?

And one thing to be remembered: it is not that the people who are poor, starving, become frustrated with life — no. They cannot become frustrated. They have not lived yet — how can they be frustrated? They have hopes. A poor man always has hopes. A poor man always desires that something is going to happen, hopes that something is going to happen. If not today then tomorrow, or the day after tomorrow. If not in this life then in the next life.

What do you think? Who are these people who have depicted heaven as a Playboy Club — who are these people? Starved, poor, who have missed their life. They are projecting their desires in heaven. In heaven there are rivers of wine. Who are these people who are imagining rivers of wine? They must have missed here. And there are kalpavrikshas — wish-fulfilling trees. You sit underneath them, desire, and the moment you desire, immediately it is fulfilled. Not even a single moment passes by between the desire and its fulfillment, no shadow between the desire and the fulfillment. It is immediate, instant!

Who are these people? Starved, have not been able to live their life. How can they be frustrated with life? They have not experienced — it is only through experience that one comes to know the utter futility of it all. Only zorbas come to know the utter futility of it all.

Buddha himself was a Zorba. He had all the beautiful women available in his country. His father had arranged for all the beautiful girls to be around him. He had the most beautiful palaces — different palaces for different seasons. He had all the luxury that is possible, or that was possible in those days. He lived the life of a Zorba the Greek — hence, when he was only twenty-nine he became utterly frustrated. He was a very intelligent man. If he had been a mediocre man, then he would have lived in it. But soon he saw the point: it is repetitive, it is the same. Every day you eat, every day you make love to a woman...and he had new women every day to make love to. But how long...?! Soon he was fed up.

The experience of life is very bitter. It is sweet only in imagination In its reality it is very bitter.

He escaped from the palace and the woman and the riches and the luxury and everything....

So, I am not against Zorba the Greek because Zorba the Greek is the very foundation of Zorba the Buddha. Buddha arises out of that experience. So I am all for this world, because I know the other world can only be experienced through this world. So I don't say escape from it, I will not say to you become a monk. A monk is one who has moved against the Zorba; he is an escapist, a coward; he has done something in a hurry, out of unintelligence. He is not a mature person. A monk is immature, greedy — greedy for the other world, and wants it too early, and the season has not come, and he is not ripe yet.

Live in this world because this world gives a ripening, maturity, integrity. The challenges of this world give you a centering, an awareness. And that awareness becomes the ladder. Then you can move from Zorba to Buddha.

But let me repeat again: only Zorbas become Buddhas — and Buddha was never a monk. A monk is one who has never been a zorba and has become enchanted by the words of Buddhas. A monk is an imitator, he is false, pseudo. He imitates Buddhas. He may be Christian, he may be Buddhist, he may be a Jain — that doesn't make much difference — but he imitates Buddhas.

When a monk goes away from the world, he goes fighting with it. It is not a relaxed going. His whole being is pulled towards the world. He struggles against it. He becomes divided. Half of his being is for the world and half has become greedy for the other. He is torn apart. A monk is a schizophrenic basically, the split person, divided into the lower and the higher. And the lower goes on pulling him, and the lower becomes more and more attractive the more it is repressed. And because he has not lived the lower, he cannot get into the higher.

You can get into the higher only when you have lived through the lower. You can earn the higher only by going through all the agony and the ecstasy of the lower. Before a lotus becomes a lotus it has to move through the mud — that mud is the world. The monk has escaped from the mud, he will never become a lotus. It is as if a lotus seed is afraid of falling into mud — maybe out of ego that "I am a lotus seed! And I cannot fall into the mud." But then it is going to remain a seed; it will never bloom as a lotus. If it wants to bloom like a lotus, it has to fall into the mud, it has to live this contradiction. Without this contradiction of living in the mud there is no going beyond.

You ask me, Sometimes when you speak, I get the vision of living a kind of Zorba the Greek life — eat, drink and be merry — lusty and passionate, and I think this is the way. Other times I feel you are saying that the way is to sit silently, watchful and unmoving like a monk.

No. I will be the last person to make a monk out of you — otherwise, why are the monks and nuns so much against me? I would like you to become rooted into the earth. I am perfectly in agreement with Friedrich Nietzsche who says: "I beseech you, my brothers, remain faithful to the earth and do not believe in those who speak of other worldly hopes!" Learn your first lesson of trust by trusting the earth. It is your home right now!

Don't hanker for the other world. Live this world, and live it with intensity, with passion. Live it with totality, with your whole being. And out of that whole trust, out of that life of passion, love and joy, you will become able to go beyond.

The other world is hidden in this world. The Buddha is asleep in the Zorba. It has to be awakened. And nobody can awaken you except life itself.

I am here to help you to be total wherever you are, in whatsoever state you are — live that state totally. It is only living a thing totally that one transcends it.

First become a Zorba, a flower of this earth, and earn the capacity through it to become a Buddha — the flower of the other world. The other world is not away from this world; the other world is not against this world: the other world is hidden in this. This is only a manifestation of the other, and the other is the unmanifest part of it.

The third question:

Osho,

> *No oasis, no deserts,*
> *no mountains, no valleys,*
> *no summer, no winter,*
> *no rain, no snow,*
> *no yes and no!*
> *No Sufi, no Zen,*
> *no tantra, no mantra,*
> *no crown, no cross,*
> *no gain, no loss!*
> *All in YOU.*
> *Infinitely, eternally*
> *yes and no! Forever with*
> *YOU!*

This is the way to understand me. I am neither Sufi nor Zen. I am neither male nor female. I am neither positive nor negative. And I am here to help you to transcend all polarities. Hence I speak on the polarities, so that you can understand them, so that you can become aware of them — so much so that you are not trapped by them.

I talk to you about Sufism and about Zen so that one day you can go beyond both. You have to go beyond all standpoints! You have to go beyond all kinds of principles, dogmas, paths, methods, techniques. To be with me is on the way towards transcendence. I am neither a theist nor an atheist, neither a Hindu nor a Mohammedan.

I am simply an awareness — full of love. You can also become that, because whatsoever I have become you can become, because wherever you are I was also there one day, with the same agony, the same suffering, with the same dichotomies — with the same problems! I was just like you. That's why I say you can also be just like me.

To be with a master is to be with a man who has been just like you, because only that man can help you who has been just like you. If a master descends from God, he cannot be of much help — because he has never been a man. If God himself comes on the earth and moves amongst you, he will be of no help at all. That's why he has never tried. Or maybe he has tried and failed, so he has dropped the whole project.

God cannot commune with you. He has never been a man. He will not know where you are. He will not know how you are suffering. He will not have any compassion for you. He will have no understanding. And he has always been there where you would like to be. The distance will be vast. Even if God confronts you, there will be such a gap between you and God that it will be unbridgeable. Hence the meaning of a master.

A master is one who has been just like you, who has arisen out of you, who has moved out of you and gone ahead. He knows all the pains of the journey. He knows the whole past of man. He understands — that's why he has compassion. And he can help, because he is still in the body. His one hand is still in the world, his other hand has reached God. He can become a bridge. A master is a bridge.

This is the way to understand me. Don't let it remain just in the mind. Let it become vibrant in each cell and fibre of your body. Let it become your heartbeat and your breathing.

The fourth question:

Osho,
Why do the mystics speak a language of their own?

They have something to say to you, to share with you, but that something has never even been dreamt by you. They have to use your language, but in such a way, with such nuances, twists and turns, that they can give you an idea of something which is not contained by your language.

That's why mystics use language in a certain way, and different mystics decide in different ways. Sufis have decided for parables; their message is all in their stories. Stories have a beauty. Even children can understand them. They can go to the lowest, who cannot understand anything higher, and even he can understand the story. He will understand according to his capacity, but if you go on meditating over the story...and one has to meditate over these stories. These are not stories that you read once and throw them away. They have great meanings hidden in them. You have to dig again and again. You have to meditate. Slowly slowly, new meanings arrive. As you grow in sympathy, in trust, in consciousness, in meditation, the meaning grows.

Sufis speak in parables. They have chosen that way because there are so many people in the world and at different stages of life, at different stations. Something has to be told which can be understood by all. Now, the parable has a beauty: it can be understood by all in different ways. It is very unlimited. Those who can't understand, even they can enjoy it. If today they enjoy it, tomorrow they may understand it.

Mahavira has chosen a different method. He does not speak at all. Language has been dropped. Silence is his language. He simply sits with his disciples. Now this will be difficult; not all will be able to understand it — only the highest. It is said about Mahavira: his first sermon, of course in silence, was understood only by gods. That's a way of saying that nobody understood it. It took years for men, a few men, to understand him.

Jainism is the smallest religion as far as the number of the followers is concerned. Why? The reason is here: Mahavira didn't choose a method that can be understood by many people in many ways. He was a very very mathematical person — that is the reason behind it. He would like to be exact. He cannot use a parable. A parable is basically inexact. A parable has to be vague. So many meanings can be in it; no meaning in particular, and many meanings in it. It has to be a magic bag: you can bring out of it any meaning that you want. It will be understood by many people. Millions will be able to understand, even children will be able to read it. And something will happen to them.

Mahavira was very mathematical. Because he was very mathematical he would remain silent — because he knew that if he said something it would not be as exact as it is in him, so it was better not to speak. Silence is his language. Only a few very evolved souls could understand him.

Zen has a different method of its own. It does not use parables. It does not remain silent either. It uses koans, puzzles, riddles, which cannot be solved by the human mind. That is its way to destroy the human mind. It takes years.

Never be befooled when you read in books about Zen that the master hits a disciple and he becomes enlightened immediately — you don't know the whole story. He was meditating for twenty-six years. That part is not told in it. After twenty-six years he has earned the blow of the master; it is not for everybody. Don't think that when you go to a Zen master he will hit you on your head and you will become enlightened. He will not hit you at all. He will be very polite with you. He will say, "Sir, so great of you to have come to me! I rejoice in your presence." Don't think that he will hit you. It has to be earned. It takes years to get that blow of the master. That blow can be given only at the last moment.

When between you and reality there is only a very very thin layer left, so just one blow and the layer is broken and the bird is out of the egg.... But the bird has to be given a chance to mature in the egg first. Don't go breaking eggs before they are ripe, otherwise you will kill the bird. You will not be of any help.

Zen has its own methodology, very crazy, but of immense power.

You ask me: *Why do the mystics speak a language of their own?*

They have to. Each mystic has to create a language according to his understanding, capacity, according to his past, his experiences. When Jesus speaks he speaks as a son of a carpenter. Whey Buddha speaks he speaks like an emperor. That is their past. When you speak you have to use your past.

Buddha cannot speak the same way as Jesus. His terminology is bound to be different. He has never been to the forest, he has never chopped wood, he has never cut wood, he has never carried logs to the father's workshop. He does not know how the freshly cut wood smells. He cannot speak that language. He cannot use the parable of the shepherd and the sheep, the lost sheep. No, he has no understanding of the shepherd and the sheep. Jesus can use that parable.

Buddha speaks like a king – the language of the court, the language of philosophy, not the language of the common person. He has not been a common person – how can he speak that language?

So each mystic has to use his own language. And remember: speaking is precarious. People talk around the subject, interrupt, change the subject, do not understand, are silent. Words heal and wound, build up and sow confusion. To use the word is to use a very very dangerous weapon. It can be used for surgery; it can also be used to cut somebody's throat. And one has to be very skillful. Many mystics have decided not to speak at all. And those who have spoken, they have also spoken continuously against speaking. And even if they were very very intelligent, very experienced with language, very articulate, then too....

The statements of the Buddha seem hard and impossible to us who are full of ideas and understanding nothing. "That art thou" – a statement like a sea. You cannot walk on it, you cannot build on it. It runs like water through your fingers. "If you meet the Buddha on the way, kill him" – a statement like a mountain. You cannot see through it, you don't know what lies behind it. You have no idea what it means, what it is all about.

Just a few days before, I received a letter from America. Somebody must have read in one of my books somewhere: "If you meet the Buddha on the way, kill him." Now he was very angry. Must be a very poor Buddhist. He was so angry and annoyed that he wrote to me in great rage: "Who are you to tell us to kill the Buddha? How can you say such a sacrilegious thing? To kill the Buddha? Buddha has to be worshipped, not killed. Buddha is the greatest man who has walked on the earth. What do you mean by saying 'Kill the Buddha if you meet him on the way'?"

He was really angry. I can understand his anger. He does not understand Buddha, he does not understand these great statements. And it is not my statement either. Zen people have been saying it down the ages; it is more than two thousand years old at least. But he may not be aware of it. He must be thinking that I am somebody who is against Buddha. But Buddha is dead! If I am against him, how can I say kill him?

These statements are like mountains, great mountains. They are like Everest, very difficult to climb too — every possibility of never reaching to the understanding of them.

He could not understand, this American could not understand, because he must have been brought up in a Christian way, and then he may have become interested in Buddha. That is the problem. No Christian can say that: "If you meet Jesus on the way, kill him." That is not their language. They will think this is sacrilegious — that's what he writes in the letter: "This is sacrilegious! You must be an atheist, an irreligious person. You must be a Satan to say such a thing as 'Kill the Buddha.'" His upbringing must be Christian; that is another kind of language. He does not know the Zen way of saying things.

It is not said against Buddha — it contains Buddha's whole message! Buddha will absolutely agree with it. That's what he did when he was leaving the world. His last statement was exactly this. He said to his disciple, Ananda, who was weeping and crying, "Don't weep and cry for me! In fact I have been the barrier to you. Now the barrier is dying, you are free, and it may become more easy for you to be enlightened. Be a light unto yourself."

And Ananda had lived with Buddha for forty years, and lived unenlightened. And after Buddha was gone, within twenty-four hours, he became enlightened. What happened? He was clinging to the idea of Buddha. That very very clinging was a barrier.

It happened in Ramakrishna's case too:

He was a worshipper of Kali — the Mother goddess. And then he came across a very strange man, Totapuri. A man like Totapuri very rarely happens in the world. He was like Bodhidharma. A very very strange man. Naked he used to walk, utterly free from all kinds of morality, ethics, rules, regulations. He was a *paramahansa*, a *jivan mukta* — he was free in his life, absolutely free. Freedom was his quality. Just wandering around the Ganges, he came to Dakshineshwar. Ramakrishna saw him, became interested in him. He had never seen such a freedom, and such grace and such beauty. And he asked him, "Help me."

He looked at Ramakrishna and he said, "Yes, I will help you. But the only thing is: you will have to destroy this Mother goddess."

Ramakrishna started shaking and trembling and perspiring. He said, "What are you saying? How can I destroy the Mother goddess? She is my Mother! She has helped me up to now. She is my all in all. She is my soul, my very heart. I will die!"

Totapuri said, "So better die, but kill this Mother. If you really want to have freedom, you have to destroy all connections and all attachments. And this is your attachment. You are not attached to your wife, so that is not a problem. You are not attached to money, so that is not the problem. You are not attached to the world, so that is not the problem. Your whole attachment is with this Mother, this idea of a Mother goddess. And I know, it is beautiful, but still it will keep you away from the truth."

Ramakrishna would sit in meditation in front of Totapuri, but the moment he would close his eyes, the Mother goddess was there with all her glory. And he would start swaying, and tears would come in his eyes. And he would forget all about Totapuri and his freedom. And Totapuri would shake him up and he would say, "You have again fallen into the dream. It is all dream! Why don't you take a sword and cut her in two pieces? Destroy her!"

It happened many times and Ramakrishna was not able...What to say about cutting? — he would forget all about Totapuri and the idea that he had given him. And he would look at the face of the Mother inside, and it was so alive and so beautiful, so full of light. It was no ordinary experience: it was the greatest vision, the ultimate vision of form, God as form, beyond which is only the formless.

Totapuri got fed up and he said, "Now, today I leave. Before I leave, you try once more, and I have brought this piece of glass."

Ramakrishna said, "For what?"

He said, "When I see that your tears start coming and you start swaying and you are feeling orgasmic, I will cut on your third eye with this glass. Blood will start coming. And I will cut deep, just to remind you that I am here! Just to remind you: take the sword and cut the Mother in two pieces."

And Ramakrishna said, "From where to bring the sword?"

And Totapuri said, "From where have you brought this Mother? From the same source — it is all imagination."

And that day Ramakrishna tried. Totapuri cut his third eye with that piece of glass. Blood started flowing, and he pushed the glass deep into the third eye. In a single moment of awareness, Ramakrishna took a sword, cut the Mother in two pieces. The Mother disappeared, and it opened the door for the formless.

For six days he was in samadhi. And when he came back, the first words that he uttered were, "The last barrier has fallen. I am infinitely grateful to you, Master Totapuri — infinitely grateful to you. The last barrier has fallen."

This is the meaning when Zen people say, or I say to you, "If you meet the Buddha on the way, kill him." In fact I should say to you, "If you meet me on the way, kill me" — because you may not meet Buddha, you may meet me. "On the way" means when you start moving from form to no-form, your master will be the last barrier. You have become so attached to the master. You have been in such love with the master. You have enjoyed so many delights and ecstasies through him. It seems sheer ungratefulness to cut him — no, it is not. But this is a Zen way of saying a thing.

Christians will feel offended, Jains will feel offended, Hindus will feel offended, Mohammedans will feel offended — this is not the right way to talk about your master!

Different mystics have chosen different ways of speaking, but if you look deep down the message is not very different. Containers are different but the content is not different. And everybody has to choose his way of speaking, and has to choose the way that his disciples will understand.

A psychology professor conducted an experiment to prove a point about work. He hired a man to hit a log with the reverse side of an axe. The man was told that he would be paid twice the amount he normally made. The fellow lasted half a day. He gave it up, explaining, "I have to see the chips fly."

Now, a man who cuts wood, if he is told to cut the wood with the reverse side of the axe, soon will lose his enthusiasm. He needs to see the chips fly — they keep his enthusiasm, they keep him moving, they keep his energy flowing. That is his language! He can work only in that language. That is his noe-sphere — without that he cannot function.

And each mystic has to speak according to himself and according to the disciples that gather around him. And each mystic attracts a certain kind of people. Can't you see it: here, a certain kind of people has gathered — the people of the future. You will not find orthodox people here, you cannot find. Impossible. You will not find the puritans here, the moralists. You will not find the hypocrites here. This is not the place for them! I am not the man for them.

One French orientalist went to see George Gurdjieff. Just once he went to see him. The orientalist used to live in Paris; Guénon was his name. And just close by, a few miles away from Paris, was Gurdjieff. But only once he went, for half an hour. And then he came back and he started talking against Gurdjieff — he talked his whole life against Gurdjieff. He used to say to people: "Flee from Gurdjieff as you flee from the plague — just flee from him! He is the most dangerous kind of disease on the earth." What happened? He was a moralist, very very puritan. And what he saw there in half an hour's time was very very different.

Gurdjieff used to force people who were not drinkers, he would force them to drink as much as possible. Now, that was his device. When a man is utterly drunk, he becomes very very real and honest. This is a very bad state of affairs, but this is how it is. People have become so false that to see their original face you have to wait...only when they are absolutely drunk. Then their masks slip by; they cannot hold them, they are so drunk. Everything becomes shaky and they start coming up in their true colors.

So each disciple had to go through that torture. It was torture for somebody who had not been drinking too much or who was against alcohol. Just think of Morarji Desai: if he had gone to Gurdjieff...! He would force people to drink so much that they would fall on the ground, start uttering nonsense, shouting, shrieking, abusing. And that was his way of watching them: then he would sit silently and watch, listen to them. Once he had understood your reality, then there was no problem – then the work started. But you reveal your reality only when you are drunk. Otherwise, you maintain your false face.

This moralist saw this happening, and he was aghast. He could not understand it. Sometimes orthodox people come here, but they escape; they never come back again. It is a different kind of commune. I can be understood only by the new man that is going to be born, that is on the way. The past cannot understand me. So I have to use the language of the future.

And you know, everybody has to use his own language.

I have heard:

If a lawyer wishes to give someone an orange, he might say, "I give you all and singular my estate and interest, right title and claim, and advantage of and in this orange, with all its rind, skin, juice, pulp and pips, and all right and advantages therein with full power to bite, cut, suck or otherwise eat the same orange, or give the same away, with or without its rind, skin, juice, pulp, pips, anything therefore or hereinafter or in any deed or deeds, instruments of what kind or nature whatsoever, to the contrary in anywise notwithstanding."

Now just one orange he is giving to somebody! But this is the way a lawyer speaks, the way of the law.

Two tramps are sitting underneath a tree. First tramp, lying on a park bench underneath the tree, "I just dreamt I had a job."
Second tramp, "Yes, you look tired."

There are languages and languages. The mystics also happen in all kinds of shapes and sizes. And, of course, they have to use the language that they know, and the language that they would like to be understood by the people. And the language that they use has to be expressive of their experience.

Kabir speaks in one way, Krishna in another, Nanak in still another — they were people of different centuries, different atmospheres, different climates, and they were talking to different kinds of people and different potentialities.

The fifth question:

Osho,
Why am I so nice to others and so hard with myself?

Let me tell you one story:

"Preacher," complained an aggravated young waggoner, "I am at my wits' end about my horses. They don't eat anything but hamburgers and french fries. Already they're so skinny I'm afraid they won't last much longer."

"Let me ask you something," said the preacher. "Do you pray every day?"

"Why, er–uh–not usually," the driver stammered.

"Do you always wash your hands before every meal?"

"Not always."

"And do you ask God's blessings before you eat?"

"No!" the driver answered tersely.

"Then all is perfectly clear," said the preacher. "It is irrevocably intertwined with the divine law of compensation. Since you eat like a horse, your horses eat like humans."

You ask, Why am I so nice to others and so hard with myself?

It is the law of compensation. If you are so nice with others, you will be hard with yourself. You really want to be hard with others, but you are hiding it, you are repressing it. It becomes accumulated in you. And you can't be hard with others; you have been taught not to be hard with others. So finally, where are you going to pour your garbage? Only you are left.

It almost always happens: people who are nice to others are hard on themselves — they have to be. There are ordinarily only two types of people: the murderers and the suicides. Murderers are people who are dangerous to others, very dangerous — they can kill. And the people who are not dangerous to others tend to be dangerous to themselves — they can commit suicide.

There is no necessity to be divided in two categories, you can go beyond them. And that's my teaching. There is no need to decide a priori that you have to be hard with others or you have to be nice with others. You have to be conscious in yourself. It is not a question of being hard or nice to anybody — you have to be conscious inside yourself. And the first effect will be that you will be nice to yourself. The first ripple of being conscious is being nice to oneself — the first ripple of consciousness is self-love.

You will be surprised to know this, because you have always been taught that self-love is a kind of selfishness — it is not. It is the foundation of all altruistic love. Self-love is the base of all possible love — love with your wife, love with your children, love with your God. Unless you love yourself you cannot love anybody else.

Meditate over Jesus' saying: Love thy neighbor as thyself. But thyself comes first. People have started loving their neighbors and have forgotten that they don't love themselves. So when you love your neighbor and you don't find him very loving — and you have to love him because you have been taught, and this is good manners, and civilization and culture, respectability comes through it, and you love your neighbor — you will hate yourself. Then the law of compensation will work.

And if you hate yourself, how can you love your neighbor? You can only pretend; only on the surface can you show. Deep down, you would like to murder him. Deep down, you are full of hate. This is the situation that has happened to humanity.

My approach is totally different: Be conscious! And the first ripple will be self-love, you will love yourself, because you are closest to yourself. And it has to start there. Just as you throw a stone in a silent lake and ripples arise, first they arise just around the stone, and then they spread towards the bank. Then they go on spreading.....

Love yourself. For that you have to be very conscious. Only a conscious person can love himself, because only a conscious person knows that "I am not there, but God is." How can you love yourself? You don't know who is there. You have not even tasted anything there, you have not seen anybody there. It is all darkness.

And you have been taught that you are ugly, that you are worthless: "Improve upon yourself! Be this! Be that!" Nobody has told you to accept yourself. Everybody has been telling you to reject yourself, so you hate yourself and then you become hard with yourself. Hatred is hard. And then whatsoever you go on thinking about that "I am soft and nice to others," that softness and niceness is hypocrisy, it is not true — it can't be true.

A real niceness for others can arise only if you are nice with yourself. Start from there. Forget all about what you have been told. Your priorities are all wrong. Don't put the other as more important than you. Nobody is more important than you. You are the most important person in the world, you are the center of the world. And I am not telling you to become egoistic: I am simply saying a truth — that each is a center to the whole world, to the whole universe. God exists in you, you have to be the center. I am not saying that others are not centers — everybody is. But how are you going to understand others' significance if you don't know your significance?

Love yourself. And out of that love a great love will arise for others, because they are also like you.

And the last question:

Osho,

What is the trade secret of the priests? How have they been able
to exploit man for so long?

It is very simple. Just a few stories will make it clear to you:

Two music students were discussing their part-time jobs. Said one, "I work in the opera at night and carry a spear in one act."

His friend asked, "How do you manage to keep awake so late at night?"

"It's simple," replied the first. "The man behind me carries a spear too."

The second story:

Preacher Pitts had undertaken that morning to describe the terrors of hell to his congregation.

"Brothers and sisters," he intoned, "some of you have seen melted iron running out of a furnace, haven't you? It's white, sizzling and hissing. Well, in the place I'm talking about, they use that stuff for ice cream."

Reverend Walker stood before his congregation and in dynamic fashion pontificated on the wickedness of intercourse. After twenty minutes of ranting about the sin of sex, he raised himself to full height, leaned over the pulpit, and boomed:

"Brothers and sisters, if there are any among you who have committed adultery, may your tongue cleave to the woof of your mowf."

And if you make people afraid, you also become afraid. It works both ways. So it is not only that the priest has made you afraid – he himself has become afraid, he is also trembling.

Fear has been their trade secret. Create fear in people, and when people are frightened they are ready to become slaves, then they are ready to do anything.

I want you to be absolutely free of fear. There is no fear. This existence is yours, there is no hell — unless you decide to create one. Then it is a private affair. Then you can create it. But there is no hell! It is all heaven. And heaven is not in the end when you reach God, no. Heaven is all the way to God. Each moment is heavenly. The whole journey is heavenly.

Heaven is a way of looking at things, and hell too. But in the past the fear has been used as a trade secret. And joined with fear is greed. That is another side of the same coin. One side is fear, another side is greed. Both have been exploited. And a really religious person is one who is free of fear and greed.

And if you are free of fear and greed, you will be free from the exploitations that have been going on and on down the centuries. Because of it, religion has not been of any help to humanity; rather, it has been a curse, it has not been a blessing. Make it a blessing. Drop fear and greed. Live joyously! Live in a heavenly way this moment, now.

Live...love...be...and forget all fears. There is nothing to be afraid of. We are part of this existence. This existence is not antagonistic to us. It is very friendly. It has created us! How can it be inimical? And there is nobody sitting there counting your sins, and nobody is there to punish you. God is not to be feared.

And if there is fear, you cannot love. Fear kills all capacity to love. In all the languages of the world, there are words like "god-fearing" — they are ugly words. Drop them. Never use them. Let this religion be a religion of love — be god loving. And then you are out of the grip and the trap of the priest.

And not only are you out of the grip and the trap of the priest — you will free the priest too. He is also suffering with you. Continuously talking to you again and again about hell and heaven, he also becomes convinced of it. It is not that only you are the victim — he is also a victim. It has become a nightmare to all.

This is what I mean by a new religious consciousness in the world: free of fear and greed. The whole energy has to be poured as celebration....

Enough for today.

CHAPTER 5

YES, JUST LIKE THAT

A Sufi teacher was visited by a number of people of various faiths who said to him, "Accept us as your disciples, for we see that there is no remaining truth in our religions, and we are certain that what you are teaching is the one true path."

The Sufi said, "Have you not heard of the Mongol Halaku Khan and his invasion of Syria? Let me tell you.

"The Vizier Ahmad of the Caliph Mustasim of Baghdad invited the Mongol to invade his master's domains. When Halaku had won the battle for Baghdad, Ahmad went out to meet him, to be rewarded. Halaku said, 'Do you seek your recompense?' and the Vizier answered, 'Yes.'

"Halaku told him, 'You have betrayed your own master to me, and yet you expect me to believe that you will be faithful to me.' He ordered that Ahmad should be hanged.

"Before you ask anyone to accept you, ask yourself whether it is not simply because you have not followed the path of your own teacher. If you are satisfied about this, then come and ask to become disciples."

What is man's basic problem? It is not ignorance, it is knowledge. Knowledge is always borrowed. It is never original. But one can believe that one knows and can befool others and can be befooled oneself.

Knowledge is the greatest deceptive force in the world. It makes people cunning, hypocrites, egoists. It gives them false notions that they know — that they know what truth is, that they know what "the true path" is. And because of this, they go on missing.

They come across truth many times, but they cannot see. Their eyes are full of knowledge, hence blind. A knowledgeable man is a blind man. He is cunning and clever, but not intelligent. Cunningness and cleverness look like intelligence, but that is only an appearance. And don't be deceived by the appearance, because it is there where man's basic confusion is rooted — in his cleverness, his cunningness, his knowledgeability.

One has to unlearn it all, then only does one become a disciple. If you know already, you can't be a disciple; your very knowledge will hinder you. How can you surrender when you know? Knowledge never surrenders. It is only innocence that is capable of that great quantum leap.

Surrender is possible only out of innocence, because out of innocence arises trust, out of innocence is faith, out of innocence is all religion.

I have heard a beautiful anecdote:

A great master, Zusya, went to suffer the exile in Germany. He came to a city of Reform Jews. When they saw his ways, they mocked him and thought he was crazy. When he came into the synagogue, some of them poked fun at him, and when the children saw their parents ridiculing him, they thought he was crazy and began to pull at him and tug at his belt. Then he beckoned to the children and said, "My dear children, gather round and I will tell you something." The children thought he would show them a trick. They all stood around him and he in the middle. And he said to them, "My dear children, look well at me, do not take your eyes off me."

The children, because they thought he was going to show them something, looked steadily at him and he also looked steadily at each child separately. After that he told them to go home.

When the children came home and were given their food, they refused to eat. One said that the meat must not be eaten. Another asked how one could eat unclean meat. And so all the children refused to eat. They said the dishes were unclean and the food was unclean.

Then, as women do, one went to another and told her that all of a sudden her son came home from the prayer house and refused to eat; whatever was given to him, he said it was unclean. Then her neighbor said that her son too refused to eat and shouted that everything was unclean and that one could not pray in her house because her hair was uncovered. Then another neighbor came in and also told such things about her son — the whole town was amazed! Then they each learnt that their sons were not the only ones who suddenly became pious. They said that the visitor whom they had ridiculed and thought crazy was none other than a saint. By looking at the children, he had instilled in them something of his being. The parents became afraid that they had shamed him and went to beg his forgiveness.

Zusya laughed and forgave them all. He wanted to look in their eyes too, but they escaped as fast as they could.

In this beautiful anecdote, what happened? The children were innocent. They were ready to look into the eyes of this strange master. They became connected! For a moment they were lost into the vastness of the master; for a moment the master flowed in them. There was a meeting and a merging, a communion.

Just looking in their eyes for a few moments, something was transferred — the purity of the man, the holiness of the man. Something of his being spilled into the eyes of the children. They were no more the same. Their vision changed.

But the grown-ups escaped. They were afraid to look into the eyes of the master. What was their fear? They were cunning, clever, knowledgeable. They must have thought, "It is a kind of hypnosis or something. This man is a magician or something." They must have thought of a thousand and one things: "The time is not ripe for us. We cannot go on this faraway journey. The moment has not come. We will have to wait. We have to do a thousand and one other things, then...."

They were not innocent. Even their apology was out of cunningness; it was not out of love and understanding. They were afraid: if the man is so strange and powerful, he may do something wrong to them. Hence the apology. Not out of understanding, not out of humbleness, but out of fear.

But the children? – they simply got in tune with the master!

Jesus is right when he says: Unless you are like small children you will not enter into my kingdom of God.

Jesus was standing in a marketplace; a crowd was standing around him, and somebody asked, a rabbi, "You talk so much about the kingdom of God, but who will be capable enough, pure enough, virtuous enough, saintly enough, to enter into your kingdom of God? What will be the characteristics of the people who will be allowed in?"

Jesus looked around. The rabbi thought he would say, "People like you." And the rich man of the town who had donated much to the synagogue and who had been a charitable man thought he would say, "Men like you."

And there was another who had practised all that has been told down the ages, all the rituals, prayers. He had followed every rule and regulation. He was a virtuous man, known as a saint. He thought, "Certainly, he is searching for me. He will say, 'Men like you.'"

But they were all frustrated. His eyes moved...he stopped at a small child who was just standing in the crowd. He took the child up and showed the people that "Those who are like this small child, they will be able to enter into my kingdom of God."

It is innocence that falls in harmony with the divine. Knowledge is a jarring note. Knowledge is a China Wall. Knowledge is an armour, your defence against the mysterious. But that's what happens.

People who are knowledgeable start searching for truth. And they have taken one thing for granted, that they already know what it is. Now it is only a question of searching. They will be able to recognize it, they know its characteristics.

It is not so. Unless you know truth, there is no way to know it. No scripture can describe it. There is no possibility of anybody giving you the knowledge of truth. A master never gives the knowledge of truth to you; he simply makes his truth available to you. If you are courageous, if you are innocent, if you are open, ready to take the jump, ready to die in the master, then you will know truth — not knowledge about truth but an experience of it. Truth always comes as an experience. It is always existential.

Remember: these are the barriers. The man who has followed all the rituals thinks he knows. He is a great yogi. He has not been missing a single rule of the yoga. He thinks now he is capable. He is not. It is not ritual that prepares you. Ritualistic people are stupid people. They follow the ritual, but the ritual is followed unconsciously. And they will find ways and means to go on following the ritual and yet remain the same.

I have heard:

A doleful-looking customer went to the bar and ordered six whiskies. The barman poured them out for him in six glasses. "Now line them up in front of me, will you?" asked the customer. He then paid for them and told him to keep the change. He swallowed down the contents of the first glass in line and then repeated the process with the third and fifth glasses. Then, saying, "Goodnight," he turned to walk away.

"Excuse me," said the barman. "You have left three glasses untouched."

"Yes, I know," he said. "The doctor said he didn't mind me taking the odd drink."

You can always find a way. The ritualistic person remains cunning.

A politician, who had been prevailed upon to accompany a

friend on a bear hunt, had concealed his nervousness manfully, although his first night in camp was a sleepless one. Starting forth in the morning, the two had walked but a short distance when they came upon fresh tracks which the enthusiastic sportsman identified as being those of a large bear.

"Tell you what we had better do," said the politician brightly. "You go ahead and see where he went and I'll go back and see where he came from!"

Remember that man is so cunning, so political, that he can always find a way out of a certain ritual, rule, discipline. And he can remain untouched by it. And he can go on doing the ritual and yet remain untransformed by it. That's why you see so many people in the world going to the synagogue, to the church, to the temple, to the mosque, to the gurudwara — and still remaining the same! Millions of people are praying, but there seems to be no prayer in existence, there seems to be no fragrance of prayer in the world. There is but hatred and hatred. There seems to be no love! How is it possible that millions of people pray every day and there is no love flowering? So many people praying and no compassion! Something deep down must be wrong, fundamentally wrong.

The prayer is false. It is being done because it has to be done. It is a kind of duty to be fulfilled, but the heart is not in it. The cunning man always keeps his heart away from everything that he does; he only pretends. He goes through empty gestures. And he is so cunning that he can always find a loophole and escape through it.

The basic problem of man is not ignorance: it is knowledge. Ignorance never makes a person cunning.

Those who are really ready to become disciples, they have to drop only one thing and that is their knowledge. They have to become ignorant again. And when you become consciously ignorant, ignorance becomes luminous. The whole point is of consciousness. You can remain unconsciously very knowledgeable, and your knowledge remains dark, dismal, dead. If you become consciously ignorant, even your ignorance becomes enlightened. It is luminous. It is full of light.

And remember: when you consciously look at your life, you are bound to become ignorant again – because knowledge as such is not possible. Life remains a mystery. There is no way to demystify it. That's what knowledge is trying to do: it is a demystification of life. It tries to destroy mystery. It makes everything clear, explained away.

The whole effort of knowledge is how to banish mystery from existence. It cannot be banished. It is its ultimate nature. It is not an accidental quality. Mystery is the very core of life. Life is mysterious – they are synonymous.

So the man of knowledge does not destroy the mystery of life. He simply closes his eyes with a very thick curtain of knowledge, and starts thinking he knows. He knows nothing.

It will look strange to you and very paradoxical, but it is so. The man who knows, knows nothing. And the man who knows that he is ignorant has started knowing. The whole point is of consciousness.

A conscious ignorance is what disciplehood is – conscious ignorance. But people are living in unconsciousness. And they go on groping. In unconsciousness they go to the masters, but in unconsciousness. They remain with the masters but fast asleep. Sooner or later they become fed up, because nothing is happening. Nothing can happen if you remain unconscious. You cannot connect with the master. They remain cunning, clever, even when they are with a master. Nothing happens. Nothing can happen in knowledgeability.

Sooner or later they decide that this is not the right master – without ever thinking, "Am I the right disciple yet?" That should be the basic question. It is none of your business who is the right master or not. And how can you decide? You don't know what a master is. You are not even a disciple yet! You have not taken even the first step and you are thinking and deciding and judging about the last step. It is better to keep quiet.

Just think about one thing again and again, remind yourself again and again: "Am I the right disciple? Am I ready to learn? Have I dropped my knowledge? Have I come with an open heart? Am I trying to become more conscious of what I am doing? Is my prayer conscious? When I sit by the side of the master, am I sitting there consciously, alert, aware? When I listen to the master, am I really listening? Or just hearing?"

Hearing is one thing: listening is very different. Hearing is simple; anybody hears. Whosoever has ears can hear. Listening is rare. When your ear and your heart are together, then listening happens. When you hear, your mind is full of thoughts; the turmoil continues, the traffic continues. All kinds of noises, thoughts, prejudices...through that crowd, yes, you hear, but you can't listen. For listening, silence is needed. There should be no clouds inside you, no thought stirring. Just a pure silence, then listening happens.

The disciple has to ask again and again, "Am I really a disciple? Am I yet a disciple?" And if you remain alert about that, you will find many masters in life. But if you are not aware of it, you may come to a Buddha and go empty-handed.

Hank was riding the range, a-singing and a-humming. Suddenly his horse reared and stopped. In front of them was a huge snake. Hank drew his gun and was about to fire when the snake cried, "Don't shoot! If you spare my life, I have the power to grant you any three wishes you make!"

"Okay," said Hank, figuring he had nothing to lose. "My first wish is a handsome face like Paul Newman. Second I want a muscular body like Mohammed Ali. And my last wish is to be equipped like my horse here!"

"Granted!" said the snake. "When you wake up tomorrow you'll have all those things."

Next morning, Hank awoke and rushed to the mirror. Sure enough, he had a face like Paul Newman and to his delight he saw a pair of massive shoulders and arms like Mohammed Ali. Then, glancing down in great excitement he let out a blood-curdling howl.

"My gawd, I clean forgot!" he babbled. "Yesterday I was riding Nellie!"

Man lives in unconsciousness, unaware. And you can even be with a Buddha and nothing is going to happen to you. Your unconsciousness will be a mountain.

The vibes of a Buddha are very delicate. They cannot penetrate your mountains of unconsciousness. If you are conscious, then only can those delicate vibes penetrate you. They are subtle, they are not violent, they are not aggressive. They will not even knock on your doors, they will not force entry into you. The vibes of a Buddha cannot rape. They come very silently. If you are utterly quiet, only then do you become aware of their presence. They come without any noise...rose petals falling on the ground. Yes, just like that.

But it is very easy to decide that the master is wrong. In fact, that helps you to remain the way you are: what can you do? — the master is wrong. And then you go on moving from one master to another and hoping.... But you remain the same! If you miss one master, you will miss all of them. In fact, the more you go from one master to another master, you are simply becoming more and more accustomed to missing, you are becoming habituated to it. You are learning how to miss. If you miss one, then to miss the other will be easier, and then to miss the third will be even easier. And if you have been moving to many masters, slowly slowly, you become so efficient in missing that it is almost certain that you will never find a master anywhere.

That's why people can't find — not that masters don't exist. Life is so rich! Existence always gives you all possibilities to grow. Masters are available, and always. In no time, in no country, is it that they are not available. In no clime. However dark is the time on the earth, the masters are always available. In fact, the darker it is, the more possibility there is of masters being available.

Krishna says: When it is dark and religion is destroyed, I will come. I always come.

So the moments of darkness, of miserable times, are the opportunities for masters to bloom. The physicians happen when people are ill. Nature always balances. It always provides for your needs.

Just watch: a woman becomes pregnant, and her whole body starts preparing for the child. By the time the child is born, suddenly

her breasts are full of milk. The child is not born yet but food is
getting ready. Nature provides all that is needed — even for a child
who has not even asked, who cannot ask. Before the child comes,
the food has arrived. Before the hunger, the food. Before the thirst,
the water.

And before the disciple, the master. So if you are a disciple, you
are bound to find a master. It has never been otherwise. If you cannot
find a master, think again, meditate over it — are you a disciple? And
you will find you are too full of knowledge. That's why you cannot
be a disciple.

A disciple means one who is ready to learn, and a man full of
knowledge is not ready to learn. He is ready to teach. He is not ready
to learn.

Are you a disciple? A disciple is one who is ready to surrender,
to bow down, to drop his head. Are you ready to die? Are you ready
to stake all that you have? Nobody seems to be ready to die. In fact,
people need a master, not to die but to live forever. They would like
to become immortals. They would like to find the elixir that will
make them immortals. They would like to find something so that
they can fight with death. Yes, that is found! But you have to fulfill
the condition first. And the condition is: only those who are ready
to die will attain to life eternal.

A very ancient story, a true story, and of great significance:

In some monastery in Tibet, a monk who was thought to be
dead was buried in a crypt. After a time he regained consciousness
and horror and mental conflict set in. The crypt was opened only
when a brother died, and it was impossible to call loud enough or
to knock hard enough to be heard. What, then, was the unfortunate
man to do? Was he to wait for a death of starvation and thirst, there
in the neighborhood of his dead brethren? He began to pray — but
was not prayer a supplication that God might grant death to one of
his healthy brethren? Because the crypt would be opened only when
somebody died in the monastery again. That was the only possibility
for him to get out: if somebody died immediately.

Against such horrible mental and physical agonies — you can

well complete the picture – our dear monk held out and remained alive. He kept himself alive by eating insects which fell down into the crypt through a small air-hole, and he licked the drops of moisture from the walls, dirty sewage water.

After many years, they found the unfortunate man wrapped in cloaks... when somebody died the crypt was opened, after many years. They found the unfortunate man wrapped in cloaks which he pulled out of the coffins, and with his white beard reaching to the ground.

He was utterly blind by now, but still alive and still hoping and praying. He was taken out. He lived at least ten years more.

Man clings to life – even if when to live is worse than death. Just think of this man! eating insects, living with dead bodies, the smell. Think of that crypt: hundreds of dead bodies around, just licking drops of moisture from the walls, and waiting and praying for somebody to die. He went blind! Years and years in that darkness, but still hoping to live.

Such is the desire for life. Such is the lust for life. And to be with a master one has to be ready to die – not physically: metaphorically. But even the idea of death makes people run away.

But to be in contact with a master, you have to slowly slowly disappear, metaphysically disappear: the ego has to die. Jesus says: Until you are reborn...but how can you be reborn if you don't die? Rebirth has to be preceded by a death. And the death has to be deeper than the bodily death, because the bodily death is not much of a death. Soon you are born again. Here you die and, within moments, you have entered into another womb somewhere else. There is not even a gap: one body you lose, another body you immediately gain.

But to die in the presence of a master is to really die, it is real suicide. The ego disappears forever. That is the meaning of surrender. It is difficult. The disciple comes, he bows down also, but that bowing is false. He says, "I am at your disposal," but that is an empty gesture.

After an hour's lecture on duty to King and Country, putting others before self and so on, the education corps captain pointed to one private and said, "Right — you! Why should a soldier be prepared to die for his country?"

The soldier scratched his head for a minute, then grinned and said, "You're quite right, sir — why should he?"

Just to think of death frightens. Don't laugh at those people who escaped from Zusya — Zusya was death. A master is death. That's what ancient scriptures say: A master is a death. Those people escaped! The children were innocent. They were not afraid because they didn't know what it is to look into the eyes of a master.

People avoid looking into the eyes of the master. They avoid getting too close, because to be too close is to melt, is to disappear, never to be the same again.

Remember these things....

The story:

> A Sufi teacher was visited by a number of people of various faiths who said to him, "Accept us as your disciples, for we see that there is no remaining truth in our religions, and we are certain that what you are teaching is the one true path."

Let us go into each important word in the story:

> A Sufi teacher was visited by a number of people of various faiths who said to him...

A Sufi teacher, a Sufi master, is not there to destroy your religion but to fulfill it. If he destroys anything, that means it is not religion — that's why he destroys it. If it is religion, he supports it, he enhances it. He is not against any path. All paths are God's paths. So if he finds somebody is following a path, he gives all his support. He will not take you astray from the path that you have been following. He will strengthen it.

A Sufi master is not a missionary. He is not interested in

converting people from one religion to another. He is interested
certainly in converting people from irreligion to religion, but not
from Christianity to Mohammedanism or from Mohammedanism
to Buddhism, or from Buddhism to Hinduism. A Sufi is not
interested in changing people's identities, superficial identities. It
never makes much difference. I have seen many Hindus who have
become Christians — they remain the same. Nothing ever changes.
It can't change! because of their conditioning.

I used to live with a friend whose father was converted to
Christianity, but they still think themselves Brahmins. Untouchables
are not allowed in his family. They are Christian Brahmins, but
Brahmins they are. The whole thing continues.

I have seen Christians becoming Hindus. It makes no
difference.

I have heard about Mulla Nasruddin, who became an atheist
in his old age. One day he was trying to convert somebody to his
atheism, and was very loud. Finally he said, "There is no God — and
Mohammed is his only prophet."

It is very difficult. You can become an atheist, but if you have
been a Mohammedan, deep down you remain a Mohammedan
— Mohammed is the only prophet.

I have heard about another atheist who was dying, and he said,
"Thank God that there is no God!"

It is very difficult to get out of your conditioning. A Sufi master is
not interested in changing your rituals, but he is certainly interested
in giving you more and more religious quality. It is not a question
of form: it is a question of quality. Whether you go to the mosque
or to the temple does not matter! The real thing is prayer — where
you pray is immaterial.

Just remember always, this is the Sufi approach: where you
pray is immaterial — prayer matters. To whom you bow down is
immaterial — bowing down matters. To whom you surrender has no
meaning — but that you have surrendered is of immense importance.

Surrender has importance and relevance. The object of surrender is just an excuse.

You can go to one master, A, and surrender, or to master B and surrender, or to master C and surrender — it makes no difference. If you are surrendered, you have started moving towards God. The master is just an excuse. Any master will do. So whatsoever is your liking, whosoever is of your liking, wherever you feel surrender is easier, surrender. The Sufi helps you to surrender, to pray. It does not matter whether you pray in Arabic or in Sanskrit or in Hebrew, but what you say in your prayer matters.

I have heard:

After five-year-old Matt gave a loud whistle in the middle of the minister's sermon, his grandmother launched into scolding.

"Why on earth would you do such a thing?" she demanded.

"I've been praying for a long time that God would teach me to whistle," he explained, "And this morning he did."

A child's prayer is a child's prayer. What can he ask? He is asking God to give him the capacity to whistle. Just look at people's prayer, what they are asking, and you will find it all childish. Somebody is asking for money.... Which is nothing but a capacity to whistle, so everybody can see who is whistling more loudly, more sharply, so you can defeat other whistlers. That's what money is all about: so you can whistle. Somebody is praying to be made a prime minister or a president. That is again the same: asking to be given the capacity to whistle so loudly that the whole country, the whole world listens.

All are asking for the ego, for some importance, for some superiority. All are wanting to defeat others, all are competitors. And how can you pray if your mind is full of competition, jealousy? How can you pray if your mind is not full of love?

The real prayer does not ask for anything. The real prayer is a thanking. It simply gives thankfulness to God for all that he has already given. There is no complaint in it.

A Sufi master is one who helps you for the essential religion. And the essential religion is one. Hinduism, Christianity, Jainism,

Buddhism, Judaism — these are forms, forms of different rituals. These are different languages, but the message is one.

> A Sufi teacher was visited by a number of people of various faiths who said to him, "accept us as your disciples, for we see that there is no remaining truth in our religions..."

Now, these people have been followers of somebody else. When you go to a Sufi master, he will not accept you so easily — because you have been a follower of somebody else. What have you been doing there? If you have missed that master, you will miss this too. What is the point of changing? Maybe you will feel for a few days that you are again on a kind of honeymoon, a new love affair. But if the old love affair is finished, this too will be finished sooner or later. It may give you a little thrill and sensation. You may start dreaming and hoping again, but nothing is going to happen. Not essentially. Because you will go on doing the same that you have done with your old masters. Unless you change. Unless you understand that there is something lacking in you, not in the master but in you. Unless you take the responsibility that "I have been missing," there is no point in accepting disciples. Sufis won't accept you. But if a disciple comes who has done all that he could do, their doors are open.

I would like you to be reminded of Gautam Buddha: he went to many masters in his search — that's how a disciple should be. And he surrendered to many masters, and he surrendered totally. He was not holding back. Whatsoever the master with whom he was at that time would say, he would do it totally.

It is said that his masters would finally say to him, "We are sorry. In fact, we have not attained it either. We are pretenders. You have exposed us. We cannot deceive you. We don't know a thing. Our deception goes on because people who come to us never listen to what we say — they never do it, so we are never exposed. You are the first person who has done whatsoever we say, and now we are feeling sorry for you. Excuse us. Forgive us!"

That's what the masters said. They were not masters. But Buddha's sincerity, his honesty, provoked even those deceivers to feel sorry. He worked so hard. And sometimes their demands were stupid.

For example, one master, so-called master, said to him, "Go on reducing your food till you are taking only one grain of rice – go on reducing, slowly slowly." He did that. He became just bones; all flesh disappeared. Just a skeleton he was. The master must have felt...he was saying this to many people but nobody had ever followed it, so there was no problem. But this man, his sincerity, his utter devotion, his trust.... When there is so much trust, even the people who exploit trust cannot exploit such trust.

It is said he fell at Buddha's feet and said, "Excuse me. Please forgive me. I have sinned against you and against God. I have committed a crime. I had never thought that anybody was going to follow what I say. And I have been making such strange demands that nobody will follow. And when nobody follows, there is no question of ever being exposed."

That's why your so-called masters go on demanding the impossible from you. They will say, "Repress sex and don't ever think of any beautiful woman, not even in your dreams." Now, first they say, "Repress sex." If you repress it, your dreams will become full of sexuality. And then they say that even to dream about sex is a sin – you will never attain to God. If you follow them, you will be in difficulty. But nobody follows.

And when people don't follow, they feel guilty that "We have not been following the master." Out of their guilt they touch his feet; out of their guilt they go on following him.

Buddha went from one master to another. For six years he travelled all around the country, and it always happened: his sincerity was such that each master told him, "Please, you forgive us and you go and search somewhere else." He searched long and went to many people, but he never left the master till the master himself said to him, "Now you leave me. It is becoming unbearable. You go on doing whatsoever I say and nothing is happening, because what I am saying is absolutely fabricated, guesswork. I have not known myself"

This is the way of a disciple. If such a disciple comes to a Sufi master, he will welcome him, he will embrace him to his heart. He will take him to his innermost bosom. But these people were not like that. They said to the master:

> "Accept us as your disciples, for we see that there is no remaining truth in our religions..."

How can you see? You are so blind. How can you see that there is no truth in your religions? This assertion is egoistic. A real seeker will say, "Maybe there is, but I am blind, I cannot see it. Give me eyes! Help me to see." A real seeker will say, "It is not that there is no truth in religions, but I have not been able to see it. It must be my fault." He will take all the responsibility on his own shoulders.

To throw the responsibility on somebody else is an old ego trick. Beware of it. It never wants to take the responsibility on itself. It always goes on complaining about others. If you are not achieving, then something is wrong somewhere, but you are not wrong.

If you go on following whatsoever you are doing, if you do it sincerely, and then you come to know that you have done it as totally as is humanly possible and nothing has happened, then it is time to move. A Sufi master accepts only those who move in such a way. But these people were saying:

> "Accept us as your disciples, for we see that there is no remaining truth in our religions, and we are certain..."

Now only stupid people can be certain about such mysteries.

Wise people will be hesitant; intelligent people will not be so certain, cannot be. How can you be certain? And they said:

> "...And we are certain that what you are teaching is the one true path."

And this they must have said to other teachers too.

Mulla Nasruddin was in love with a woman. One full-moon night, sitting on the beach, he told the woman, "You are the most beautiful woman in the world. Never has there been any woman so beautiful, never will there be ever."

The woman was thrilled. Her ego swelled up. And Mulla looked at her — she was a transformed being, and Mulla said "Sorry, excuse me. But let me remind you of one thing: this thing I have been telling to many women before, and I cannot promise you that I will not say it to other women again. You are not the only one I am saying this to — this I say to every woman. This has been my usual practice."

These people who are saying to this master, "You are the only true path," must have said it to others too. Their words have no meaning, no significance. They have been used again and again. They are really saying, "We are so intelligent that we can see where truth is, who is true, who is really a perfect master. We are so intelligent that we know that you are the only true path."

They are not saying anything about the master or the truth or the true path. They are simply saying in an indirect way, "We are so intelligent that we can understand who you are." But you cannot deceive a master. Whatsoever you say, he will see through it.

To encounter a master is to encounter a mirror. You cannot bribe a master. You cannot because he has no ego. You cannot buttress him. Now, this was something great they were saying. It is almost like saying to a woman, "You are the most beautiful woman in the world." When you say to a religious teacher, "You are the true path," it is almost the same.

That's what the so-called teachers go on hankering for. They wait for somebody to say it. If the master had been a bogus one, he would have cherished these disciples. He would have declared to his other disciples, "Look! These are the real people I have been waiting for! These are the people who understand me." But because a master has no ego, he has not any self left — Sufis called it *fana* — he has disappeared. A master is really a true absence, a nothingness. He reflects the disciple. There is no way to provoke his ego, because there is none.

The Sufi said, "Have you not heard of the Mongol Halaku Khan and his invasion of Syria? Let me tell you.

"The Vizier Ahmad of the Caliph Mustasim of Baghdad invited the Mongol to invade his master's domains. When Halaku had won the battle for Baghdad, Ahmad went out to meet him, to be rewarded. Halaku said, 'Do you seek your recompense?' and the Vizier answered, 'Yes.'

"Halaku told him, 'You have betrayed your own master to me, and yet you expect me to believe that you will be faithful to me.' He ordered that Ahmad should be hanged."

A strange story to tell to those people who are declaring, "You are the true path, you are the true master." But a master has to say the truth as it is. He has to be absolutely frank. He cannot afford politeness. If it has to be hard then it has to be hard. If it hurts, so it hurts. But the master has to say it as it is.

Now, he is saying, "You have betrayed your old masters, and you come to me — how can I trust you? that you will not betray me? You have not followed your old masters, because I can see that you are carrying junk. If you had followed any master, you would have become unburdened of the junk. I can see the garbage of your knowledge.

"If you had followed any master, then the first thing would have been to drop knowledgeability. You have so much knowledge, and because of that knowledge you are saying what is true and what is not true, and what religion to follow and what not to follow, and what is the right path and what is not the right path. It is according to your knowledge. You are so full of this bulls hit! How can I think that you have followed any master, that you have been disciples to anybody? You have never been disciples. That much is certain. Whether those masters were true or not, that is not your business. One thing is certain and that is your business: that you have not been disciples at all. And the same you are going to do to me too. How can I accept you? For what should I accept you? Just to be betrayed again?"

There is a Sufi story:

A man was in love with a woman, so much so that he was ready to do anything. And the woman was demanding, very demanding. Finally she said, "There is only one condition more to be fulfilled, only then will I be yours. You are too much attached to your mother — unless you kill her and you bring her heart on a plate as a present to me, I cannot be yours. This is my last condition."

He had fulfilled many conditions.

He rushed home. He killed the mother. He took out her heart. And when he was coming back, he was in such a hurry, he was in such a passionate blindness, that he stumbled on the way. The plate fell and broke and the heart also fell and broke into many pieces, but from those many pieces only one voice came: "My son, walk a little more consciously."

He gathered the pieces. He was not in any mood to listen to it.

He gathered the pieces, he rushed to the woman, he offered the heart. The woman looked at it — she was aghast. She said, "It is finished! If you can kill your own mother, I cannot trust you. You can kill me for any other woman. You are a dangerous man. You simply get out of my house! Never come back again. The relationship is completely finished. If you had said no, I would have been yours, but you missed."

The story is the same, with the same flavor and the same meaning and the same message. If you can betray your old masters so easily and can condemn them so easily, how can the Sufi trust you? You will do the same to him.

Do you see the point? If a man who is a Hindu easily becomes a Christian, the Christian missionary is simply deceiving himself — because if he was not a true Hindu and he could deceive, how can he be a true Christian? And a true Christian and a true Hindu are the same. The difference is only between the untrue Christian and the untrue Hindu.

Truth is one and the true path is one. It does not belong to anybody. It is nobody's property. It is not my path and Buddha's path and Krishna's path and Zarathustra's path — it is just the path. Buddha, Zarathustra, Lao Tzu, they have all walked on it. It is only one! There are not many paths really. Many people walk on the path, but the path is one. And it is so vast that they may not even meet each other.

The demand of the Sufi master is very significant. You have to understand it. He says, "You have betrayed your own master — you can betray me too. And I don't want anything to do with people such as you. Go back!"

And he tells this story:

> " The Vizier Ahmad of the Caliph Mustasim of Baghdad invited the Mongol to invade his master's domains."

He betrayed his master. And now he wants to be rewarded. Halaku Khan did well with him. This is the reward.

> "He ordered that Ahmad should be hanged."

"This man is not trustworthy. He has betrayed his master who has trusted him for so long, maybe for years — how can I trust this man? I cannot leave him alone; he is dangerous. He can do the same to me and more easily, because I am a stranger. He was not even true to his master, who was not a stranger, who had taken him so close to himself that he could betray him and help me to destroy his master. And now he has come to be rewarded. This man is a traitor!"

The Sufi said:
> "Before you ask anyone to accept you, ask yourself whether it is not simply because you have not followed the path of your own teacher. If you are satisfied about this, then come and ask to become disciples."

Not that he is saying, "I will not accept you", but he makes a simple condition, "Have you followed your old master? Have you done what he was telling you to do? Have you practiced it in any way? If you have practiced, if you have done it, if you are certain about it, that you did it and it didn't work, you did all that you could and it didn't work, you were not half-hearted in it, you were not holding back, you were not clever and cunning, you were not just a spectator but you had participated in the being of the master, if you can be certain about this, if you are satisfied with your performance as a disciple — then come to me. I will accept you."

But that is something very important. This is happening nowadays very much in the world. People go on moving from one master to another; like driftwood they knock on many doors. But they never knock long enough, so the door doesn't open. They have no patience. They don't do a thing. They are simply rushing here and there — as if somebody else is going to give them the truth. Truth is not a thing to be given. It cannot be transferred. You have to earn it. You have to become pregnant with it. It has to be born in you. You have to become a womb for it. It is something alive. You have to pour your life energies into it. You have to revive it within your being. You have to create it. God is not sitting there somewhere so you can go and discover him. God has to be created!

So those who are looking for God as if he is hiding somewhere, and they will go and search and find him, they are looking in vain. You are not only to discover God: you have to create him. Each prayerful heart creates God again and again. It is your creation. But people go on thinking of God as if it is something like a commodity, that you can purchase it.

A man came to Mahavira, a king. His name was Presenjit; a very famous king of those days. And he was going to many masters. He had been to Buddha, he had been to Ajit Keshkambali, he had been to Prabuddha Katyana, he had been to Makkhli Goshal, he had been to Sanjay Vilethiputta — to many teachers. Then he came to Mahavira, and he asked Mahavira, "Give me what you call meditation, Mahavira, give it to me! And I am ready to pay for it. Whatsoever the price."

A worldly man — only knows how to purchase a thing, thinks of everything as if it can be purchased. If he falls in love with a woman, he purchases the woman and misses thereby — because love cannot be purchased. You can purchase the body, but not the soul. Love has to be earned. You have to become worthy of it.

Now, he comes to Mahavira and asks such a stupid question. Mahavira must have laughed. He said, "Listen. Why did you trouble to come so far into this forest? In your own capital there is a man — my disciple he is, a very poor man — and he would very much like to sell his meditation. He is so poor. Just go to him! I don't need what you can give to me, so I am not in any mood to sell my meditation to you. Go and purchase it from a very poor man. He may decide to sell it."

It was a joke. Presenjit rushed in his chariot, went to the poor man's hut. It was such a poor hut that he thought, "Certainly this man will sell. I can even purchase this man — what about the meditation!"

And the man came, a very poor man, almost naked, but utterly beautiful and graceful, a great light within his being — you could see it. And the king felt, "Mahavira is right — this man has got it.

Look at his face — so luminous!" And he said, "just tell me what you want. I have come to purchase your meditation, your samadhi. And I am ready to give anything you ask."

The man hesitated. What to say to the king? And the king thought, obviously, "He is hesitating about the price." So he said, "Don't be worried. You can say any amount."

But the man said, "It is not a question of price."

The king said, "Don't be worried about it at all. I can give my whole kingdom to you, because when once I decide to purchase a thing, I always purchase it. Just say!"

But the man said, "I am sorry to say...I don't want to say no to you, but what are you asking? It is absurd! I cannot sell it. It is not a thing. It is not anything objective. It has happened to me. Mahavira must have played a joke with you. You go back to the master. He has simply sent you here so that you can understand that even if you give your kingdom to a poor beggar, he cannot sell his meditation or samadhi. There is no way to purchase it. It is invaluable. And it is not a commodity at all."

But people go on thinking God is a commodity, samadhi is a commodity, enlightenment is a commodity: "Give us...!" It is not! You have to become it. You have to be transformed. And only your effort can transform you. The master can show you the way, but you will have to follow.

The Sufi said:

"Before you ask anyone to accept you, ask yourself whether it is not simply because you have not followed the path of your own teacher.

"That you have missed and you are not ready to say that you are not a disciple. That you have not been a disciple. Instead you are saying that the master is wrong. Instead of saying 'I have not followed the path,' you are declaring that the path is wrong and there is no more truth on it.

"If you are satisfied about this...

"...that you have done all that you could, and more is not possible for you, and nothing has happened there, then come to me; Then I am ready to help you. But be satisfied about that."

This has to be understood by every disciple, every seeker. You are with me here. If you don't go into that space that I make available for you, sooner or later you will start thinking, "Nothing is happening. What am I doing here? I must go and seek some other door. I must go and beg from somebody else. I must go and learn from someone somewhere else." But the space is available to you. The door is open. And you are not walking in. You remain hanging outside. You go on pretending in a thousand and one ways that you are moving, but you are not moving.

The moving is possible only when you are totally with me — if even a small part of you is not with me, it is impossible to move in the door. You will have to move as a total organic unity. You cannot leave your left hand outside. You cannot leave anything outside. You will have to move in totally! Only then can you move. You cannot move in partially, remember it.

So those who are totally with me, they have moved. And those who are going to be totally with me, they will move. But there will be many also who will simply be here partially. A little bit. Trying to judge whether it is worth taking the risk. Hanging around. Calculating. If you are calculating, you are not a disciple. If you are trying to figure it out, you are not a disciple. Because it is not a question of figuring it out. It is so immense, you cannot figure it out. It is so enormous, you cannot calculate about it. It is bigger than you, so you cannot hold it in your hands. You have to be ready to disappear, to evaporate. You have to die, and only then...the resurrection.

The disciple has to become the mythological bird, the phoenix: he has to disappear into the fire, and out of the ashes the new will be born.

Those who are ready, those who can take the risk, those who are courageous, only they will attain. And the remaining ones will start thinking, "Maybe this is not the right door, this is not the right path, this is not the right master. I should go somewhere else. Why am I wasting my time here?" And you will do the same somewhere else too. And you can go on and on, life after life, wandering and wandering, and never arriving.

This is what you have been doing in your past lives! You are not new, nobody is new. All are old-timers. You have been here forever and ever, from the very beginning you have been here. I know people are here who have been with Buddha...and missed. I know people are here who have been with Rumi and missed. And I know, there are many people here who have been with Jesus and missed.

It is not new. It is not that you are for the first time with a master. You have been many times. And each time you missed, you condemned the master rather than rethinking about your own self.

The calculating people are always ready to listen about the truth, but it has to be abstract. When you come to the details, when they have to do something, when the truth starts becoming a pragmatic reality, then problems arise.

There is a famous statement of Ludwig Wittgenstein: Don't look for the meaning, look for the use. And in the same way, thousands of years before Wittgenstein, Lao Tzu says: The meaning is the use. The use is the meaning. When you look for it, you cannot see it. When you listen for it, you cannot hear it. But when you use it, it is inexhaustible.

A master is not there to give you a doctrine but a discipline. A doctrine is an abstract thing. It is about God. A discipline is not about God: it is about you.

A master is not there to philosophize, because we have more philosophy than we need, already too much. A master is there to help you walk. You are cripples. A master is there to heal, to cure you, your crippledness, your blindness, your paralysis. He is a physician, he is not a philosopher. But people are always ready to listen to abstract things, because those abstract things never touch your life.

I have heard – this story comes from the heart of China:

In a small church in a remote village, the people came to the minister complaining that the wife of a deacon was stealing chickens from her neighbor. They said, "You've got to do something about it."

He said, "All right, I will." That Sunday he preached on the text "You shall not steal." At the close of the service the deacon came to him and said, "Excellent sermon, Pastor."

But in three or four days the people came and said, "That sermon didn't do any good at all – she's still stealing."

So the next Sunday, the minister got more specific. He said, "You shall not steal your neighbor's goods." At the close of the service the deacon shook hands and said, "That's a much better sermon. You've really got to speak specifically."

However, during the week the people said, "That didn't do any good – she's still stealing."

So the minister took courage in both hands and said, "You shall not steal your neighbor's chickens."

The deacon came to him and said, "Now look, you're not supposed to be all that specific in the pulpit."

When it comes to the small, real details of your life, you stop hearing. When it is about abstract worlds of paradise, God, Nirvana, you are all alert. It doesn't matter. It is beautiful philosophy. You cannot lose anything. You can become a little more knowledgeable. But when it comes to the stealing of your neighbor's chickens, then it touches your life. There you become alert. There you stop listening.

Remember: a master is not to impart abstract truths to you but something that has to be practised in life, something that has to become your lifestyle.

Great courage is needed, and great endeavor, and great discipline, to change and transform one's way of life. If you cannot, don't condemn the path you have been following because really you have never followed it.

A man went up to the salesman at the Rolls Royce stand in the motor company's show and asked the way to the gents' toilet.

The route was a bit complicated and the salesman deserted his post to escort the man to the door of the toilet. Thanking him, the man asked why he had gone to so much trouble.

"Because," answered the salesman, "yours was the first genuine inquiry I've had all day."

If you really want to be with a master you will have to become a genuine inquiry. Not philosophic curiosity, but an inquiry in which your life and death are involved. An inquiry which is going to transmute you. An inquiry that is going to become a metamorphosis.

You are capable of flying into the sky, but you are hiding in your cocoons. Those cocoons have to be broken — and it hurts. And it hurts because you think those cocoons are your defence, your safety, because you think those cocoons are your homes. They are your prison cells.

The master has to destroy the prison cell so the prisoner can be freed. But the prisoner has become too identified with the prison cell, so he decorates it. He may even hang the picture of the master in the prison cell. He may worship the master, but in the prison cell. He will not listen to the master that the prison cell has to be broken. And unless you destroy the prison cell, and cooperate with the master in destroying it, you will not be free.

And to be free is the only way to know what truth is. Freedom is truth. Freedom is God. Freedom is Nirvana.

Enough for today.

CHAPTER 6

ONLY ONE ECSTASY

The first question:

Osho,

How does the internal world of experience relate to external reality?

There are not two realities. All duality is only in conceptualization. Reality is one. It is mind that divides: the lower and the higher, the good and the bad, the internal and the external, heaven and hell. It is mind that divides! But reality remains undivided. It is all one. You cannot demark where the inner ends and where the outer begins. There is no possibility of demarcation.

The internal is the external, and the external is the internal. They are absolutely one.

To see this is to be free of all division and of all schizophrenia.

It is good to divide for intellectual purposes. It is good to categorize to understand things. But to know reality one has to drop all categories, all mind concepts, because they limit. They have to limit to define. You cannot define the unlimited. You have to divide and cut into pieces. Only parts can be defined: the whole cannot be defined.

But the moment you cut the whole into pieces, it is no more real. The whole remains the whole.

Just listen to these words of Lao Tzu:

> *The great Tao flows everywhere,*
> *to the left and to the right.*
> *All things depend upon it to exist,*
> *and it does not abandon them.*
> *To its accomplishments it lays*
> *no claim.*
> *It loves and nourishes all things,*
> *but does not lord it over them.*

The Tao goes on flowing — to the left, to the right, to the sinner, to the saint, it is available. It goes on raining on all. It makes no distinctions of higher and lower, of the accepted, the chosen, and the rejected, the condemned. The great Tao flows everywhere.... It knows no boundaries. It jumps from one thing into another. From man into woman, from yin into yang. The yin goes on yanging and the yang goes on yinning.

There are moments...have you not watched in your own being? You may be a man ordinarily. Sometimes you are not a man at all: you are a woman. You may be a woman ordinarily, but sometimes you are a man. The Tao goes on flowing. Nothing can obstruct it. There are female moments in every male's consciousness, and there are male moments in every female's consciousness. Man and woman are together, undivided, two aspects of one coin.

> *The great Tao flows everywhere,*
> *to the left and to the right.*
> *All things depend upon it to exist...*

It is an invisible ocean of energy, of consciousness, of bliss — sat-chit-ananda — it is truth, it is consciousness, it is bliss. But even these three words are not three things. The idea of the trinity in Christianity, is beautiful, but there are not three Gods — there is only one God. Three faces. The Hindu idea of Trimurti is even more beautiful: one God with three faces. In fact, the God has as many faces as there are people.

The God means the whole. Where are you going to put the God? In the external reality or in the internal? When you love, your beloved becomes part of your internal reality. Is he or she external to you? Are you external to him or her? All those old categories start disappearing — that's the beauty of love, because it makes you aware of the invisible unity of all.

To its accomplishments it lays no claim.

God remains silent. Tao remains silent. It lays no claim.

It loves and nourishes all things,
with no distinctions,
but does not lord it over them.

That is another thing so nice about Tao, about the real God: it is not bossy! The moment your God becomes bossy, your ego has entered in your God, you have falsified God. That's how many Gods have become untrue Gods. Your mind has corrupted them. You have brought all your nonsense to the concept of God. You have poisoned the very concept.

The Tao loves and nourishes all things,
but does not lord it over them.

Thus the Tao is something purely helpful — never coercive. The Taoist never speaks of obedience, but only of being in harmony with the Tao. The internal and the outer are in harmony, in absolute harmony. They are notes, two notes, of the same music — two musical instruments in the same orchestra, in absolute harmony: Being in harmony is the way of Tao.

In the moment of awakening to the real, one realizes, not that one should not rebel against Tao or God, but that one simply cannot.

You cannot be otherwise! Notwithstanding what you go on believing. You may think of yourself as an individual — you are not, because you are not separate. Your thinking is just your thinking. It is a private idea. It corresponds to no reality at all and, hence, it will create misery for you.

This idea of internal and external has created much misery for man, because then people start dropping the external. That's how the idea of renunciation arose: "Renounce the outer and be the inner!" But how can you do it?

There is an apple on the tree. It is external. If you eat it, it becomes internal: it will be your blood, your bones, your marrow. When does it become internal? How does the external become internal? And one day you will die, and all that was inside you will be again outside, back into the earth. It will nourish some apple tree, more apples will grow.

You breathe in and it becomes internal. Then you have to breathe out. Where does the breath become internal? Watch. That's what Buddha says: Watch your breathing — and see where it becomes internal and where it becomes external again. Just watching your breath, all distinctions will disappear. You will see it is the same circle. The internal is the external, and the external is the internal.

The moment you see this in your breath circle, you have solved a great problem, a great dichotomy is dissolved. Then you are no more a body or a soul. Then you don't talk about these words. Then all these words are just childish — maybe useful, but they have no reality, no truth. Just useful, utilitarian.

You ask me: *How does the internal world of experience relate to the external reality?*

It does not relate! Because they are not two. They are one. It often becomes a great question. But the question is basically false, so all the answers that have been given are false. Once you start by a wrong question, you will arrive again and again at wrong conclusions.

For at least five thousand years, man has been puzzled by one thing: the body/mind problem. How do they relate? First you divide...division is false. There is no body and no mind separate. It is body mind. It is one entity. The mind is only a way of looking at the body, and the body is also a way of looking at the mind. It is the same reality looked at from different angles. It is not two. But once you have thought that body and mind are two, then the problem arises: How do they relate?

Just watch a small action: you think to raise your hand – how do you do it? Such a simple phenomenon, raising your hand up – how do you do it? Philosophers have been puzzled and have not been able to answer it, how it happens, because of this internal and external: they are the mind and the body is being raised – how can the body follow the order from the mind?

Mind is invisible, immaterial; body is visible, material – how can matter follow mind? What is the link? How is it translated into body language? How does it correspond? But to me, basically the problem is wrong: there are not two entities in you – it is all one. Then the problem disappears.

You ask me how the internal relates with the external reality. There are not two realities. There is no question of internal and external. They don't relate. They are one. How do two lovers relate with one another? If they are lovers, they don't relate – they are simply one. In love they know the unity. If they are not lovers, then they relate. Then relationship is not much. It is more conflict and less relating. It is more fight than being together.

If love has happened, in that moment it becomes absolutely clear that there is no division. Then they start functioning in a harmony. And not that the harmony has to be imposed from the outside. No, it comes of its own accord, with no effort, with no cultivation, with no conditioning. It simply happens. As trees grow upwards...just like that. As birds can fly...just like that. As flowers can bloom...just like that. It is natural.

The internal and the external are in absolute harmony. There is no division. But man has created the division and has created much anxiety about it. Drop the division, and go beyond anxiety.

Dropping dualities one becomes religious. Don't think yourself separate from the world. That's why Zen people say: The world is Nirvana. There is no other enlightenment.

That's why the other day I was talking about Zorba the Buddha. Zorba is extrovert, Buddha is introvert. Zorba has no idea who he is, Buddha has renounced the world, he only thinks about who he is. His whole consciousness moves inward. Zorba is interested in women and wine and dance and song; his whole energy moves outward.

To me, the perfect master will be one who has no divisions. He flows in all the directions — internal, external — because there is no problem at all. It is all one flow. To be in this one flow is to know God.

The second question:

Osho,
I have fallen in love with a friend's wife who is in love with my wife — is it not strange?

t is. This whole life is strange. Things happen here, strange things. I can understand your problem. No husband can ever believe that anybody can fall in love with his wife — although he can fall in love with somebody else's wife and there is no problem. But somebody falling in love with his wife? and he is so fed up with the woman? and he cannot see any beauty in her? and all ugliness has surfaced?

A man came home and saw his partner making love to his wife. The partner was very much afraid: "Now there is going to be trouble."

And the man came and tapped on his shoulder and said, "Come with me to the other room. I would like to have a word with you."

And the partner was trembling: "Now there is going to be danger — maybe some fight or something." And the man took him into the other room and closed the doors and said, "Tell me one thing: I have to, but why you? What has happened to you? Have you gone crazy or something?"

I can understand your problem: somebody falling in love with your wife? Let me tell you one anecdote:

Two men were playing golf one morning, but could not play as quickly as they wanted because there were two women playing the hole ahead of them who were moving too slowly.

Finally, out of their frustration, one of the men began walking towards the women to ask them to stop gossiping so much and to play golf, or to please get out of the men's way.

He got within a hundred feet of the women and all of a sudden stopped, turned around and ran back to his friend.

"You'd better go," he said. "One of them is my wife and the other is my mistress."

So the second man started walking towards the women. He got within a hundred and fifty feet of the ladies, and he too turned around and ran the other way. He got back to his friend and said, "Small world!"

The third question:

Osho,

Jewish religion, like Zen, is based only on the formless and doesn't permit the worship of forms. But ever since I have been in India these last eight years, I've moved away from this idea and have fallen in deep love not only with your form, but also with Hindu religion, its multitude of mythological figures and the stories around them – Ram, Krishna, Shiva, etc. I love keeping my room decorated with pictures of your form and of all these as well, and

*immersing myself in the feeling of being surrounded by an Indian
mythological world of gods and goddesses, though intellectually I
know the illusion of it.*

*I also love form by way of the Indian trees, skies and nature, as
well as the Indian people – in general and in particular – and I
seem to come alive here in India in a great heart-throbbing dance
of joy as I never could feel living in the West.*

*My head knows the truth of the concept of the formless and
of the idea of "killing the Buddha", but my heart is absolutely
immersed in the love and worship of form. I even have no desire
for enlightenment any more and would rather love Buddha than
become him, in these my own ways.*

*Does this mean I am stuck somewhere and need you to be a
Totapuri to cut my forehead, or is it okay for me to remain in my
present ecstatic, heart-throbbing world?*

Ananda Prem, the Jewish concept of God as formless and the Zen
concept are not the same. Zen has no concept of God – because
how can you have a concept of a formless God? That is absurdity! The
moment you have a concept you have created a form. That's why Zen
never talks about God, Buddha never mentioned God at all. He has
been asked again and again, but he keeps mum, he will not say.

If you talk about the formless God, what are you saying? What do
you mean by "formless God"? If you contemplate on the formlessness
of God you will be surprised: either you have to drop the idea of
God like Buddha, like Zen, or you have to create some form. Either
the formlessness can remain and God has to go, or God can remain
but then the formlessness has to go.

So remember it: Zen has no idea of God. Formlessness cannot be
called God. The moment you call it by any name, you have given it a
certain form; the formlessness is falsified, is destroyed. It is no more
formless. About the formless God you can be only silent. You cannot
even say that much – that God is formless. That is profane! that is
sacrilegious! You cannot define in any way. Not even are you allowed
to say that God is indefinable because that becomes a definition. You

have said something, you have already said something. And you are
saying nothing can be said.

Buddha is very logical in that way. Zen is very clear. Judaism is
not so clear. It is against creating forms of God, that is true — but
its being too much against simply shows it is obsessed with the idea
of form. That's how Mohammedans are also obsessed, because they
are an offshoot of Judaism.

Judaism is obsessed that there should be no statue of God in
any temple. And Mohammedans have gone one step further: that if
you find any statues, destroy them! free people of the forms of God!
As if you can free anybody from the forms of God — because forms
exist in the mind, not in the temples. They are not in the statues but
in the intellectual visualization of God.

Why should Judaism not permit the worship of forms? The very
effort to deny forms shows that somehow you are still attached to
the form. It is not formlessness! It may be an anti form attitude, but
not formlessness.

Zen is really formlessness. And because of this, just as Prem
says:

> Jewish religion, like Zen, is based only on the formless and does
> not permit the worship of forms.

If God is formless, who are you to permit or not to permit? The very
idea of permitting is destructive to freedom. Judaism has not given
freedom to people. It is not just an accident that all the revolutionaries
have come from the Jews. It is a rebellion. From Jesus to Freud,
all the revolutionaries have come from the Jews. Why? No other
religion has created so many revolutionaries — no other religion is
so restrictive.

If a religion is free, the revolutionary has nothing to do there.
Hinduism has not created any revolutionaries. Buddhism has not
created any revolutionaries. Why? Because the freedom is so total!
What is the point?

If Jesus had been born in India, nobody would have thought about him that he was a revolutionary. People would have allowed, because there is no question — who is there to allow or not to allow? It is everybody's own choice.

Because Jews have not been allowing forms, Jesus was born. And Jesus became the form of God for Christians, for millions of people. And then it has been happening again and again.

Marx comes out of Jews, and Albert Einstein, and Sigmund Freud. Why? The religion is very restrictive. It does not have the flavor of Zen.

And when I am talking about Jews, I leave aside the Hassid masters. They have the flavor of Zen. But Jews don't accept them either. They are thought to be rebellious. And whenever a religion becomes too much interested in permitting and not permitting, it becomes ritualistic, dull, dead. It becomes formal.

Just see the point: Jews talk about the formlessness of God and their whole religion has become absolutely formal! Just ritualistic. Nothing of the interior, nothing of the heart. Just a social formality.

I have heard:

The couple were registering at a small hotel in Vermont. They were asked to show their wedding license. The man flashed a fishing license to the near-sighted clerk and laid it on the desk.

After the couple went upstairs the clerk examined the license more carefully and rushed up after them. He banged on the door shouting, "If you ain't done it, don't do it! This a ain't the license for it!"

Who can permit? Who can give you a license for anything? If there is any possibility to know God it is through freedom. It is through absolute freedom.

You say: *"But coming to India, I have moved away from this idea...."*

It is good that you have moved away from this idea — that was just an idea, not your experience. But now you have moved to another idea, just the opposite. That's what has been happening to Jews down the ages. When they rebel, they move to the opposite idea. Just the opposite. It always happens. You react, and you move to the other extreme.

Now, Prem says she has moved away from this idea. You may have moved, but you have moved in the opposite direction. Now she is surrounded by all kinds of gods and goddesses: Ram and Krishna, Shiva.... In India you have millions of gods. They say there are more gods than people in India.

I have known people whose whole day is lost into worship ping. I used to stay with a man. He had at least three hundred statues in his small temple, his own temple. Three hundred statues of all kinds of gods and goddesses. And from four o'clock early in the morning he would start worship ping — you have to take care of three hundred gods. Half the day was wasted in it. And he was in such a hurry he could not worship even one, because he knew, "Now there are still two hundred and ninety-nine waiting," and he had to rush to everybody. And he had to be careful, otherwise somebody may have become angry — those three hundred jealous gods. You have to pay the same attention to each.

He was getting crazy! I said, "You will go mad! Three hundred gods are too much."

Now Prem says she is feeling ecstatic. Yes, you will feel ecstatic because you have moved to the opposite polarity. It gives freedom. But this is not true freedom — soon you will lose it. Soon you will become tired. And then there is every possibility the mind will start moving to the other extreme again. And the truth is just exactly in the middle, remember. The truth is just exactly in the middle.

In ancient Greece, on the temple of Delphi, there were two inscriptions. One is very well known, the other is not so well known. There must be some cause why the other never became so well known. One was: Know thyself. And the other was: never in excess. But the other is not so well known, and they both are together. They each are as important as the other, of the same plenitude, of the same potential.

One can know oneself only if one lives a life of no excess, if one moves just in the middle. Otherwise, one becomes a victim of extremes.

Now, from the idea of formless God you are becoming a victim of thousands of forms. Just exactly in the middle, where gods disappear; neither form nor formlessness, when there is utter silence — there is the home.

And Prem says: *I even have no desire for enlightenment any more and would rather love Buddha than become him...*

Reading your question, Prem, I started becoming worried about Buddha. It is perfectly okay, you will love Buddha — but what about Buddha? Your love will be your love, with all its poison. In fact, your love is not love at all. Only through light does love arise. Only after enlightenment does love flow. Before that it is just a false illusion of love.

You can go on loving Buddha, but you will never know what Buddha is — how can you love? Your love will be nothing but a kind of illusion, a hallucination.

You have loved people before, now you project the same illusory energy on Buddha. And if Buddha is alive he won't allow it. He will try to destroy it in every way, because he will think of you in this illusion, in this dream. You may feel good, but this is a dream all the same. Sooner or later you will awake and then you will see that you have been wasting your life.

Yes, there is excitement but there is no ecstasy. And don't think your excitement is ecstasy. They look alike. And the greatest danger in life is from things that look alike. Excitement looks like ecstasy — it is not. Ecstasy has no excitement. It is a very tranquil state. Ecstasy is absolute silence, nothingness. It is enlightenment!

Now, you say: *I even have no desire for enlightenment...*

In a way that is good, because if you don't have any desire for enlightenment, enlightenment becomes more possible. But the way you are speaking it seems that you are clinging, you are afraid. It is not just a statement of no-desire: it is a statement of rejection. You are afraid of enlightenment, you are afraid to become so conscious — because then all these illusory loves will disappear and all these mythological gods that you are surrounded with will look stupid. You will have to throw them down in the river. You will have to get rid of them, because they are unnecessarily occupying space.

You cannot love Buddha unless you become a Buddha! And to become a Buddha is what enlightenment is, and that's what ecstasy is.

Prem, you are not in an ecstasy. You may be in a heart-throbbing excitement, you may be enjoying this trip, but for how long? And these gods that you are surrounded with are all nothing but your projections. You have created them. You can put your energy into Ram, and then he becomes alive, but it is your energy.

Why not become alive? Why put it in Ram and make him alive? Why go that far? And you say:

> Does this mean I am stuck somewhere and need you to be a
> Totapuri to cut my forehead?

I am not a Totapuri. Ramakrishna was too much attached to form, and Totapuri was too much attached to formlessness. I am not attached at all! To me both are the same. Attachment to form or to formlessness is the same. I am not giving you a formless god, I am not trying to substitute form by formlessness — no, I want you to drop both form and formlessness and just be...free of all illusions. In that just being is freedom. Meditate on these lines of J. Kerouac:

> There is no way to lose.
> If there was a way,
> then

when the sun is shining on the pond
and I go west, thou east,
which one does the true sun
follow?
Which one does the true one borrow?
Since neither one is the true one,
there is no true one way.
And the sun is a delusion
of a way multiplied by two
and multiplied millionfold.
Since there is no way, no Buddhas,
no dharmas, no conceptions,
only one ecstasy,
and right-mindedness
is mindfulness
that the way is no-way
anyhow some way.

Only one ecstasy. Ecstasy has nothing to do with form or formlessness. Ecstasy has nothing to do with Judaism, Hinduism, Buddhism. Only one ecstasy. And what is that? I teach you only that, and what is that? That is being so utterly quiet, unmoving, not going anywhere, not desiring anything, not dreaming anything — gods or no-gods, forms or no-forms — no thought at all. The thought of form, the thought of formlessness, are all the same. Can't you be in that mirror like silence? nothing is reflected even! The mirror is empty. That is the one ecstasy.

That one ecstasy is God. The taste of it is God. God is not a person with form or without form. God is the taste on your tongue of that moment — of that moment of bliss, of that moment of Tao, of that moment when all stops, time stops, and the world stops.

I am not a Totapuri at all. He was very much obsessed with the formless, otherwise why should he bother to cut Ramakrishna's forehead? I would not have done that. For what? I am not in any way interested in changing you from one position to another position, from one philosophy to another philosophy. They are all points of view. My effort is to make you free of all points of view — Ramakrishna and Totapuri both.

And what happened? do you know? And that's what I am afraid of, Prem, it can happen to you. Ramakrishna said after those six days, "The last barrier has fallen," and then he lived at least ten more years — and continued to worship Kali. And the day he died, he died with the name of Kali on his lips: "Jai Kali, Jai Kali!" The day, the moment he died, it was not the formless, it was again the form. What happened? For a few days he remained in that excitement of the formless, then he became tired and moved again.

No excess. No extreme. Be in the middle. Exactly in the middle is the door. If you think of time, then in the past there is no door, in the future there is no door — but in the present, because that is exactly in the middle. If you think of form and formlessness there is no door, but exactly between the two. Neither this nor that — neti, neti — just exactly between the two. Neither the soul nor the body. Don't become a spiritualist or a materialist. Don't think of the external reality or the internal. Just exactly in the middle!

Always go on thinking of the middle, and slowly slowly relax in the middle and let the extremes dissolve. And you have arrived home.

The fourth question:

Osho,
Kindly tell me — have we met in a past life?

Chidvilas, we have not even met in this life. What are you talking about — the past life? You have been here, I have been here, but meeting has not happened yet. I go on trying to meet you, and you go on escaping. You are very artful, skillful, clever. And you know it! And to avoid this encounter you are interested in thinking about past lives.

Ask me why we have not met in this life. How is it going to help whether we met in the past life or not? Now we cannot go back to it; we cannot make anything out of it. It is finished. But this is how mind works. It escapes from the present. It finds ways either in the past or in the future. Those are tricks, strategies of the mind to save itself. Why should you be interested in "past life"? It is finished, it is gone, it is no more! It has no existence anywhere, no validity. Even if we did meet, it matters nothing.

The only thing that matters is: I am here and you are here, but the meeting is not happening. If the meeting happens, you will become enlightened. And let only that be decisive. The day you become enlightened, the meeting has happened. Otherwise, what is the point?

And I know that you know it, because you have also asked another question which will make it clear. Chidvilas asks:

> I strongly feel to go through that beautiful initiation ceremony again! What am I missing which I got while you allowed me to enter your kingdom? Please throw some light on this feeling, and on missing.

You know it! You are missing. The initiation ceremony is not going to help — no ceremony is going to help. It is not a question of any ceremony. It is a question of risk. You have to be courageous enough to encounter me, to face me, to face the reality that I am making available to you. And you go on dodging. This way and that you go on running.

And your mind is full of knowledge. So you can always find excuses, explanations, rationalizations. That's why the meeting is not happening. Now this is another effort out of your knowledge: you want to know whether we have met in some past life.

If I say yes, your ego will be strengthened. You will start thinking yourself very special. That is the desire in it. So even if we have met, I am not going to say it. All I am going to say is: Meet me now! because there may be no other life for me again. You may not meet me again. No possibility. Don't miss this opportunity.

And remember: the initiation ceremony is not going to help. It has not to be just a ceremony — it has to be existential. You are initiated as a sannyasin, but that has not helped either. Just by becoming a sannyasin you don't become one. It is just a preliminary. It helps. It brings you a little closer. It makes you a little more open, a little more trusting. But it is not the end!

The real initiation is going to happen some day when you drop all your mind and you just look into me with no idea, with no knowledge, with innocence.

Remember Zusya and those children who looked into his eyes. The day you look into my eyes as if you are a child, innocent, with no past, with no future, then the meeting will happen.

And that meeting is going to transform you. I am waiting for it. I am working for it. I am surrounding you from everywhere. But up till now it has not happened — because of you. You go on escaping.

Stop escaping.

The fifth question:

Osho,
Why are the psychotherapists called shrinks?

Because they are. The word exactly describes what the Psychotherapists are doing – they shrink people. They shrink people from persons into patients. That's their work. They reduce.

When you go to a psychotherapist, you go as a person, with dignity. They reduce you immediately to labels: you are a schizophrenic, paranoid, neurotic. Immediately you are reduced! You are no more the same person with the dignity. A label has been put on you. You are a disease! You have to be treated.

By reducing you to a patient, the psychotherapist has become much bigger. The more he reduces you to smallness, the bigger he feels.

This is an old trip, only the names have changed. In the past it was the priest, now it is the psychotherapist. In the past, the priest was shrinking you – trying to create the guilt feeling, trying to create the feeling that you are wrong somehow, that you need to be changed, that you are not acceptable as you are, that you are getting ready for hell.

The whole effort of the priest was to reduce you to criminals, sinners. The priest was creating a kind of guilt feeling in you. Now the work has been taken up by the psychotherapist. The psychotherapist is the priest of the new age. He reduces you, he does not enhance you. He does not give you splendor, respect for your being. On the contrary, he makes you feel worthless.

And that's why we are trying to create a new kind of therapy here – in which you are not reduced to diseases, but enhanced, expanded. The psychotherapist is not there to label you as ill, but is there only to help you to know that you are not ill, that who says that you are ill? that you are carrying wrong notions about yourself. Who has told you that you are worthless? You are immensely valuable.

That is my whole effort here: to help you expand.

The psychotherapist and the priest and the so-called gurus, they have all been doing the same thing to people: they have been shrinking them. They have reduced humanity to worms, crawling on the earth, ugly, afraid of seeing their own faces in the mirror. Afraid to look into their own beings, because there is nothing but all that is wrong. Wounds and pus.

Here the effort is to create a totally different kind of therapy, true to the very meaning of the word. The meaning of the word "therapy" is that which heals. And what heals? Love heals. Love is therapy. Nothing else is therapy. Not psychoanalysis, not analytical psychology. Only love heals. Healing is a function of love. But love expands your consciousness. It allows you to go higher and higher and touch the stars. It makes you feel respected. It makes you feel that you are needed in existence, that without you there will be something missing in existence, there will be a hole without you, unfulfillable. You are a must. This existence cannot be the same without you. You are not just an accident. You are essentially needed.

Let me remind you of Zusya again: Zusya is one of the most beautiful masters — you can call him the perfect master. One day he was caught praying in the synagogue. Why caught? because the people felt very offended. He was saying to God, "Listen, I need you so you need me. Without you I will be nothing. And I say to you: without me you will be nothing. I am me because of you; you are you because of me."

The people were offended. They said, "What are you saying Zusya? Have you gone mad?"

He had not gone mad. This is the way one should have a dialogue with God. This is not ego! not at all. This is a simple fact. Even a small leaf of grass is as valuable as any star. There is no hierarchy in existence, nobody is lower and nobody is higher. We are all joined into one organic unity.

This is real therapy. Therapy when it is real will be nothing but love. Therapy when real will help you to regain your confidence, will help you to bloom.

The word "Buddha" comes from a root "Bodha". In the ancient days, the word "Bodha" was used for the opening up of a bud. It comes from the world of flowers; then it was taken over. "Bodha" means originally opening up of a bud and becoming a flower. Then it was taken in a metaphoric sense: when a man opens up, blooms, releases fragrance and color and dances in the sky, he becomes a Buddha — he has opened up.

Real therapy does not shrink you: it opens you up. It makes all that is yours available to you. It gives you your lost treasure. But as far as the modern psychotherapy is concerned, people are right in calling psychotherapists shrinks — they are.

And a strange thing is this: that they are as ill as the people they are treating. Sometimes even more so. I have never come across a psychotherapist who is not mentally in some disturbance. Maybe just to avoid his own mental disturbance he has become interested in other people's mental disturbances, and he is playing superior. And he is getting more and more ill every day.

I have heard:

A motion picture actor told his psychiatrist, "I'm attracted to men instead of women."

The shrink replied, "You've come to the right place, handsome!"

They are suffering from the same kind of problems, pretending to help people. Psychotherapy is one of the most bogus things that has happened to this age. But a totally different kind of orientation is needed.

People get in trouble — not that people are wrong but because people are brought up in wrong situations. Everybody is born perfectly healthy and normal, but is born in a neurotic society, where parents are neurotic, teachers are neurotic, priests are neurotic, politicians are neurotic. And they all jump upon the small child, and they start manipulating him. They drive him crazy.

We have not yet been able to develop a right kind of upbringing. The science remains very rudimentary, primitive. We have come from bullock-carts to jets, but as far as the rearing of a child is concerned, we are as primitive as ever. We have not evolved in that. Parents go on pouring their diseases into the children. And children are helpless victims. And in their own turn they will have nothing to give to their children — they will have to give their illnesses. That's all they have.

People are not neurotic: it is a neurotic atmosphere.

And, just by analyzing people's neuroses you are not going to transform them either. Just by analyzing, at the most you can help them to become a little more adjusted. You can make them feel that that's how life is. Freud says: There is no possibility of enjoyment in life — one can only endure it.

If you go through psychoanalysis, sooner or later you will see this is what life is: all this nonsense, all this rubbish, all these neurotic desires — this is what life is! One starts settling with it. One loses hope, becomes settled. What is the point of raging against it? It is to no purpose. There is no enjoyment possible.

Psychoanalysis is very pessimistic. It is very strange! People say Buddha is pessimistic, even Freud and people like that say Buddha is pessimistic. This is really strange. Buddha is not pessimistic, neither is Shankara, nor is Rumi. These people are not pessimistic, although they say that life is full of misery. But they say it only to make you aware that it should not be so, that it need not be so.

Life is misery, they say again and again, because life can be bliss. They simply provoke you to take your life in your own hands. It can be transformed into bliss. But they are not pessimists.

Freud is a pessimist. Psychotherapists are pessimists. They have accepted this is all that life is supposed to be; one has to live with it, one has to endure it somehow. They make people capable of coping with it, but this is not much. Just to cope with it — and then comes death...?

No, life can be a dance. Life can be a song. A real therapy will not only help you to cope with life: it will help you to become more alive. It will help you to gain life abundant. It will help you to move towards sat-chit-ananda — it will help you to attain to eternal bliss. Only then is it therapy. But then it is no more a kind of shrinking — then it is expansion.

In fact, the original Hebrew word for heaven means expansion. When Jesus says: the kingdom of heaven is within you, he is saying metaphorically that if you expand, if you expand to the very ultimate limits of existence, this is what the kingdom of heaven is.

Real therapy will be of a totally different color, shape, flavor.

This is why I am so much interested in therapy. You will not find anybody else in the whole of India so much interested in therapy. To have therapies in an ashram is unheard of, but my interest is deep in it, because I know therapy is doing much wrong to people. It has moved in a very pessimistic dimension.

And therapy is the religion of the modern man. Just to go on talking about the Bible and the Koran and the Vedas is almost out of date, it is meaningless. It has no relevance. One has to talk relevant to the situation and to the real problems people are facing in their lives.

Therapy is one of the things that has to be changed, transformed, so that it can become a healing force, so that it can bring you towards more wholeness and holiness.

The sixth question:

Osho,

Do real problems exist? Are all problems just mind games? Does awareness make problems disappear? Or is there a possibility that awareness brings repression? If find that whenever I feel a little more centered and aware than usual I don't feel any problems, but when I am no more centered all the old problems are back and they look even bigger. Is this repression?

Ratna, all problems are out of unawareness. Unawareness creates problems, is the only problem really. So when you become alert, aware, problems disappear — they are not repressed! And if you repress them you will never become aware, remember it; because a person who represses his problems will be afraid of becoming aware. The moment one who has repressed problems becomes aware, those problems will come up. Awareness will bring them to light.

It is as if you are hiding rubbish in your house: you will be afraid to bring light in, because then you will have to see all that you have been hiding there. You cannot bring light in.

I used to live in a village once, for a few days. There was a river, so dirty — just such a small river that you cannot even call it a river. And there was no other way, no other water supply. A guest came to stay with me. Now, I was a little puzzled: how to take him to that dirty river? So I took him early, four o'clock in the morning, and we enjoyed and we talked about the beauty, because the moon was there and the river was really looking beautiful. And he enjoyed and he said, "I have never seen such a beautiful spot."

I said, "That's perfectly okay, but never come in the day."

He said, "Why?"

I said, "Just don't come."

Naturally, he rushed, in the morning he went back. And he came from there saying, "Such a dirty place!"

But it was looking so beautiful.

If you repress, you will be afraid of becoming aware. That's why millions of people are afraid of becoming aware. Awareness will bring light into you, and then you will see all the scorpions and the snakes and the wolves...and that is frightening. One keeps oneself in darkness. At least one can go on pretending that there is no problem.

Awareness will release all that is repressed. Awareness never represses — on the contrary, it releases repressions.

But Ratna's experience is true. If you become aware, problems disappear. Naturally, the question arises: Is not awareness repressing those problems? — because how can they suddenly disappear? And when awareness is lost, centering is gone, and you are no more so conscious, again the problems pop up — and they are bigger than ever! So the natural conclusion is: awareness repressed them. It is not so.

When you are unconscious, you create problems. Unconsciousness has its own language — that is the language of problems. It is like when you are groping in darkness. One thing falls, you stumble upon another thing. These are problems because of the darkness. If light comes, you will not stumble upon the table, and nothing will fall. You can move easily now. You will be able to see. But when it is dark, try to move in your own house and many accidents will happen. You may not be able to find the door in the night. You may not be able to find where things are.

In darkness, the way you live creates problems. Darkness or unconsciousness only understands the language of problems; it has no solutions. Even if a solution is given to you, in your unconsciousness you will make a problem out of it. That's what goes on happening: if I say something to you, you understand something totally different. You understand from your standpoint.

A spinster schoolteacher on her summer vacation was visiting the reservation at Yosemite. She spotted a big brave standing against a tree and became very curious about his sex life.

"How does a great big man like you get satisfaction up here where there are no young squaws?" she asked.

The Indian stared at her unbelievingly and then said, "You see cow?"

"Yes, I see cow...you don't mean?"

"Yes," said the brave, "me make love to cow. Also, you see horse?"

"Yes," said the spinster, horrified. "I see horse."

"Me make love to horse."

"Oh, dear!" cried the distraught old maid.

"No," grunted the Indian sadly. "No make love to deer. Run too fast."

Unconsciousness understands in its own way. That's why Buddhas are always misunderstood. That's a natural fate. It can't be avoided. It is very difficult to understand a Buddha. It is very easy and natural to misunderstand him. To understand him will require great awareness on your part — because he lives in the world where there are no problems! where there are all solutions and solutions and no problems, all answers and no questions. And you live in a world where there are only questions and questions and no answers. You live so far away...as if you are living on different planets.

He goes on shouting from there, but whatsoever reaches to you is totally different. And you can always find rationalizations for whatsoever you understand. You can become very argumentative, defensive too.

Gilliam was seated in the witness stand. He had already calmly answered all the questions of the prosecuting attorney. Now it was the judge's turn.

"Does the defendant really expect this court of law to accept his story that the completely assembled still on his property was not being used for the purpose of producing illicit whiskey?"

"That's right, Your Honor!" said Gilliam. "I bought that as a novelty, a conversation piece. I do not now, nor have I ever, operated it as a still to produce whiskey."

"Hogwash!" howled the magistrate. "As far as this court is concerned, possession of the equipment is proof enough of your guilt!"

"Then, Your Honor, I guess you'd also better charge me with raping your daughter!"

"What!" screamed the judge. "Did you rape my daughter too?"

"No, sir," said Gilliam. "But she was at my place last night – and I sure got the equipment for it!"

Mind is very cunning and clever. It can argue in clever ways. It can even find rationalizations and proofs; it can give you the feeling that you have understood rightly.

But Ratna's question is of immense importance. It is of importance for everybody who is here. Because this is a place where you have to become more and more aware. Awareness has to become the climate.

Do real problems exist?

They exist only when you are unconscious — then they are real. If unconsciousness is there, they are real. Just as dreams exist when you are asleep — are they real? Yes, when you are asleep they are absolutely real. But when you are awake, you know they are unreal, they were unreal. They were part of sleeping consciousness. Exactly like that — problems exist if you are not centered, not alert. If you become centered, alert, watchful, a witness, problems simply dissipate, evaporate.

Are all problems just mind games?

Yes. They are all mind games. And "mind" is nothing but another name for unconsciousness.

Does awareness make problems disappear or is there a possibility that awareness brings repression?

It depends on you. There is a little danger of it. If you force awareness upon yourself, it will be repressive. If you allow awareness to take possession of you, it will be non-repressive. If you practise awareness, stubbornly, if it is a kind of will, then you will repress. Will always represses. Will is the source of repression. Wherever will is, there will be repression.

So your consciousness has not to be out of will-power. It has to be out of understanding. It has to be relaxed. It has to be a kind of let-go. Not enforced. That is one of the most essential things to understand. If you try to become aware, you will repress.

For example, anger has arisen, and you try to become aware of the anger — stubbornly, forcibly, violently, aggressively actively, with will. With that effort, anger will recede. It will fall into the reservoir of your unconscious. It will move into the basement of your being, and will wait there. When your effort is gone...and effort cannot be continuous, because effort tires. You can make effort, will for a moment, for a few moments, for a few hours, or for a few days, but sooner or later you will need a holiday. You will be tired of the whole effort. And the moment you are on a holiday, the anger will come back, and with greater force — because while it was repressed it became pressurized. And whenever any energy is pressurized, it gains energy, it becomes more condensed. So whenever the lid is off your effort and will and the weight is removed, it will explode into violent rage.

That's what happens to people who cultivate things. They can repress their anger but they will be creating only rage. Anger is momentary. Rage is chronic. Anger is nothing to be worried about — it comes and goes. It is just a breeze. But rage is dangerous. It becomes part of you. It becomes your foundation. It is always, there. Don't you know people who are always angry? And they may not show their anger at all, and they are always angry. Whatsoever they do, they do in anger. The anger is constantly flowing underneath them like an undercurrent. It has become underground. But it affects their love, it affects their friendship, it affects their very vibe. They become repulsive, they become ugly. And they may not be angry at all, not showing anger.

Ordinarily what happens is that people who become angry for small reasons are good people, they are never in rage. You can trust them: they cannot murder or commit suicide. They will never gather that much poison. Small poison is created, thrown away. They are always fresh, healthy. Situations create anger, but they don't collect it, they don't accumulate it — they are not hoarders.

The so-called good people, respectable people, saints, etcetera, they are the really dangerous people — they go on accumulating. One day it is going to explode. And if it is not going to explode, it has to become their very life-style. Chronic it will be.

Never bring awareness through will-power. Anything brought by will-power is going to be wrong — let that be the criterion. Then how to bring awareness? Understand. When anger comes, try to understand why it has come; try to understand without any condemnation, without any justification either, without any evaluation. Just watch it. Neutral you should be.

Just as you watch a cloud moving in the sky: in the inner sky an anger cloud moves — watch it. See what it is. Look deep into it. Try to understand it. And you will find there is a chain: the anger cloud disappears, but because you looked deeply into it, something else has been found — maybe ego was hurt, that's why you become angry. Now watch this ego cloud, which is more subtle. Go on watching it. Get deep into it.

Nobody has ever been able to find anything in the ego. So if you go deep into it, you will not find it; and when you have not found it, it is no more. Then suddenly there is a great light — out of understanding, out of penetration, out of witnessing, with no effort, with no will, with no conclusion that it should be like this or should be like that. A neutral witnessing. And awareness arises. And this awareness has beauty and benediction. This awareness will heal you

And if this awareness comes, you will never be tired of it, because it has not been forced in the first place. So there is no need for any holiday!

Just think: the Christian, the Jewish God, after six days was tired and had to rest on the seventh day. In the East we don't have any conception for God's rest. Why? It looks a little hard on him. The Eastern God goes on working, goes on working — no holiday. Why is there no holiday in the East for God? In fact, the holiday that happens here in the East, in the offices, in the schools and colleges, has been brought from the West. Otherwise, there was no question of holiday at all, because life was seen from a totally different vision. It is play, not work.

The Jewish God must have got tired. Six days work, such a long work, and such a failure! Must have got tired. And finally, in the end, he created man, and since then he has not created anything. It indicates what has happened to him: he became so fed up with his own creation that after man he stopped it. He said, "Enough is enough!"

But the Eastern God is a continuum of creativity. It is play — leela. Then it is possible. Let your awareness be a play. Effortless, relaxed, and then it can become a continuum, it will be there, it will not be lost.

My feeling is that Ratna must be making this effort too much. That's why she says:

> "I find that whenever I feel a little more centered and aware than usual, I don't feel any problems, but when I am no more centered, all the old problems are back and they look even bigger. Is this repression?"

There must be a little bit of it, otherwise those problems will never come back. Once you have looked into any problem deeply, relaxedly, it is finished forever. Because all anger is the same. If you have looked into one anger situation deeply, you have understood it forever. It is finished, you are freed from it And all that energy that was getting involved in anger will be yours. And all that energy that was getting involved in greed is yours. Suddenly one finds oneself a great reservoir of energy. Then one can dance, overflow, with joy. Then life is no more an endurance but becomes enjoyment. Then life is a celebration.

Unless your awareness is without will you will be repressing. And repression can be very subtle. Then always, when the awareness is gone, the repressed thing will come, and in a bigger form, with vengeance. It will take revenge.

Ratna, don't force awareness on yourself in any way. Let it grow. Become more relaxed, calm, quiet, accepting. One has to accept all – the good and the bad, success and failure, love and hate. All one has to accept. In that acceptance, relaxation happens. And awareness is nothing but the fragrance of relaxation. It is the flowering of let-go.

Then problems disappear and disappear forever....

The last question:

Osho,
What's it all about?

I don't know, and I don't think anybody knows, or anybody has ever known. Buddha, Christ, Krishna, nobody. And it is beautiful that nobody knows, because once it is known all joy will be lost. It is a mystery. It is infinite mystery. There is no way to demystify it. There is no way to know what it is. All knowledge fails. Innocence succeeds, because innocence can say, "I do not know."

Enough for today.

CHAPTER 7
IT WILL DEVOUR YOU TOO

It is related that a dervish once stopped a king in the street. The
king said, "How dare you, a man of no account, interrupt the
progress of your sovereign?"

The dervish answered, "Can you be a sovereign if you cannot
even fill my kashkul, the begging bowl?"

He held out his bowl, and the king ordered it to be filled with
gold.

But, no sooner was the bowl seen to be full of coins than they
disappeared, and the bowl seemed to be empty again.

Sack after sack of gold was brought, and still the amazing bowl
devoured coins.

"Stop!" shouted the king, 'for this trickster is emptying my
treasury!"

"To you I am emptying your treasury," said the dervish, "but to
others I am merely illustrating a truth."

"And the truth?" asked the king.

"The truth is that the bowl is the desires of man, and the gold
what man is given. There is no end to man's capacity to devour,
without being in any way changed. See, the bowl has eaten nearly
all your wealth, but it is still a carved sea-coconut, and has not
partaken of the nature of gold in any respect.

"If you care," continued the dervish, *"to step into this bowl, it will devour you, too. How can a king, then, hold himself as being of any account?"*

Man is always in a state of becoming. Man is not a being but a process of becoming. Hence there is so much misery, anxiety, anguish. Animals are, trees are, mountains are, God also is — man is not. Man is an effort to be.

Trees are not trying to be, they simply are. God also is not trying to be, he is one with isness. Man is just in between the two — of course tense, pulled apart, torn apart. A part of his being wants to become one with the animals, another part of his being wants to rise high into the sky and become God.

Man remains in this tug-of-war.

Walt Whitman says: "There have been many moments in my life when I had the desire to become an animal again, because they are so free of desire, so free of anguish, so free of competition, so free of ambition."

Look into the eyes of a cow, or into the eyes of a cat or a dog — all seems to be so quiet and silent. As if this moment is all! But look into the mind of man and you will find a maniac. And not one but a crowd, not one but the whole madhouse inside. So many madmen shouting, desiring, asking and asking. And the desires are contradictory. If you fulfill one, necessarily the other becomes impossible to fulfill. If you fulfill the other, then something else becomes the problem.

You cannot satisfy man! There is no communication between his parts. One hand wants to do one thing, another hand may want to destroy it. A part of you is constantly hankering for the past that is lost; another part is striving to reach to the future. How can you be at ease? How can you be at home?

Listen sometimes to what goes on inside your mind.

Just the other night I was reading a passage from Ionesco's play, The Bald Soprano:

Two couples — the Smiths and the Martins — sit in a room

engaging in small talk which does not communicate. A weird clock on the wall which strikes at any time does not communicate either.

At one point in the play, the four characters angrily shout meaningless insults at each other: "Cockatoos, cockatoos, cockatoos.... Such coca, such coca, such coca.... Such cascades of cacas, such cascades of cacas, such cascades of cacas...."

When the Martins fall into bored slumber, the maid addresses the audience: "Elizabeth is not Elizabeth, Donald is not Donald. It is in vain that he thinks he is Donald. It is in vain that she thinks she is Elizabeth. But who is the true Donald? and who is the true Elizabeth? Who has any interest in prolonging the confusion?"

Ionesco is telling us in this play that loss of self is the loss of communication, and the loss of communication is the loss of self.

Have you watched inside yourself what goes on? No communication! between one fragment of your being and another fragment of your being. What to say about communion? There is no communication even. You are not one: you are a multiplicity. And you are a multiplicity because of the multiplicity of desires. You want to become so many things.

In the first place, the moment you want to become something you are losing your being. In the clouds of becoming, the being is lost. The moment you start thinking in terms of what to become, you are no more aware of who you are. When becoming is dropped, energy turns back upon itself.

That's what Jesus calls conversion — returning to the source. That's what Patanjali calls pratyahar — coming back to oneself. That is what Mahavira calls pratikraman — turning back to one's own being.

We are all rushing — rushing for somewhere there in the future. We are all rushing so fast because life is short and time is fleeting. And we go on rushing, and where do we reach? We reach only our graves. Nothing ever is fulfilled, because those desires are by their very nature unfulfillable.

Try to understand the nature of desire. That is the only deception there is, the only mirage, the only illusion. If one understands what desire is, one becomes a Buddha. Seeing the futility of desire, desire is no more valid for you. That dimension simply disappears. Becoming aware that no desire is ever fulfilled, cannot be fulfilled by its very nature, it is intrinsically unfulfillable, you need not then renounce it.

Those who renounce have not understood. Those who have understood, they don't renounce – there is nothing to renounce! Simply, the desire is no more relevant. It slips out of your hands – not that you renounce it. It simply becomes utterly meaningless. In that very understanding you are free of it.

The whole work of sannyas is to understand the nature of desire. What is the nature of desire?

First thing: it always hankers for that which is not. Now, look into it, meditate over it. This is the very nature of desire: asking for that which is not. How can it be fulfilled? When you have it, your desire will have moved away.

You see a beautiful house, and you desire it and you long for it and you dream about it, and you work hard for years. And then one day the house is yours. But you are surprised, a revelation: the moment the house is yours, the desire is no more there for it. It has already moved. It is never in the present. It can only be in the future. Future is its space, its soil; it grows there. Present is not its soil. In the present it dies – immediately dies. So when the house is yours, and you have moved into the house, suddenly you are surprised: where are those beautiful dreams that you have been dreaming about the house? House is yours, but where are those dreams? They have flown away.

The English poet, Byron, was in love with a woman. He was in love with many women, it is said near about sixty women – and he didn't live long. And to each woman he was saying, "Without you I cannot live." And he was deceiving. And the deception may not have been conscious, because he was a good man. It may have been unconscious. He may not have been doing it on purpose, but it was happening. Whenever he became interested in a woman, the whole world would disappear. That woman would be his target.

And he was a beautiful man, talented, a genius. And women are always interested in people who have some kind of talent, some kind of genius. Women are always interested not in the physical beauty as much as in something inner. And Byron had it! that magic touch, that magnetism. So it was very easy for any woman to fall in love with him. But the love would not last for a few days, at the most for a few weeks, and Byron would move to somebody else.

When he fell in love with one woman, she was very insistent: "Unless you get married to me I am not interested. You say you are ready to die for me — I don't want you to die for me. I simply want you to get married to me."

Now, that was a bigger demand. It is very easy to die — it is so poetic, so romantic — but to live with a woman and to get married is so unpoetic, so unromantic, so utterly meaningless. Byron tried to avoid and avoid, but the woman was also very clever. She had learnt many stories about Byron, that this was happening: "Within weeks, within days, his interest simply disappears. He starts looking at the woman as if he has not known her at all, as if she does not exist."

The more the woman avoided Byron, the more he became infatuated. That is the nature of desire. The more the woman looked unapproachable, the more mad he was. The more the woman created hindrances, the more he was bent upon it to get her. He was ready to do anything — even marriage. They got married.

The day they got married...Byron and his wife are coming down the steps of the church, the wedding bells are still ringing, guests are still in the church, coming out, Byron is holding the hand of the woman for whom for months he has been dreaming and has not been able to sleep, has not been able to think of anything else. She has been for these few months his whole life.

And suddenly he saw another woman pass by...and for a moment he forgot the woman to whom he had just got married. His hand slipped out of the hand of the woman. The woman saw what was happening. Those eyes were focused on the movement of some other woman, and she asked Byron, "What are you doing?"

And Byron said, "I am sorry, but I have to be true to you. When I saw this woman, my whole energy moved towards her. I forgot about you, completely. It is not conscious that I have taken my hand out of your hand. You ceased to exist in that moment. And I know I was mad after you, but the moment we were married something disappeared. The oasis is no more an oasis. You are an ordinary woman."

And you will see this happening to you again and again, if you are alert. You strive for a certain thing – and you get it one day! But all joy is in the waiting, dreaming, fantasizing. When you get it, it is finished – because desire cannot live in the present. Desire cannot live with that which is available to you, which is yours. Desire lives only in that emptiness....

Whatsoever you have is never an object of desire – how can it be? What you don't have is the object of desire. So whenever you have it, the moment you have it, it ceases to be an object of desire. This is the intrinsic nature of desire. Hence desire just drives you and drives you...to no point! It is a vicious circle. You go on moving, much movement...Much Ado About Nothing! A tale told by an idiot full of fury and noise signifying nothing – that's what desire is.

But that is where man is caught. Man is not caught in the world. Don't renounce the world. The world has nothing to do with it. There are thousands of people who have renounced the world without understanding the nature of desire – they remain the same. They can move to the Himalayas or to a monastery – Catholic, Hindu, Christian, Mohammedan – they can go to Tibet, but nothing is going to happen.

In fact, this is again another game of the desire. Now, they are not desiring the things of the world – they are desiring things of the beyond. Now they desire God, they desire paradise, they desire heaven, they desire Nirvana, enlightenment. But they go on desiring! And desire is the problem, not what you desire. The object is irrelevant. Desire can live with any object. It can live with money, it can live with power, prestige, respectability; it can live with God, it can live with enlightenment. Any object will do.

If you don't understand desire you will go on changing your objects of desire. And the desire will continue the same. And you will be in the grip of it.

This is a very unconscious state. You are suffering from desire, but you think you are suffering from things. People think they are suffering from their wives, from their husbands, children, society, people. No. Not at all. You are suffering only from one thing: desire.

Come to the root cause of it, and try to understand the root cause. And my emphasis is on understanding. I am not saying do something about it. I am not saying don't desire — no, not at all. I will be the last person to say don't desire. I am saying something totally different: Look into desire. Meditate on desire. Go deep into it. See it as deeply as possible. Layer upon layer, penetrate into it. Penetrate to the very core of it.

In that very penetration there comes a renunciation which is not of your making. There comes a renunciation which is a gift. And because it comes out of understanding you need not cultivate it, you need not practice it. Its very coming is transforming. You go through a mutation.

Let this be your criterion forever: that that which you do is going to remain superficial — you are superficial, how can you do anything in depth? Your doing is not going to help. Your doing has been your undoing up to now. No more of it. Now change the emphasis. It is not a question of doing.

Sannyas is not a question of doing: it is a question of awareness, understanding, observation, witnessing. Witness desire.

Below man, there is no desire. There are needs. They are momentary. The tiger is hungry, he searches for the prey. When he is not hungry, there is no desire.

One day, a tiger and a hare entered into a restaurant. And the tiger asked for Coca-Cola. The waiter asked the hare, "What would you like? And your friend has asked only for Coca-Cola — is he not hungry?"

The hare said, "What are you asking? If he was hungry, should I be here? He would have breakfasted long before. He is not hungry — that's why I am with him."

If a tiger is hungry, he eats! But when he is not hungry, he does not hoard. He never thinks of the future. Tomorrow does not exist for him. When the spring comes, trees bloom; they don't prepare for it, they don't fantasize about it, they don't have great desires of blooming. They don't go through rehearsals; they don't cultivate. They don't do yoga. When spring comes they bloom! It is simple, it is spontaneous. It is not out of desire — hence the beauty of nature, hence the immense silence of nature. There is no desire. The desire has not entered yet. It cannot enter, because for desire to enter a little bit of consciousness is needed — otherwise, how will you think of tomorrow? How will you think of death? How will you think of beyond? How will you plan for the future?

A little consciousness is needed — but only a little, because we have seen Buddhas who are fully conscious: again desire disappears. A Buddha again lives spontaneously, like a tree, like a rock, like a river. Of course, there is a great difference. The difference is that the Buddha is conscious and the tree is unconscious. But there is a great similarity too: both are utterly in the moment.

Buddha is in the moment because he is fully conscious; the tree is in the moment because it is fully unconscious. One thing is similar, that both are non-dual, a single phenomenon. Buddha is pure consciousness — consciousness and only consciousness. *Chinmatram* — just consciousness. There is no duality involved in it. And the tree is unconscious — *Achinmatram* — just unconsciousness, no duality involved, purity, one.

When the dual comes, tension comes. With the dual, the tug-of-war. Man is dual. A part has become conscious, and the greater part has remained still unconscious. Man is like an iceberg — only the tip of the iceberg is conscious, one tenth. Nine tenths is underneath the water, unconscious. Between these two there is bound to be conflict, a civil war.

Man is a constant civil war. The conscious says, "Do this," the unconscious says, "Do that." They are totally different phenomena. They can't understand each other. There is no possibility of any communication. One says one thing, another says another thing. There has never been any communication between them.

Because of this split, man remains in a turmoil, and remains absolutely unconscious of who he is. If he listens to the conscious he is one thing. If he listens to the unconscious he is totally another. That's why man is divided in many ways. Not only psychologically — biologically, physiologically man has divided himself. The upper part of the body seems to be higher; the lower part seems to be lower — not just lower, but low in an evaluating sense. You are identified with the upper part of the body; you are not identified with the lower part of the body. The lower seems animal. And you are constantly repressing it.

Because of these repressions, there has arisen a China Wall and you are not one. And without being one, there is no possibility of peace.

The animals are in peace, in utter peace. The Buddha is in peace. Man? Man is just in misery.

Sometimes man decides, as Walt Whitman says, just to become an animal. That's why there is so much attraction in drugs: they help you for a moment to lose your consciousness. You are again one. It may be alcohol or it may be modern drugs, but they give you a release — a release from the tense life. You relax, you become calm. Suddenly you are one again. And life seems to be no more a continuous fight in which failure is absolutely certain.

When you are drunk, you can dance again, sing again, be loving again. There is no more competition, no more politics. But how long can you remain in a drugged state? You have to come out of it. It cannot become a permanent state. And when you come back, those worries, those anxieties, are waiting for you — and they jump upon you with a vengeance. Then it becomes a vicious thing: when you become too tired of the worries, you fall into a drugged coma; and then you come again and the worries are there — they have grown meanwhile. When you were fast asleep in the coma, they were growing, they were multiplying. They don't wait for you. When you come back they are there to be taken care of.

Man constantly wants to fall back but cannot. All his efforts, at the most, can succeed for a few moments. But this is easier – to fall back. It is always easier because it is downhill. The other way to be blissful is to become a Buddha, but that is an uphill task; one has to grow, grow in consciousness. That is the only growth, remember! To grow in consciousness is the only growth. To transform your dark continent inside into an eternal light, to fill your whole being with light and awareness – that's what growth is.

Just watch your life, how conscious you are. You will be surprised – it is negligible, it is almost zero. It is very fragile, your consciousness. It is not even skin-deep. Somebody insults you and the consciousness is gone, and you are boiling with anger, mad. Somebody praises you, and the consciousness is gone, and you are puffed up and your ego becomes huge. Just small things!

Just two persons standing by the road when you pass by start laughing, and you are hurt. They may not be laughing at you – there are millions of things to laugh at. You are not the only person to laugh at. They start whispering something, and you start thinking they must be whispering against you, otherwise why should they whisper? Why can't they talk loudly? And suspicion has arisen. And you are in a turmoil. What is your consciousness?

Rena went into the City Clerk's office to report the birth of her sixth child.

"But, miss, this is your sixth child by the same father," said the clerk. "Why don't you marry him?"

"Are you jivin'?" replied Rena. "I don't even like the sonuvabitch!"

Then why do you go on making love to this man? But you should not ask the question. People go on doing a thousand and one things, not knowing why they are doing them, for what. They are simply doing them because they have nothing else to do; they are simply doing them to keep themselves occupied.

A man was getting married, and his friends asked him, "How come? Because you were introduced to this woman only two, three days ago. Have you fallen in love or something?"

And he said, "Nothing of the kind! We were dancing in the club and after a few minutes I could not find what to say to her, so I proposed."

You can laugh at it, but think of your own proposals...were they out of your consciousness, or just because you couldn't find anything else to say? And one has to say something. Just think: when you talk with a friend or your wife or your husband, are you really talking, or is it just that one has to say something? Silence seems so embarrassing.

And just because something has to be said, you say it, and then it creates trouble. Ninety-nine percent of your troubles will disappear if you stop talking too much.

I have heard:

A hunter went into the jungle. He found there a skull. He was just sitting by the side of the skull, underneath the tree – he was tired and exhausted. Nothing else to do, and there being nobody else he just said "Hello!" to the skull – just by the way.

But he was surprised: the skull said "Hello!" He was shocked too. He said, "Can you talk?"

The skull said, "Yes!"

And the man asked, "What brought you here, to this situation?" The skull said, "Talking, too much talking."

He was scared. He ran away from the place. He could not believe it. He immediately went to the king, because this was a miraculous phenomenon. And he told the king, "Something one will not believe I have seen, I have heard with my own ears a skull talking! I said 'Hello!' because there was nothing else to do and there was nobody else either. Just the skull was Lying by the side of the tree. I never thought...but the skull said 'Hello!'"

He was still trembling.

"And I asked the skull, and she answers! She says, 'Yes.' She can talk."

The king said, "You must be joking."

He said, "No! I bet!"

The king said, "Okay, I will come."

And the whole court followed, and the king went there, and of course the skull was there, and the man went close to the skull and said, "Hello!" And she didn't reply. He said, "Hello!" loudly, and the skull remained silent. He said, "What has happened to you?" But no answer.

And the king said, "I knew it before. Either you are a madman or you have some deceptions in your mind. Cut this man's head!"

The head was cut and thrown there, and the king returned. When the king returned, the skull said to the head "Hello!"

He said, "You fool! Why didn't you speak that time?"

And the skull asked, "What brought you here?"

And the head said, "Too much talking."

Ninety-nine percent of your problems will disappear if you don't talk too much. But what else to do? Life is so empty! One fills it somehow, patches it, stuffs it, makes it look as if it is full. Desires help you infinitely. They keep you on the go. They make you feel that something is happening or is going to happen. They keep you hoping. They keep you on the move; otherwise, how will you move? how you will live? But all those desires are unconscious. You don't know from where they come, how they take possession of you, where their source is.

Armstrong was brought into court for non-support by his wife.

"Young man," said the judge, "your wife says you have twelve children and you don't support them. How can a man who doesn't support his family want to have so many children?"

"Your Honor," said Armstrong, "when I get that feelin', I feel I could support the whole world."

But from where does that feeling come? It comes from somewhere in your innermost core, but it is dark and you have never groped for it, from where it comes. The only thing that a man has to do to get out of the misery that is created by the unconscious and the problems that are created by the unconscious is one, the only one key: become more conscious.

What do I mean when I say become more conscious? De-automatize your habits. Remember this: de-automatize your habits. You are walking, it is an automatic habit; you need not be aware of it. But bring awareness to yourself. Walk fully conscious.

Buddha says: When you stand up, stand up consciously; when you sit down, sit down consciously. When you say something, say it very consciously. When you listen to something, listen consciously. When you are eating, eat consciously.

It happened once:

Buddha was not yet enlightened, was coming closer and closer and closer. Maybe ninety-nine percent of his being was almost light; only one percent remained dark. He was just on the verge of enlightenment. It was just a few days before he became enlightened that this incident happened.

They were moving — he had five disciples with him. A fly came and sat on his forehead. Just out of unconscious habit, he waved his hand, the fly went away, but he stopped himself in the middle of the road with the five disciples watching what happened. Now, there was a fly, but he took his hands again, very consciously, slowly, waved at the fly — which was not there!

The disciples were puzzled, they said, "What are you doing? The fly is gone! When you first waved your hand, the fly went away. What are you doing now?"

Buddha said, "I did it unconsciously. It is automatic. It was robotlike. Now I am doing as I should have done. The fly is not there — that is not the point — but now I am doing as I should have done. Consciously I move my hand, slowly, with full awareness, attentiveness. My mind is nowhere else. My total mind is focused on this simple act — the hand is moving, and then I wave, with great compassion for the fly.

"The first time, I was walking, I was looking around, and the fly came. And the robot part of my body worked, but I was not in it."

That's what happens when you have learnt something. If you start learning to drive, in the beginning you have to be very alert — alert about many things: the wheel, and the accelerator, and the brake and the clutch, and the people on the road. You have to be conscious of all these things. Slowly slowly, once you have learnt to drive, you need not think of anything at all. Everything has become automatized. Now you can sing a song, smoke a cigarette, listen to the radio, talk to the friend — you can do anything! Now, that part, the driving part, needs no attention, your attention is free.

This is a necessity of life, otherwise you will not be able to do many things. So whatsoever you have learnt is always transferred to the robot. Then the robot does it and you are free to learn something else. This is perfectly okay in ordinary life, but, slowly slowly, the robot becomes bigger and bigger. And your tiny consciousness remains tiny.

The work that one has to do upon oneself consists in taking back from the robot, de-automatizing processes. And you will be surprised: if you de-automatize any process, great awareness is released.

Just walk consciously for half an hour, and you will be surprised how quiet, how peaceful and serene you look and you feel. Just sitting in your chair, watch your in-going, out-going breath, silently — the breath goes in, and you know, you watch, it is going in. Each step of the breath: it has touched your nostrils, the inner side of the nose, it is moving, it has touched your throat, it has moved, it has gone deep into your lungs; you can feel the belly coming up. And then you feel for a moment it has stopped. No movement. And then the return journey: the belly falls back, the air is going out; again you feel the same route. It leaves your nostrils...and again a moment's gap. And then again new fresh air moves in.

If you simply watch such a simple process, you will be surprised: one hour's watching of breath will bring you so much silence and so much alertness, as you have never felt in your life. And that makes a difference. That is the difference that makes the difference, that transforms your whole life, slowly slowly. Then you can change everything: eating, walking, breathing — even making love can become a very conscious, alert phenomenon.

And then from everywhere, consciousness goes on pouring in. And, slowly slowly, the balance changes: you become more conscious than you are unconscious. Then you start leaning towards God, farther and farther away you start moving from the animals. When a man is really conscious, all desires disappear just as dewdrops disappear when in the morning the sun rises.

Desires have not to be dropped, they have also to be used to grow in consciousness.

Now this famous Sufi story — it is one of the greatest gems:

> It is related that a dervish once stopped a king in the street. The king said, "How dare you, a man of no account, interrupt the progress of your sovereign?"

We will go into each important word:

> It is related that a dervish...

A dervish is one who has attained. A dervish is one who has arrived. A dervish is one whose journey is complete, whose circle is complete. A dervish is one who no longer has any desires, a state of desirelessness. But the state of desirelessness is the state of bliss — satchitananda — it is the state of bliss, of consciousness of truth. The dervish is the highest point of growth.

> It is related that a dervish once stopped a king...

Now, the dervish looks like a beggar, and is really the king. And the king looks like a king, but is nothing but a beggar. The dervish has nothing, but has all; in having nothing he has become capable of having all. By becoming empty of all desires he is full of God. There is no need to ask for more. More cannot be conceived.

The dervish lives like a beggar, but only from the outside. If you can look into him, if you have eyes to see, if you have a little alertness, you will find him luminous, you will find in him all the grandeur of God, all the splendor of existence. He is the richest man there is.

Swami Ram used to call himself an emperor. When he went to America, people could not understand. In the East we know; in the East this has become now a definite conclusion. Thousands of years of experience have proved it again and again, that only people like Buddha are real emperors. And the so-called emperors are just beggars somehow hiding their inner emptiness.

The kings, the presidents, and the prime ministers are nothing but people suffering from inferiority complexes. Hence creating much noise around themselves to show others that "We are not nothing. We are somebodies!" A man who tries to prove that he is somebody is simply showing that deep down he is afraid of his nobodiness. If he becomes the president of a country, of course he can prove — at least to the fools he can prove that he is somebody. And looking in the eyes of those fools, he himself can believe, "When so many people believe that I am somebody, I must be somebody. How can so many people be wrong?" He deceives others and is deceived in return. It is a self-deception. The East knows it.

The East has known real emperors. And it has known a long long series of beggars too. You will be surprised: the East has never been interested in writing the history of emperors, prime ministers and all those kinds of neurotic people. The East's interest has been in Buddhas, Ramas, Krishnas.

The West is very much puzzled why we have not been interested in history. We have been writing real history — because the real history consists of the evolution of human consciousness. The real history has nothing to do with money, the real history has nothing to do with power-politics. The real history has only to do with one thing: that is who comes in the world with light, religious light, bliss, consciousness; takes humanity a step further into growth.

But when Swami Ram went to America, people were naturally puzzled. He was a beggar, and he called himself an emperor! People started asking him, "Why do you call yourself an emperor? You don't have anything."

And he laughed, and he said, "That's why — because I don't have anything, because I don't need! I am an emperor, because all that I need I have. And your emperors are not emperors, because they will never have all that they need. Their desires will go on multiplying themselves. They will live the life of a beggar, and they will die the life of a beggar."

Look into the hearts of the rich people — they have to be pitied. They are poorer than the poor. It sometimes happens that in a poor person's heart you may find a jewel, luminous, but rarely in a rich man's heart, because to become rich he has to sell his soul. To become a prime minister or a president he has to destroy his self, he has to compromise. He has to adjust to the demands of the stupid humanity, the majority. He can lead people only if he follows them — so your great leaders are nothing but great followers of the masses and the mob.

It is related that a dervish once stopped a king in the street.

And why in the street? Because the king is always and always moving. He is always searching for more; he is always in the street, he is always on a journey, because there are many things yet to be attained.

When Alexander came to India, Diogenes asked him — a very rare man, Diogenes.... Naked he lived, like Mahavira, an utterly blissful man. He asked Alexander, "Where are you going?"

Alexander said, "I am going to conquer the whole world!"

And Diogenes asked, "Then what? Then what will you do?"

Alexander was a little puzzled because nobody had asked this: "Then what?" He shrugged his shoulders, and then said, "Then I will rest."

And Diogenes started laughing — that mad laughter. Only

enlightened people can do that. Embarrassed, Alexander said, "Why are you laughing?"

He said, "I am laughing because I am resting right now!"

He was Lying down on the bank of a river, naked, it was early morning. Fresh air, and the sun was rising and the birds were singing, and it was all beatitude. And he said, "You fool! I am resting, and you will rest when you have conquered the whole world, then what is the point? If I can rest without conquering the world, why can't you? Come on! Lie down by the side of me! And this bank is so big, it can take both of us. There is no problem, no competition."

Alexander was hypnotized by this man. He said, "You are right. Nobody has dared to say such things to me. I see the point, but right now I cannot stop because I am in the middle of my journey, I am on the road. I have to conquer and finish things, then I will come."

Diogenes said, "You can go. But remember: this road is endless. You will never be able to come back."

It is never completed. Who has ever been able to complete it? Death comes before! And it happened exactly like that. Alexander could not come back. He died. He never came back to his country; he died in the middle. And the moment he was dying, only Diogenes was in his mind. In that moment, just think how poor he must have looked to himself, and how rich Diogenes was — how beggarly he was. Begged and begged and begged...and to no point! And was dying.

It was because of the memory of Diogenes that he told his generals, "When you take my body to the cemetery, let my hands hang out in the procession — out of the casket."

"Why?" the generals asked, "because we have never heard of any tradition like that."

He said, "So that everybody can see that Diogenes was right — I am dying empty-handed. Let them see my hands! My whole life was empty and I am dying empty-handed, nothing in my hands."

Every king is in the street.

It is related that a dervish once stopped a king in the street. The king said, "How dare you, a man of no account interrupt the progress of your sovereign?"

It is very difficult to see who is the man of account and who is the man of no account. It takes great insight to see it. Those who appear on the surface men of account are not. They are just pretenders. And those who don't appear at all as men of account are. But appearances won't help.

The dervish answered, "Can you be a sovereign if you cannot even fill my kashkul, the begging bowl?"

Now the Sufi master is creating a situation. Great must have been his compassion. He is creating a situation, and a rare situation. He says, "You and a sovereign? And you think yourself a man of account? If you are, then do this simple thing. I have got this begging bowl, this kashkul, can you fill it?"

The king must have laughed: "This man is mad. Such a small begging bowl I cannot fill?"

He held out his bowl, and the king ordered it to be filled with gold.

But no sooner was the bowl seen to be full of coins than they disappeared, and the bowl seemed to be empty again.

Sack after sack of gold was brought, and still the amazing bowl devoured coins.

"Stop!" shouted the king, "for this trickster is emptying my treasury!"

Still he could not see the point. It is so difficult to see the point. The master was confronting him. The master has come to the disciple. The master is creating a situation in which even a blind man will be able to see, in which the deaf will be able to hear, and the heartless will start feeling again. But people are stubborn — stubborn in their idiocies, stubborn in their ideologies, stubborn in their conceptions and prejudices.

"Stop!" shouted the king, "for this trickster is emptying my treasury!"

The master looks like a trickster, as if he is after his treasury. He is after him, certainly, but not after his treasury. A master is always after the disciple. But you can miss, because sometimes the situation may be such that your whole mind will interpret it in a wrong way.

The king knows only money and money and money. He understands only one language — the language of money. Now, certainly, this man is cheating. He can see only some device: "The begging bowl is a trick. It cannot be filled and he will empty my whole treasure. And he has caught me — he has provoked me and now he is cheating."

"To you," said the dervish, "I am emptying your treasury..."

*"...*because you cannot see beyond that. Your eyes are focussed on money. You can only think of money. All is always translated by you in terms of money — as if money is all. Life is much more: money is nothing."

"To you I am emptying your treasury," said the dervish, "but to others I am merely illustrating a truth."

Who are these others? The dervish must have been Surrounded by his disciples. It was a situation for the king, and it was a situation for his disciples too. To those disciples he was illustrating a truth. What truth was he illustrating? And the king asked:

"And the truth? What truth?"

"The truth is that the bowl is the desires of man..."

The bowl is made of the mind of man. The bowl is made of the skull of man. It represents man's mind — his constant hankering to become this, to become that, to gain, to profit. It represents greed. It represents that constant effort to be something other than you are, to be somewhere else, to be more, to have more. This madness for more is represented by the bowl.

"The truth is that the bowl is the desires of man, and the gold what man is given...."

And God has given much more than you really need, much more than you deserve. God has been a showering, a constant showering, of gifts on you. You have not earned them. But look at the thanklessness of man. Even to thank God seems to be impossible. We go on complaining to God. We go on asking for more. All your prayers are nothing but demands for more.

Have you ever prayed without demanding anything? directly, indirectly?

A woman, a young woman, heard a mystic say, "You should not ask God anything for yourself. Ask for others, then the prayers will be heard. Ask because of compassion."

The woman was young but was very much worried...in fact she had come to the mystic only to be blessed. She wanted a husband, and it was getting late. Must have been homely, ordinary; must have been poor or something. But now the mystic says, "Ask not for yourself, only then will the prayers be fulfilled." So what is the point in praying? But then she found a way.

She went into the temple and prayed to God, "God, give my mother a beautiful son-in-law."

Directly or indirectly, all your prayers are demands. And a demand poisons the prayer and kills it, cuts its wings. Then it cannot reach to God. Only prayers which have no demands are weightless enough to fly into that plenitude.

"The truth is that the bowl is the desires of man, and the gold what man is given. There is no end to man's capacity to devour without being in any way changed...."

And man goes on devouring. You can go on giving. The more you give, the more demand comes, but the frustration continues. The gap between the man and his desire remains constant. It is one of the constants in the world, unchanging.

The difference between you and the horizon remains constant. You can go on and on, and whether you go on foot or you rush in a plane makes no difference — the horizon remains there, always there, never here. The closer you come to the horizon, the more it goes on receding. You never come close.

It is not that man is not given anything. Just think of this beauty! of this benediction of existence, of this silence, of this joy, this celebration! Have you ever thanked God for a rose flower? If not, then when are you going to thank him? Have you ever thanked God for the dewdrops slipping so quietly from the grass leaves in the early sun, so pearl-like? And sometimes when the rays penetrate them, a small rainbow arises around them. Have you not looked at this beauty? at this poetry? at this constant celebration of existence? When are you going to thank God? For what are you waiting? Have you forgotten to thank? Have you forgotten to bow down in gratitude?

Those who know, they always thank and praise, even in moments when you will not think that praise is possible.

Let me remind you of Zusya, the same mad mystic who would run and jump and dance into the synagogue, so madly, so wildly, that everybody else who was in the synagogue would escape, because he would turn tables upside down. And whosoever would come in between him and his dance would be thrown. His dance was of such abandon that he would forget everybody! He would forget himself — only God existed in those moments.

Zusya's son died, his only son and he had loved the son tremendously. And do you know what? He danced! He danced all the way to the cemetery. He was dancing and tears of joy were flowing from his eyes. And he was saying to God, "Look! You had given me such a beautiful and such a pure soul, and I am returning the beautiful and the pure soul as beautiful as it was. It has not been contaminated at all. Can't you see?! I am returning your gift back to you. I am happy that for these few days you have given this gift to me. I am immensely grateful. It must be time that the child has to go back home."

If you see, then all and everything becomes a cause to celebrate. If you can't see, then everything is a cause for a complaint.

> "The truth is that the bowl is the desires of man, and the gold what man is given. There is no end to man's capacity to devour, without being in any way changed."

And things go on showering on you, and you never change, you remain almost the same! You devour everything, but nothing transforms you.

> "See, the bowl has eaten nearly all your wealth, but it is still a carved sea-coconut, and has not partaken of the nature of gold in any respect."

Remember this. If you start feeling grateful, you will be transformed. You will start changing your being from baser metal into gold – this is what alchemy is all about, and this is what sannyas is all about. Sannyas is the purest alchemy, the new alchemy, the science of transforming the baser into the higher. And the bridge is gratitude.

Feel grateful! Search for causes to be grateful, and you will find infinite causes. In the morning the sun rises and there is enough cause, more than enough, to dance and sing. God has risen in the sun. And by the evening when the sun is setting, sing and dance!

Soon the night is coming with its beautiful darkness and all those stars. Soon the mystery will surround you, the mystery of darkness and the coolness of darkness and the silence of darkness and its infinite music.

Just go on looking for reasons to celebrate, and you will become religious. And, slowly slowly, each gratitude felt deeply transforms you. Desires never transform, only gratitude transforms – and they are diametrically opposite. Desire means: "Give me more! I am complaining. I am demanding." Gratitude says: "You have given me so much that I never deserved in the first place. I am grateful, I am thanking."

See the point. Desire says: "Give me more!" Gratitude says: "You have given already so much! Nothing more is needed. It is enough for me to live with it for eternity." Desire takes you into the future. Gratitude makes you still, in the present. Gratitude is meditation. It is being silently herenow...and the whole opens up. And thousands of lotuses bloom in your being.

That fragrance transforms you. That fragrance will fill your begging bowl. You will become an emperor. You will not be a beggar any more.

This is what I would like to give to you here. But if you desire, it cannot be given. If you don't desire, it can be given. If you ask for it, you will miss. If you don't ask for it and you celebrate, you have got it already!

"If you care," continued the dervish, "to step into this bowl, it will devour you too. How can a king, then, hold himself as being of any account?"

*Y*es, that's what happens really. This more, this constant desire for more, this obsession for more, devours all that you go on collecting, and finally devours you too. That's what death is: devoured by your own desiring, eaten up by your own hungry mind. That's what death is. Sooner or later, you will step in the bowl. That bowl is your grave.

And the dervish is right:

*"If you care to step into this bowl, it will devour you too. How
can a king, then, hold himself as being of any account?"*

"What are you talking about?" the dervish said. "Do you think
yourself of any account? You cannot even fill this small begging
bowl, and you think you are a king? Forget all about this nonsense.
Your kingdom is not worth anything; it cannot even fill the begging
bowl of a beggar. What worth does it have? Even if you step in it,
you will disappear. You are less than the begging bowl of a beggar.
What nonsense are you talking about that you are of some account?
You are not."

A man becomes only of some account when he stops desiring.
The moment you stop desiring, you are yourself. Suddenly you
become awakened to your innermost being.

A famous ancient parable:

Once ten men forded a swift and dangerous river. Upon reaching
the shore, they counted to see if all had arrived safely. But each man
could count but nine. A passerby, hearing their wailing over the loss
of a comrade, counted the men and discovered there were ten. He
then asked each man to count, and when he counted, he counted
only nine. The stranger touched him on the chest and said, "You
are the tenth!"

That's the function of a master: to put his hand on your heart
and to say to you, "You are the tenth!"

You go on searching everywhere, except in your own being.
You count everybody else, but then it only comes up to nine, one is
missing. And you can go on looking for that one forever and ever,
and you will not find — because that one is you!

A man becomes an emperor the moment he finds himself.

In the same way, a great scientist, A.S. Eddington, says: "We
have found a strange footprint on the shores of the unknown. We
have devised profound theories, one after another, to account for

its origin. At last we have succeeded in reconstructing the creature that made the footprint. And, lo! It is our own."

You are the tenth. If this simple key becomes available to you, you are the emperor. Then all the treasures of life are open for you, and all the mysteries therein.

But everybody is rushing to find where it is...and it is inside you. The sought is not outside, the sought is in the seeker. The God is not outside, the God is in the seeker. Seek, and you will seek in vain. Stop seeking, and look within, and you have found it: And, lo! It is our own footprint.

The tenth is missing, and the tenth is you.

Enough for today.

CHAPTER 8

THE GRASS GROWS BY ITSELF

The first question:

Osho,

What exactly do you mean by "conscious ignorance"? Is it the recognition that one is ultimately, fundamentally ignorant? Or is there more to it?

Conscious ignorance is not ignorance at all. It is the ultimate state of consciousness — how can it be ignorant? It is pure knowing. Of course, there is no knowledge, hence it is called ignorance. But there is knowing, utter knowing, clarity, transparency. No knowledge is gathered, but all is known.

Conscious ignorance means innocence and conscious. If innocence is unconscious, sooner or later it will be corrupted by knowledge. Unconscious mind is always ready to be corrupted, polluted, distracted.

Consciousness means centering, awareness — you cannot be distracted. You remain in your knowing, but you don't accumulate knowledge. Knowledge is always of the past: knowing is in the present, is of the present. Like a mirror: the mirror reflects if something comes before it, but when it passes the mirror is empty again. This is conscious ignorance – not that the mirror does not reflect: it reflects, but it doesn't gather. It is not like a photoplate.

A photoplate becomes knowledgeable. The moment something is reflected in it, it catches hold of it. It becomes attached to it. The mirror remains unattached – available, open, vulnerable, unprotected, with no defence, yet always virgin. This is virginity: when nothing corrupts you. Things come and pass.

> You ask me: *What exactly do you mean by 'conscious ignorance'?*

It is consciousness, knowing consciousness. Ignorant I am calling it because it cannot claim any knowledge – that's why. It cannot say "I know."

When the Emperor Wu asked Bodhidharma, "Who are you?" he simply said, "I don't know."

This is conscious ignorance. We misunderstood him. He thought, "Then what is the point? If you don't even know who you are, then what is the difference between me and you? I also don't know who I am."

We are simply ignorant. Bodhidharma is consciously ignorant. And that word "consciousness" makes all the difference – all the difference that there is in the world. It transforms the whole quality of ignorance. Ignorance becomes luminous. It is full of light – not full of knowledge but full of light.

> You ask: *Is it the recognition that one is ultimately, fundamentally ignorant?*

No. One is not, so how can one be fundamentally and ultimately ignorant? To think that one is you have already gathered knowledge, you have already claimed. You have already declared to the world that "I am!"

Those who know, they know something totally different. They know that "I am not — God is." They know that "My existence is arbitrary. My existence is a make-believe. 'I' as a separate entity has never existed. I am just a wave in the ocean."

But when the wave is arising and reaching to the clouds, it can believe that "I am." And the ocean meanwhile is laughing and roaring, and knows that this wave has gone crazy. Soon the wave will disappear in the ocean again. Even when it is there, it is not separate from the ocean. You cannot separate a wave from the ocean! Can you exist even for a single moment without the universe surrounding you? Not for a single moment.

So who are you? what are you?

Is it the recognition that one is ultimately, fundamentally ignorant?

No. The conscious ignorance knows that one is not. There is utter silence inside. Nobody has ever been there. You have dreamt about it; it is your dream. You are nothing but a construct of your dreaming mind.

And, secondly, ignorance does not mean that one is ignorant. It simply means that life is ultimately mysterious. The emphasis is not on your ignorance, remember it, because the ego is very cunning. It can survive even on the idea of ignorance. It can say, "I am ignorant — fundamentally, ultimately I am ignorant. But I am."

First it was claiming its existence through knowledge: "My knowledge is valid. Nobody else's knowledge is valid." Now it claims, "No knowledge is valid — I am ignorant. But I am." Now, behind ignorance, the I is hiding again. It has taken another face, a new mask, a new persona, but it is the old game being played with new rules. The form has changed but the content is the same — the same dream, the same stupid dream. The same arbitrary ego claiming absoluteness about itself.

No. When I say ignorance, my emphasis is never on I. My emphasis is on the ultimate mysteriousness of existence. Ignorance is ultimate because existence cannot be reduced to knowledge. It is irreducible. It is a mystery, and remains a mystery. You cannot demystify it.

In fact, the more you try to demystify it, the more and more mysterious it becomes. It gathers new dimensions of mysteries.

Just watch: five thousand years of human mind's evolution — has it helped in any way to demystify existence? Existence has become far more mysterious than it has ever been before. Go back five thousand years: there was a limited number of stars, because by the bare naked eye you cannot count more than three thousand stars in the night. When the night is dark and full of stars and there are no clouds, at the most you can count three thousand stars, not more than that, by the bare naked eye. How many stars are there? Now they say, "We have counted three thousand billion stars. We used to see only three thousand, now there are three thousand billion stars. And this is not the end: this is just the beginning of the counting."

The existence goes on and on. There seems to be no possibility that it will be ending somewhere.

When the Vedic mystics looked at the sky, it was mysterious. When you look at the sky it is far more mysterious. Medic mystics will feel jealous of you — but you don't look at the sky.

For thousands of years man believed that life, existence, consists of matter. Now physicists say there is no matter — all is energy. They have not been able to solve the mystery of matter. The mystery has become very deep. Now there is no matter — it is all energy.

And what is energy? Now, even to define it is becoming difficult — because it was possible to define it in contrast with matter. Now there is no matter. How to define it? Definition is lost. It is there in its sheer mystery. And the efforts that have been made to define it have made it look even more mysterious.

If you go into modern physics, you will be surprised. Mystics look not so mysterious now — with all God and heaven and angels and souls, even then they don't look so mysterious. The modern world of physics is far more mysterious, incomprehensibly mysterious. And the infinite space....

And Albert Einstein says it goes on expanding...into what? And he says, "We don't know yet into what. But one thing is certain: it goes on expanding."

Existence is expanding, into what? Naturally, the question arises. There must be some space beyond it, but that cannot be said. By the very definition of existence that is prohibited, because when we say "existence" we mean all that is, space included. All that is. Then how does it expand? into what? There is nothing left outside it!

It is almost as mysterious as one day you go to the market and you keep yourself in your own pocket. It is possible to keep yourself in your own pocket? It should be — if existence can expand without there being anything to expand into. All space is in, in its pocket, and it goes on expanding into its own pocket! Looks absurd. Zen koans are nothing compared to it.

Albert Einstein says the world is finite. That too is mysterious. If the world is finite, then there must be something to define it. There must be a boundary! If you call it finite, then there must be a boundary to it. But to make a boundary you will have to accept something beyond the boundary, otherwise the boundary cannot be drawn. The boundary can be drawn only between two things!

You can have a fence around your house because of the neighbor. If there is no neighbor, nothing exists beyond your fence, how are you going to put the fence and where? And how will you decide that "This is the place where we should put the fence," that "This part belongs to me and there is nothing outside it"?

But Albert Einstein says this is how it is: "We can't explain it, but this is how it is. The world is finite and yet there is no boundary to it. Unbounded finiteness!" Absurd! Illogical!

And not only that: this unbounded finiteness is round in shape — because everything is round. How can an unbounded thing be round? Who will give it the shape of roundness?

The mystery has thickened every day. And Albert Einstein is just on the threshold of existence. It is maddening.

So when I say "conscious ignorance," I don't mean that you are ignorant: I mean that life is so vast and existence so infinite that there is no way to fathom it. You cannot measure it; it is immeasurable.

What exactly do you mean by "conscious ignorance"? Is it the recognition that one is ultimately, fundamentally ignorant? Or is there more to it?

If there is not more to it, then the mystery is solved. There is always more to it! and there will always be more to it. Whatsoever can be said will never be satisfactory — there will always remain more to it.

And I am not saying that what is not said and you understand inside is enough — even that is not enough. Nothing is enough. That is the meaning when I say existence is mysterious. It simply cannot be understood.

To see this point makes one feel humble. To see this point, to let it sink in your heart, one feels like bowing down. To bow down before this mystery that is unfathomable — not only unknown but unknowable — is prayer.

The second question:

Osho,

> *I remember.*
> *I let go.*
> *I forget.*
> *I let go.*
> *My love affair with life*
> *keeps deepening.*
> *Still, I am not without doubts.*

But the plunge forward!
A dance unpredictable.
And I allow all around...
Dissolve in through sound...
Ahh, Osho – thank you.

A question on polarities:
man-woman, Zen-Sufi...
Can any one being encompass it all?

Yes, I am encompassing it all – so can you. Because being is vast. Being is neither male nor female. Bodies are male and female. Psychologies are male and female. But not being. Being is simply being.

At the very core of your existence, there is no man, no woman. The consciousness is beyond polarity. When you are witnessing your body, if you are a man you will see a man's body there as an object; if you are a woman, you will see a woman's body as an object. But the witness is the witness, man or woman. The witness is neither. The witness is simply there – a witness, that's all. A consciousness, an awareness.

That awareness comprehends all. When you become a witness, when you become a Buddha, all is comprehended. Then there is no question of polarities.

The world is not just polar. That is the meaning of the Christian idea of the Trinity and the Hindu concept of Trimurti. The world is not divided in two – world is divided in three. The three is very fundamental. The two is on the surface and the three is at the center. Man-woman, on the surface. Zen-Sufi, on the surface. But as you move deeper, as you dive deep into your being, and you reach the center, all disappears. One simply is. A kind of purity, a pure existence.

It is possible – not only possible, it has to be made possible. That's my work here. On the path, be a Sufi or a Zen. When you reach the center, forget all about it. When the goal is reached, the path has to be forgotten. These are divisions of the path.

One can climb up a mountain from many sides, can choose different routes. And when you are moving on different routes, you look as if you are moving in different directions, sometimes opposite also. One is going to the north, another is going to the south, but ultimately, when you reach to the peak, you will have come to the same place.

At the peak, Buddha is Christ, Christ is Krishna, Krishna is Mohammed, Mohammed is Zarathustra, Zarathustra is Lao Tzu. At the peak all distinctions dissolve.

So, right now be Zen, be Sufi, and when you have reached to the peak be Zen / Sufi — then forget all about it! But on the path...one has to move on some path. And all paths are good, because they all lead to the same goal. All doors are good, because they lead to the same shrine.

You say:

> I remember.
> I let go.
> I forget.
> I let go.
> My love affair with life
> keeps deepening.
> Still, I am not without doubts.

Don't be worried about it! Doubts are perfectly natural on the path. If you are without doubts, that means you have reached the peak. They disappear only at the peak. They have a certain purpose — they goad you, they keep you going.

Doubts are not necessarily hindrances. It depends on you, on how you use your doubts. They can become hindrances. If because of doubt you simply stop moving, you say, "Unless my doubt is dissolved I am not going to move," then the doubt has become a rock. But if you say, "The doubt is there, but in spite of the doubt I am going to move, because that is the only way to resolve it.... Unless I reach higher I cannot resolve this doubt" — a better vision, from a height, will help.

Doubts are not resolved if you remain clinging to the same space where you are, because those doubts are created by that state of mind. If you remain clinging to that state, the doubts will persist; they will become stronger every day.

Doubts are not resolved by somebody else answering you. These are not philosophical doubts – these are existential doubts. They are resolved only by experiencing. When you move a little higher, they disappear. You have reached to another state of mind. In that state of mind they cannot exist. Suddenly they disappear, as if they have never been there.

In spite of the doubt, one has to go on moving. In fact, one has to use the doubt as a goading to move. Listen to the doubt and say to the doubt, "Okay, I will remember you, but the only way to solve you is that I should go a little higher in my consciousness. I should become a little more alert. It is my unalertness that is creating you. It is my unconsciousness that is creating you, that is feeding you, nourishing you. It is my state of mechanicalness that is the cause of it."

If you try to solve your doubts where you are, you can gather many many answers from many many sources. They will make you knowledgeable, but not really – they will fill you with information. But the doubt will remain somewhere. On the surface, you may start pretending that you know, but you will know that you don't know. And it will gnaw at your heart.

You can learn the answers, you can start telling those answers to others, but your very existence, your very life-style, will show that you don't know.

That is the difference between the Western and the Eastern philosophies. They should not be called by the same name, because their approaches are so basically different, so fundamentally different, so diametrically opposite.

The Western philosopher thinks, but never changes his state of awareness. He thinks where he is. He thinks hard, he thinks very logically. He tries in every way to solve the problem, and he finds many solutions. But those solutions don't help his life. If they don't even help his life, how can they help somebody else's life?

For example: the English thinker and philosopher, David Hume, arrived at the same conclusion as Gautam Buddha, exactly the same. Had he been in the East he would have become a Buddha, but unfortunately he was in the West, in the very thick of the Western noe-sphere.

He arrived at the same conclusion, not by changing his consciousness, but only by logical argumentation. Buddha became enlightened, Hume remained unenlightened. Buddha arrived at a state of bliss; Hume remained crawling on the earth in the same way as of old. Buddha created a new tradition which has remained alive even today; twenty-five centuries have passed. Many people have bloomed because of Buddha.

What did Hume create? Hume also created great argumentation, and even today books are written on Hume, and the argument continues. But it is only argumentation; not a single human being has been transformed by it.

And the irony is that the conclusion is exactly the same. Buddha came to see that there is no self; that was his realization. He meditated. He went deeper and deeper into his being. He searched inside, each nook and corner, and he didn't find anybody there. That was his release. The ego disappeared, and with the ego all its miseries and hells.

The ego was not found, so all the problems that were created by the ego evaporated. When the source evaporated, all the by-products evaporated of their own accord. When the ego was not found, there was silence — and that silence is beatitude, and that silence is benediction.

When the ego was not found, there was all light, radiant. The whole existence flowed in. Buddha became a void capable of containing the whole existence. He himself became transformed. And thousands of other people became transformed from his insight. Remember, it was an insight.

What happened to David Hume? He also came to the same point, but it was not an insight — it was an outlook. Remember these two words. Literally they are significant: insight, outlook. He arrived at the same conclusion, as an outlook. He discussed, argued, pondered, thought, contemplated, concentrated – did everything on the problem, but never went in.

And he came to the point, exactly the same, at least in appearance the same, that there is no self. The self cannot exist. But it was not a great revolution in his life; it was just a beautiful conclusion in his treatise. But he remained the same man! Before the conclusion and after the conclusion there was not a bit of difference in the man. He continued to behave in the same way.

If you had insulted him he would have become angry, but not Buddha. That is the difference. He would have become angry, although he says there is no self. He would have forgotten all his philosophy. That philosophy was not his insight. He would have said, "That is philosophy – that is aside. But when you insult me, I am insulted. And I am going to take revenge. You have to be answered!"

When Buddha was insulted, he smiled. He said, "You came a little late. You should have come ten years before, then I was there, very much. Had you insulted me ten years before, I would have reacted madly. You come a little late. I feel sorry for you, because now there is nobody to react. I hear what you are saying, but it simply passes through me. It comes in through one ear and it goes out through the other ear. There is nobody inside to catch hold of it. I am sorry. I feel compassion for you."

This is the difference between the Eastern and the Western approaches. Western philosophy is rightly called philosophy – love of knowledge, love of wisdom. For Eastern philosophy, Hesse has coined a word which I like. He has coined a new word; he calls it *philosia* – it means love of seeing. *Sia* means to see. That is exactly the translation of the Eastern term for philosophy, *darshan* – to see. It is philosia – it is insight, it is seeing in.

Western philosophy is a search for knowledge, and Eastern philosophy or philosia is a search for knowing. Knowledge looks out; knowing looks in. Knowledge gathers information; knowing does not gather anything – it simply goes in to see who is there. "Who am I?" Its inquiry is not objective, its inquiry is subjective.

Doubts will persist. They leave you only on the last rung, never before. Use them creatively. Each doubt has to be transformed into a goading. The doubt simply says you have to go a little further, a little ahead, a little higher. The doubt says, "I do not feel satisfied — whatsoever you have now is not satisfactory. You have to go a little deeper."

Don't be stopped by the doubt; that is not the function of the doubt. And don't start arguing, and don't start thinking, because by thinking you will become a David Hume, you will remain the same person.

My effort here is to create Buddhas. And unless you become a Buddha, doubts will continue. You can solve one doubt, it will assert itself from another corner. It is the same doubt in a new shape, a new form. You repress it here, it pops up there. You will go mad. No need. Take note of the doubt, thank the doubt, and say, "Okay, so I will go a little further so you can be solved."

It is like this:

A man was sitting on a tree. His friend was sitting underneath the tree. The man on the tree was picking some fruits, and the man underneath the tree was waiting for the fruits and collecting whatsoever was falling. The man on the tree said, "I see a bullock cart coming." He was high on the top of the tree; he could see far away.

And the man underneath the tree looked to the side where the man was pointing and he said, "I doubt — I don't see. There is no bullock cart. What are you talking about? Can you deceive me? I have eyes, I am not blind. There is no bullock cart coming!"

And the man on the top said, "Yes, it is coming!"

And they started arguing. Is the argument going to help? Can the man on the tree convince the man who is not on the tree that the bullock cart is coming? Howsoever clever he is in his arguments, how can he prove to the man who cannot see the bullock cart?

What did the man do? First he argued, tried in every way, saying, "It is coming. It is painted red. One bullock is black one bullock is white, this and that," and everything he described. "And the man has a beard," and all. But it was in vain.

Then he recognized the truth: "How can he see? His vision is limited." So he called him; he said, "You come up. You climb up the tree, and I will show you the bullock cart."

Now, if the man underneath the tree says, "I will come up only if you convince me that the bullock cart is there," then there is no way. But he climbed up the tree, and he saw the bullock cart, and the doubt was resolved. And there was no more argumentation. He apologized. He said; "I feel sorry. I unnecessarily argued with you. It was not a question of argument. You had a far better vision from here."

This is what the Buddhas have been doing down the ages. They say, "We have a far better vision from here. From this vantage point you will be able to see what is. Come closer to us. Don't go on arguing."

Not that Buddhas cannot argue — they can certainly argue and they can argue better than you. But it is pointless! They can silence you through their arguments, but they cannot convince you. They can destroy all your arguments, but even that will not help — you will not be able to see the bullock cart. And the whole point is how to see it, because only seeing is believing.

Go on climbing the tree. I am calling you. I can see. You cannot see yet. Doubts will persist. Let those doubts help you to climb up faster, sooner. Let it become an urgency, those doubts, make it an urgency. Doubts in themselves are not wrong — it all depends on how you use them. They can become blessings.

The third question:

Osho,

How is anxiety related to desire? It seems easier to see that one is desiring than to see that one is "anxieting" – in fact, there is no verb form for anxiety, at least not in English. Am I desiring my anxiety or anxieting my desire?

The desire is nothing but an escape from the state of anxiety. Desires don't create anxiety, as ordinarily is believed. Anxiety creates desire.

Man is anxiety.

Just the other day I was telling you: animals have no anxiety, because they don't have to become – they are. A dog is a dog, and a tiger is a tiger, and there is no problem! The tiger is not trying to become a tiger. He is! He already is! There is no becoming involved.

In the world of animals there is no anxiety. In the world of Buddhas again there is no anxiety, they have arrived, they have become. They are *siddhas* – they are beings. Now there is no goal left, no movement. The journey is complete. They have arrived home.

Hence the similarity in the eyes of the animals and the eyes of Buddhas. The same silence! The same innocence. The same depth. The same purity. Yet the difference is also great: animals are unconscious, Buddhas are conscious. Hence animals' eyes are innocent, but not luminous. There is no anxiety, but there is no celebration either. There is no despair, but no ecstasy either. In the eyes of the Buddhas you will not find anxiety, you will not find agony; you will not find the constant urge to be this, to be that. The fever of becoming you will not find. But there will be a constant overflowing ecstasy – peaceful, blissful, a well-being.

Between these two is man: half animal, half Buddha. And that is where anxiety exists. Anxiety is this tension. A part of you wants to go back to the animals. It goes on pulling you backwards. It says, "Come back! It was so beautiful – where are you going?"

The other parts goes on hoping for the future. In some indirect way you know perfectly well that to be a Buddha is your destiny. The seed is there! And the seed goes on saying to you, "Find the soil, right soil, and you will become a Buddha. Don't go back. Go ahead...."

This tug-of-war is anxiety. Anxiety is one of the most important words to be understood, because it is not only a word: it is the very situation man finds himself in. This is the human dilemma. The most fundamental dilemma is anxiety: To be or not to be? To be this or to be that? Where to go? Man is stuck on a crossroads, all the possibilities open. But if you choose one, you have to choose against other possibilities — hence the fear. You may be choosing wrong. If you go to the right — who knows? — the path going to the left may have been the right path.

And there are people, shopkeepers, who go on calling, hawkers, who go on calling, "Come to the right! This is the right way." "Come to the left — this is the right way!" "Come our way, this is the only way!" "Follow Christianity, or Hinduism, or Buddhism...all others are wrong. You will fall in hell."

Man is paralyzed! Standing on the crossroads, listening to all these people, he is paralyzed. Where to go? Whom to listen to? Whom to believe? How to be certain that you are going on the right track? Great suspicion, great doubt, great anxiety.

And deep inside you, something is pulling you back: "Better become an animal again. Fall into drunkenness. Take drugs, or become a sex maniac. Or become violent — kill people!" Why is there so much violence in the world? The animal past goes on pulling you back. Your humanity is only skin-deep. Any moment you can become a wolf, you can become a tiger; you can tear the other into pieces. Any moment! Any moment you can kill.

And not only can you kill others: you can kill yourself too. Suicide and murder, constantly pulling you. Destruction calling you, alluring you.

And then there are Buddhas...once in a while you see a man and you are enchanted. He has that enchanted space in him. He has that magic by which your future suddenly becomes your present. At least in his presence, at least when you vibrate with him, you forget all your animal past. You start flying like angels in the sky. Those people are also there.

This is the anxiety: Where to go? What to do? And whatsoever you do, anxiety will remain. If you become an animal, the Buddha part will go on rebelling against it. Go and do something that your animal part feels good doing, but your Buddha part starts creating guilt in you. Even the greatest murderer, before he murders anybody, feels the pangs; a great pain arises in him. His Buddha part tries to stop him, "What are you doing?" He may listen, he may not listen — but he will repent! For years he will repent for what he has done. He should not have done it.

The thief, before he moves into somebody's house, is again and again warned by the Buddha part, "Don't do it. There is still time — escape!" If you do it, you feel guilty. If you don't do it, you will feel guilty. Because if you don't do it, and you leave and you come home, then you cannot sleep, because the animal part goes on saying, "You are a fool! So much money, and it was so easily available, and there was nobody in the house, and the whole neighborhood was fast asleep, and there was not a single chance of your being caught — you are just an utter fool! Why have you come back? There is still time — go again!"

If you follow one part, the other part makes you feel guilty. And vice versa. This is anxiety. And this anxiety is very existential. It is not that somebody is suffering it and somebody is not suffering — no. It is existential: everybody is born into it. Humanity is born into it. Human beings are born into anxiety. That is their challenge. That is the problem they have to solve — that is the problem they have to transcend.

Now, there are two ways to transcend it. One is the way of the world — you can call it desire. Desire is the way to hide this anxiety. You rush into earning money, madly. You become so absorbed in earning money that you forget all existential anxiety. Then there is no point, no time, to think about real problems. Then you put aside everything and you just go into the search for money, more money. And as you get money, more and more desire arises. This desiring for money or political power is nothing but a cover for your anxiety.

That's why people are very much frightened when they are left alone and nothing is there to be done. That's why retired people become very uneasy, uncomfortable. They die fast. It is said — now psychological research has proved it — that a man who is retired is going to die ten years earlier than he would have died if he had remained employed. Ten years earlier? Why? Because the anxiety that he has been repressing through his job asserts itself. He was running after money, chasing after political power; there was no time to give to anxiety.

Now there is all the time and nothing to do. Sitting in his armchair he does only one thing — anxieting. Nothing else to do! Now all the repressed anxieties of his whole life — that denied existential part takes revenge. It kills. He becomes ill, heart attacks come, he becomes paralyzed. But there is more possibility that all this is happening because of the psychology, not because of the body.

When a person is succeeding and his desires are taking him farther and farther away, he remains healthy. Politicians are almost always healthy when they are in power; when they lose power, they suddenly become old. When a person is earning and earning and earning, he remains healthy. When he becomes a failure, when he goes bankrupt, then suddenly, yes, in a single night all his hair can turn white — literally.

Desire is a way to avoid anxiety, but only to avoid. You cannot destroy it by desiring. And desire gives you small anxieties, remember, very small anxieties, which are not existential. Of course, when you are earning money you will have a few anxieties: the market and the share market, and things like that, and prices. And you have put so much money — are you going to earn out of it or are you going to lose? These small anxieties. These are nothing compared to the real anxiety — these are tricks to avoid the real.

Of course, when you are ambitious for politician power, you will have anxieties, a thousand and one. But they are nothing! they are play-things compared to the fundamental anxiety.

You ask me: *How is anxiety related to desire?*

Desire is a cover-up for anxiety. It is a trick, a strategy. And meditation is to uncover it.

That's why people can't sit silently even for a few minutes. Because when they sit silently, anxieties start raising their heads. They become very much afraid. That's why people ask, even in meditation, "What should we do? Can we chant a mantra?" Then it is okay; then the mantra becomes your cover. Then you can repeat, "Ram, Ram, Ram," and you can go on repeating. This repetition keeps your anxiety repressed.

Real meditation is Zen, *Vipassana*. Real meditation is nothing but to sit silently, doing nothing. Just doing nothing, sitting silently, that is real meditation. There is no other technique, no technique at all in it. No mantra has to be repeated. No prayer has to be done, no God's name to be pronounced. You simply sit...but that is the hardest thing to do in the world. Looks so simple!

When I say again and again:

> *Sitting silently,*
> *doing nothing,*
> *and the spring comes*
> *and the grass grows by itself...*

You think it is very easy: "We can sit and the spring will come and the grass will grow by itself." This is the hardest and the most difficult and the most arduous thing in the world: to sit silently, doing nothing. And this is the greatest meditation.

What is meditation? Just allowing your existence as it is without covering it in any way. So the Transcendental Meditation of Maharishi Mahesh Yogi is not meditation at all. It is neither meditation nor transcendental. It is just a strategy to befool people.

And America needs such people to be fool them. America needs something to cover its anxiety. Because money is there now, so money, and the search for money, cannot become a cover-up for long now. Society is affluent. People have all that you can desire. Now what? Now the anxiety is knocking on the doors, and the anxiety is saying,

"Okay, now you have a two-car garage — now what? Let me come in! Now you have a house in the hills, another house on the beach, a beautiful yacht, what else?...now let me come in! You were telling me, 'Wait! First let me have a house in the hills, another house on the beach. First let me purchase a beautiful yacht.' Now you have all that — now let me come in. I can't wait any more!"

Anxiety is knocking on the American door. It always knocks when a society is rich. When a society is poor, Transcendental Meditation is not needed. That's why in India nobody bothers about Maharishi Mahesh Yogi. Who bothers? People have so many ways to cover up their anxiety so easily.

But when all the desires are coming to a completion, what to do? Something new is needed. Then in many directions new doors have to be opened: Go to the moon! One company is selling tickets for the moon. Of course, it has to be a Japanese company — '85, 1st January. People are purchasing. It is already booked. Tickets are being sold on the black market.

"What to do? Let us go to the moon! At least we can cover up with that. We have to go to the moon. We can say to the anxiety, 'Wait! First let me go to the moon, then I will look at you. Wait a little more.'" Or do Transcendental Meditation. Any foolish word, repeat it, call it a mantra. Go on repeating it. That becomes a blanket cover.

Real meditation is not a technique. Real meditation is just relaxing, sitting silently, letting it happen, whatsoever it is. Allowing the whole anxiety to come up, to surface. And watching it, watching it. And doing nothing to change it. Witnessing it is real meditation.

In that witnessing your Buddhahood will become more and more powerful. Witnessing is the nourishment for your Buddhahood. And the more powerful your Buddhahood is, the less anxiety there is. The day your Buddhahood is complete, all anxiety is gone.

How is anxiety related to desire? It seems easier to see that one is desiring than to see that one is "anxieting."

*Y*es, it is easier to see that one is desiring because this is what you are doing. Anxiety is not something that you are doing: you are born in it. It has nothing to do with your doing. You are born as anxiety! That's why it is difficult to see — one reason.

And the second reason: you don't want to look at it. It is scary. One feels that one will go mad. It is better to avoid it, to keep it at the back, never to encounter it.

It happens every day.

One very beautiful man took sannyas a few months ago. He has been a con man. The moment I looked into his eyes he became afraid of me. I said, "What kind of con man are you? Now I am going to con you." I gave him a few groups — he escaped without those groups. He became so frightened! For months nothing was heard about him.

Then he sent his lawyer to watch here — a con man is a con man — to find out "What is really happening here? Is it okay to get into things?" The lawyer came here. He watched. He must have reported that "There is nothing to fear, you can go." He gathered courage and came back.

And I told him, "You are a coward. What kind of con man have you been? And this time don't try to escape." And I gave him a few groups again — and he disappeared!

Now I have received a letter from Singapore. He says, "Osho, I am reading your books here and listening to your tapes, but I became so much afraid because you have given me these groups again — and I will have to expose all the rubbish that I am carrying within myself. I will have to expose my whole being. I will have to be nude and true and authentic, and that frightens me. But I will come...I am reading, I am listening, I am gathering courage again, and I will come."

It happens to many people: I give them groups; one day, two days, and they escape from the group. It becomes too much. What fear arises? The fear of exposure. Not that they will be exposed to others: the fear basically is that "I will be exposed to myself," that "I will have to see what I have been hiding all along." And once you have known it, it will be impossible to hide it again.

That's why before I tell you to meditate, I send you into Primal Therapy, into Encounter — I send you into different groups. So that, the first thing: your cover is taken away; you are left naked, spiritually naked. Then meditation becomes easier, because meditation is nothing but to be with yourself in your totality.

Yes, I understand, to see desire is easy:

> It seems easier to see that one is desiring than to see that one is "anxieting."

To see that one is anxieting needs guts. It is really only for those who have courage.

> In fact, there is no verb form for anxiety, at least not in English.

Our languages are as false as we are. Our languages are made by us. They reflect us. In fact, a real language will not have any nouns, will have only verbs. If it has to be true to life, it can only have verbs, not nouns.

When you say, "This is a tree," you are falsifying, because there is no static tree anywhere. A tree is a treeing. It is growing, it is constantly moving! A new leaf has come up, and the old leaf has fallen. A new bud is opening. When you are saying, "This is a tree," it is no more the same tree. Your statement is already out of date. This is another tree!

When you say, "This is a river," what do you mean? River is a riveting; it is constantly flowing. And so is a man and so is a woman. All are processes, dynamic. Everything in existence is a verb. But our languages are as false as we are. They have to be — they are our languages.

It is no wonder that Buddhas always feel it difficult to say the truth to you — because they have to use your language, and your language is so against truth. Why do we use so many nouns when no noun is true? Life is not life but living, and love is not love but loving, and death is not death but dying. Why do we use nouns at all? It gives us a feeling of control. Nouns can be controlled; verbs cannot be controlled. Verbs are beyond you. Nouns are static, dead, you can manipulate them. Verbs are alive. They will slip out of your fingers; you cannot hold them in your hands.

Loving has to be transformed into love – then it is easy to tackle. If a man says to a woman, "I am in a state of loving towards you," just see how much difference it makes. And then he says, "I love you." When he says, "I love you," he is saying something static. Implied in it is that, "Tomorrow also I will love." It is a static phenomenon: "I love you." It is definite, it is absolute. There is not going to be any change in it.

But if a man says, "I am in a state of loving," you will be afraid, because "state of loving"? – it is a process. Morning it may be there, evening it may be gone. Then what?

And when somebody says, "I love you," the noun is addressed to you. When somebody says, "I am in a state of loving," it is not addressed to you. He may be loving to somebody else too! It is dangerous. You cannot possess it.

Nouns can be possessed, hoarded. You can become masters. But verbs cannot be possessed. They go on and on...they go beyond you; they go beyond all your comprehension. They remain unpredictable. Nouns are predictable. Verbs are unpredictable. They are like a cloud changing its form every moment.

You cannot depend on a cloud's form. There may be an elephant in the cloud – it looks like an elephant. By the time you call your child, "Come here! Come out! There is an elephant in the sky!" and by the time the child comes, it is no more an elephant. The elephant has dissolved. The cloud is not a fixed phenomenon. Now what to say to the child? He will say, "You have been lying. Where is the elephant?"

In fact, there was no elephant – the moving cloud was just elephantine. Sometimes it is horsing...it is unpredictable. And we are very much afraid of the unpredictable. And life is unpredictable, so we go on keeping ourselves surrounded by nouns. It feels safe.

Our languages reflect our minds, our ignorance, our unconsciousness, our stupidities, our jealousies, our fears, our obsessions, our neurosis. Our language represents all that we are. It is a reflection of our mind — it is a mind product.

That's why there is nothing like "anxieting." "Anxiety" — then it is fixed. Then you can label it: This is anxiety. You can label: This is love. But if you watch real love, it changes sometimes into hate — real love changes into hate. Now it will confuse you, so you label differently: This is hate — this is love. And you bypass the link. You never look into the link. Love becomes hate: hate becomes love. Friends turn into enemies: enemies turn into friends. Everything is moving into everything else! It is all one! Things are not divided by water-tight compartments.

The earth becomes the tree...the tree becomes the air...it goes on melting into each other...the air is breathed by you...it becomes your blood...everything is moving into everything else. Nothing is unrelated. It is all one process.

When you stop manipulating life, when you sit silently and simply watch, you will see all this tremendous beauty, this tremendous unpredictable process of life, this dynamism.

And this is God! This wholeness. This interdependence. This inter linked existence, where everything is changing into everything else. This fluid energy is God.....

The last question:

Osho,
Do you ever get bored? Why not drop the ashram and live in the forest?

What are you talking about? What ashram? I am living in the forest! These people are my trees — orange trees, aflame with flowers. Can you find a more wild jungle than this?

And how can I be bored with so many beautiful people around me? with such a celebrating existence? If you feel bored, that simply shows you must be insensitive, you must be thick. Your skull has to be broken. Otherwise, where can you find a better existence than this? This is the only existence there is, and the perfect one. All is as it should be. Trees are green, and roses are red. All is as it should be! How can you get bored?

Boredom comes out of insensitivity. Because you are insensitive you cannot see the subtle changes that go on happening around you. Hence it looks repetitive: "The sun rises every morning, the same sun — how can one remain without being bored?" But it is not the same sun! It is constantly changing. It is fire — how can the fire remain the same? Watch fire...it is constantly changing. Flames are changing. It is constant flux. Sun is a liquid fire. It is never the same.

But, thinking that it is the same, you don't look at the morning, and the clouds are new every day. Their forms are new. They take new colors. Every day they celebrate the coming of the sun. And the birds and the trees and the whole existence every moment is new, and fresh — as fresh as a dewdrop in the morning. And so are people!

But you are dull, you are insensitive. You think it is the same woman you have lived with for twenty years. You have stopped looking at her. You have not looked at her for many years, not into her eyes. You have not touched her. You have forgotten her body smell. Then it is boring; then it is the same woman again and again.

It is not really boring — it is just that your eyes have collected much dust. Life becomes boring the more dust you collect in your eyes. The life becomes just formal, a ritual, empty. You go on doing things. Slowly slowly, all your acts become mechanical, robot like. Then life is boredom.

But I have never seen two moments alike. Each moment has its own beauty. Each moment is only for once. If you miss it, you miss it forever; it will not be repeated again. God is not repetitive. God is very original — he never sings the same song again.

If you hear the same song again, then something must be wrong with you.

It happened:

A woman was singing, it was her birthday. She sang late in the night. Her voice was just horrible, but the neighbors were somehow tolerating it because it was only once in a year that her birthday used to come. So they had become tolerant about it. But that night she continued and continued...it was getting really late, two o'clock in the night. And a man just in front of her house could not sleep; tried in every way — tried all the tricks. Tossed and turned and did TM...etc., but nothing helped. She was driving him crazy, so he opened his window and shouted at her, "Lady, now it is time. You stop! Otherwise I will go mad."

The woman opened her door and said, "What are you talking about? It is almost one hour since I stopped!"

But what happened to this man? He was already mad. One hour before she had stopped, but he was listening, listening, listening...it was something in his mind. It was his inner gramophone.

Just watch: when you see a rose flower, your inner gramophone says, "You have seen it before. It is the same rose flower, nothing special about it. I have seen better." You look at the moon and the inner gramophone says, "So what?! This is the same moon, and we have seen it many times."

There are millions of people who never look at the sky. If suddenly one night all the stars disappear, they will not become aware of it. It may take a few days for them; when the news comes in the newspapers that "All the stars have simply disappeared from the world," then they will look at the sky. And then they will miss them, and they will make much fuss and they will say, "How unfortunate! And we had not seen the stars for many years and they were here."

You are bored because of your inner gramophone. I have none in site me. Each person is fresh, each moment is fresh. They are not repetitions — they are all unique. And I remain thrilled, I remain ecstatic.

Your life, must have become an empty ritual. You must be moving through things, dragging. Not even understanding the meaning, why you are doing these things. You come home and you kiss your wife — you have to, but there is no kiss, there is no kissing, there is no ecstasy in it. Just a dull phenomenon. And if you feel tired and bored, I can understand.

Life, slowly slowly, becomes so mechanical that it loses all meaning. All meaning oozes out of it. Then it is just a dull ritual. To live this way is to live irreligiously. That's my definition of religion: to live joyously, ecstatically, thrilled by each moment that knocks on your door, is to live religiously.

Religion is nothing but the alchemical process in which all your insensitivity dissolves, and you become utterly sensitive, delicate, vulnerable. Then each moment is samadhi, is God, is enlightenment.

Enough for today.

CHAPTER 9

HAIL GREAT SCHOLAR!

Nawab Mohammed Khan, Jan-Fishan, was out walking in Delhi one day when he came upon a number of people seemingly engaged in an altercation.

He asked a bystander, "What is happening here?"

The man said, "Sublime Highness, one of your disciples is objecting to the behavior of the people in this quarter."

Jan-Fishan went into the crowd and said to his follower, "Explain yourself."

The man said, "These people have been hostile."

The people exclaimed, "That is not true: we were, on the contrary, doing him honor for your sake."

"What did they say?" asked the Nawab.

"They said, 'Hail, Great Scholar!' I was telling them that it is the ignorance of the scholars which is often responsible for the confusion and desperation of man."

Jan-Fishan Khan said, "It is the conceit of scholars which is responsible, quite often, for the misery of man. And it is your conceit in claiming to be other than a scholar which is the cause of this tumult. Not to be a scholar, which involves detachment *from the petty, is an accomplishment. Scholars are seldom wise, being only unaltered people stuffed with thoughts and books.*

"These people were trying to honor you. If some people think that mud is gold, if it is their mud, respect it. You are not their teacher.

"Do you not realize that, in behaving in such a sensitive and self-willed manner, you are acting just like a scholar, and therefore deserve the name, even if it is an epithet?

"Guard yourself, my child. Too many slips from the path of Supreme Attainment – and you may become a scholar."

Existence is – unexplained, unexplainable, unknown – not only that, but unknowable also. There is no way to know it, because there is nobody who is separate from it. Knowledge needs separation. You can love existence because love depends on union, and we are already united with it. But you cannot know it, because knowledge needs division, and there is no way to be divided from it.

Knowledge means the knower is separate from the known. We are not separate from existence – we are it. It is our suchness – how can we know it? The claim to know is the greatest conceit. The claim to know is the greatest ego there is. Hence the knowledgeable man goes on missing it. Only lovers know, scholars never. But to be a lover needs courage – you have to dissolve and disappear.

To be knowledgeable needs no courage. That is the hiding-place of the cowards. All cowards become scholars. Because they cannot love, the only thing left for them is to try to know. And because knowledge is impossible in the very nature of things, all that they claim is false.

All knowledge is false, absolutely false. Not even a bit of it is true. It cannot be true. Only love is true, only love can be true.

Do you see the point? The way of love is the way of union, and the way of knowledge is the way of separation. Love is marriage: knowledge is divorce. Love understands: knowledge only pretends.

Remember it, because the mind is always trying to become knowledgeable. It is always collecting information and avoiding transformation. Information is a way of avoiding transformation. You go on collecting...you can become a walking encyclopedia, but still you will remain the same, exactly the same. Because this is not the way to grow in being, this is not the way to become wise.

The knowledgeable man is never wise, he cannot be. He collects rubbish and thinks it is precious. But the first step has been wrong so the whole journey goes wrong. The more he thinks he knows, the less he knows. The more he thinks he is coming closer to knowing the truth, the farther away he is moving from truth.

Existence is. If you are also in that state of isness you will understand what it is. But that is not knowledge. That's a totally different dimension. You will know, yet you will not be able to reduce it to knowledge. You will see, but you will not be able to describe it. The mystery will not be demystified by your knowing it — it will be deepened, it will be thickened. Life will become more joyous.

One cannot know, but one can dance it. One cannot know, but one can sing it. It can never become knowledge, but it can become ecstasy, great ecstasy. A great orgasmic life is possible.

The Sufis say: Avoid being scholars, pundits. Avoid! Because sometimes it has happened that sinners have reached, but scholars never. Sin is not that big a thing as knowledgeability. Seen rightly, knowledge remains the ultimate sin.

The biblical story is to be remembered again: Adam falls from grace — not because of any sin but because he has eaten the fruit of the tree of knowledge.

There were two trees, special trees, in the Garden of Eden: one was the tree of knowledge and the other was the tree of life. He became interested in the tree of knowledge. It looks foolish to us when we read the story. Why should he not go and eat from the tree of life? But that's what everybody else is doing too — nobody wants to eat from the tree of life, because to eat from the tree of life first one has to pass through a kind of death.

The moment you eat the fruit from the tree of life, you will die as you are. You are momentary. Your being now is temporal. You will die in time and you will be born in eternity. That's what life is!

— life abundant, life eternal. You will die as a tiny being, you will disappear as a drop of water, and then you will appear as the ocean. Oceanic will be your resurrection! But before that, the dewdrop has to disappear.

That is the fear. Because of that fear, Adam never went close to the tree of life. That's why you have not gone close to it. That's why millions of people go to the universities, to the libraries, but avoid going to a master.

A master, a Perfect Master, is a tree of life. He is not a teacher. A teacher means the tree of knowledge: a master means the tree of life.

A master does not impart knowledge, he imparts being. He stirs your heart, makes it more alive. He breathes in you, gives you a new rhythm. He touches you in your deepest core and creates a dance there.

Adam avoided the tree of life, so everybody else is doing it. Down the ages, people have been following Adam. But the tree of knowledge attracted him immensely. The temptation from the serpent was: "If you eat from the tree of knowledge, you will become as wise as God — you will become a god." That's the temptation of knowledge. One thinks, "If I can know more, then I will be more — I will become like a god." By knowing, nobody becomes a god, but only by being.

The serpent is deceiving you too. The serpent is not something outside; it is another name for your mind. The mind says, "Know more — if you know more you will be more." It convinces you very logically.

Once Adam has eaten from the tree of knowledge, his eyes are closed towards eternity. He becomes caught up in the net of time. And time means death. And God has told Adam, "If you eat from the tree of knowledge, you will start dying. You will lose eternity. You will lose the quality of deathlessness. You will become a mortal!"

This parable is immensely beautiful. I take it again and again — it has so many aspects. To me this seems to be the greatest parable ever — it has so many meanings.

If you eat from the tree of knowledge you will become mortal

— because you will become more and more confined into time, into mind. Time and mind are synonymous. It is mind that creates time — psychological time, I mean, not the chronological time. The more you become mindless, the less you are aware of time. When you become perfect, you become constantly, completely unaware of time. Then all is eternity.

Once a Buddhist monk came to see me. He had come from a very far off place, Kalimpong. He travelled for many days to see me. He said, "I have only one inquiry to make, and only for that have I come."

"What is the inquiry?"

He said, "My inquiry is this: since you became enlightened, what has been happening? What experiences have you been going through since you became enlightened? What has been occurring? What more? What new experiences after enlightenment?"

I said, "You don't understand the word "enlightenment". After enlightenment, nothing happens. All happening stops, disappears. One simply is."

He could not believe it. He said, "I cannot believe it. Something must be happening. Twenty years have passed…something must have happened! How can it be that nothing has happened?"

I said to him, "You will be puzzled, but let me say it as it is: Before enlightenment nothing had ever happened, because all that had happened was just writing on water. After enlightenment also nothing has happened, because time has disappeared. So the first happening and the last happening was enlightenment. Before that, all that happened was valueless; now it makes no sense, it was like a dream. And once you are awakened, nothing ever happens again. Not that the sun does not rise, not that the night is not full of stars, not that the flowers don't bloom any more — all this goes on! But nothing happens in you. All remains calm and quiet."

After enlightenment there is no biography. After enlightenment all is silence — because all is eternity. Things happen in time. Mind creates time because mind hankers for things to happen; mind hankers for excitements, something has to happen. If nothing is happening, mind becomes very uneasy. If good is not happening, let it be bad. If happiness is not happening, then let it be misery. But something must be there so one remains occupied. If nothing is happening, then you are at a loss — then why exist at all?

So mind goes on creating new ways, goes on projecting new events. "Tomorrow I have to do this, the day after tomorrow I have to do this." Mind cannot remain without events, so it projects events. And when events are projected time is created — psychological time. When nothing is projected, time disappears.

That is the meaning of the parable. God is right when he says to Adam: Don't eat the fruit from the tree of knowledge, otherwise you will become a mortal. Then you will have to live in time! And you will become corrupted — knowledge corrupts. You will not be innocent any more. You will lose trust, because knowledge creates doubt. And doubt is the thorn in the soul; it hurts, it wounds.

Still Adam ate the fruit of the tree of knowledge, and since then every Adam has been doing it.

Sufis say we have to reverse the whole process. We have to vomit what Adam has eaten. We have to throw it back. We have to become pure of it. It has not to be allowed to circulate in our systems any more. With knowledge goes time, with time goes mind — it is all entangled with knowledge. And once there is no knowledge, no mind, no time, you are back home.

Let me repeat: Sinners have reached, but scholars never.

I have heard:

George Santayana, a great American philosopher, remarked once during World War II, "I am reading the Upanishads...to take the bad taste out of my mouth."

The Upanishads? Why should he read the Upanishads to take the bad taste out of his mouth? The Upanishads are not knowledge: they are statements of pure joy, they are euphoric statements. They are ecstatic ejaculations, assertions of mad mystics. You cannot become knowledgeable by reading the Upanishads. They don't argue, they don't prove — they simply declare!

That's what Lao Tzu does, Buddha does, Plotinus, Eckhart, Rumi, Al-Hillaj — all the mystics have been doing that. What they say is not knowledge: what they say is just an overflowing joy.

When Aristotle says something, it is knowledge. When Plotinus says something, it is not knowledge. You have to make that distinction very clearly. When Jesus says something, it is not knowledge; it is just his ecstasy. It is not that he is saying it — it is said through him. God is speaking through him. He is possessed by God. What he is saying is not knowledge. It is his declaration: "I have come home." It has to be declared. It has to be declared from the housetops. It has to be shouted in the marketplaces. But it is not knowledge! And the difference is very clear.

If you read the Upanishads, you will see it. No argument is proposed, no syllogism, no proof, is given. Simply, the seer says: That art thou — Tat-tvam-asi. Finished! He does not give any argument for it. He does not try to explain it. He does not propose a philosophy around it. Such a potential statement, bare, naked.

When the Upanishads were for the first time translated into non-Indian languages, it was a problem for the translators: These people go on asserting without giving any proof — what kind of philosophy is this?" It is not philosophy really. It is religion. And that is the difference between philosophy and religion.

Philosophy proves, argues, proposes, fights, debates: religion declares. Religion says: God is! No proof is given. If you ask a mystic, he will say, "Look into my eyes. Come, hold my hand! Feel it!" But is this an argument? And it is not going to convince the skeptic. He will look into the eyes and will not see anything. It can convince only the trusting. It can convince only the disciple.

Santayana was bored with all the knowledge that the West has produced in these days, and could see perfectly well that "It is because of this knowledge that this world war is happening." Knowledge creates hate in the world, because it creates separation.

Love is not possible out of knowledge, because love is a diametrically opposite dimension. Hence he is right to say, "I am reading the Upanishads to take the bad taste out of my mouth" — the bad taste of knowledge, the ugly knowledge that has created the ugly war, the murderous knowledge.

I have also heard: when Arthur Schopenhauer for the first time came across a translation of the Upanishads, he danced – actually! With the Upanishads on his head, he danced in his garden.

His students were a little puzzled. They said, "Has he gone mad or something?" And they inquired, "What is happening?"

He said, "This is something I have been searching for – this is not knowledge, this is knowing. This is authentic!"

When he was just about to die, he said, "The Upanishads have been the solace of my life, and will be the solace of my death."

What happened to Arthur Schopenhauer? What is the beauty of the Upanishads? What is the beauty of Sufism? What is the beauty of Zen? What is the beauty of Hassidism? The beauty is that they are not knowledge – of course, great knowings, but not knowledge at all. Great insights are there, but no philosophy is proposed to be believed in. You don't become more knowledgeable through them: you become more innocent.

Religion is existential, philosophy is analytical. Knowledge has to be analytical; it can't be existential. Knowing has to be existential; it can't be analytical. If you want to know, forget all about analysis; otherwise, you will come across much knowledge but never will you become a knower.

If you want to know a flower, don't dissect it – otherwise you will destroy it. Be with it, in absolute quietness, with a throbbing, loving heart. Breathe it in, dance around it, sing a song, or be silent! Play upon a guitar, or on a flute. These are the ways to become friendly to the flower. When you are playing on a flute, the flower starts leaning towards you, the flower becomes open. He understands...a friend has come. He knows when the cuckoo calls, he knows when a peacock dances – he will know you too if you sing a song or play on the flute or dance a dance around it. Those are the languages he understands. Or silence he understands – the silence of the stars and the earth.

Just be silently with the flower! Or let tears flow, let your tears drop on the flower. He understands that language too. When it rains and it has a contact with the clouds.... But be existential, don't be analytical, and the flower will release its secrets to you.

Secrets can be released only to friends. When you are analytical, you are an enemy. When the scientist goes to the flower, he goes in a very antagonistic mood, very egoistic, self-willed, adamant, stubborn. He goes like a rapist. Science is a kind of rape on nature.

Be a poet, be a painter, be a musician — these are existential ways. And the flower, slowly slowly, will gather trust in you, will know that "This man is not dangerous, he is not a scientist. He is not after knowledge. He will not rape me. He is a lover." And the flower will drop all protections, defences, armours. And suddenly there is a meeting — and a kind of knowing which is not knowledge.

That's how one comes to know God.

Remember these two words: analytical and existential. Never be analytical. That is the path of knowledge. Be existential — that is the path of knowing. Knowing is loving: loving is praying: and one thing leads to another.

It is a well-known fact of history that in Greece, Aristotle formulated the syllogism as a way to explain and examine valid reasoning. He was the father of logic in the West. But at the same time, almost exactly the same time, another man in India was working on the same lines — but in a totally different dimension, with a totally different quality. His name was Gotama — the founder of Indian logic. But the difference is great. Their syllogisms are almost the same, their logic is almost the same — it has to be — but the difference is in their goals.

Aristotle says: it is to explain and examine valid reasoning. Gotama created similar syllogistic forms, but as he stated at the beginning of his Naya Sutras, the purpose of the study was to aid human beings in the attainment of supreme felicity — liberation, moksha, ecstasy, samadhi.

The difference is clear. Even if reason has to be used, it has to be used with full awareness to help ecstasy, to help supreme felicity, ultimate liberation. For no other reason.

Philosophy is not an end in itself: it is a means. If it helps, good; if it doesn't help, throw it away, it is garbage. Use your mind to go beyond mind. Let philosophy commit suicide in you.

That is the message of this small story.

Nawab Mohammed Khan, Jan-Fishan, was out walking in Delhi one day when he came upon a number of people seemingly engaged in an altercation.

He asked a bystander, "What is happening here?"

The Sufi masters believe in situations. Nobody else believes in situations so much. But the Sufi master and his approach is that you can teach your disciples only in a certain situation, in a certain context. If the context is not there, the teaching will be lost.

You can beat iron only when it is hot, and you can give it a shape and a form. But when it is cold, it is impossible. A situation is a hot state of affairs. Sufi masters watch always for particular situations to give particular lessons. It may take years, but they never speak out of context — never.

So, to be with a Sufi master needs great patience, because he will not speak unless the situation has arisen and things are hot and he can give a shape and form. He can teach you something only when the situation is ready.

The master is passing, a crowd is there.

He asked a bystander, "What is happening here?"
The man said, "Sublime highness, one of your disciples is objecting to the behavior of the people in this quarter."

Now, this almost always happens to knowledgeable people. They become haughty, they become egoistic. They carry that air around themselves of holier-than-thou. They are always putting everybody else right. They are always searching to condemn, to make people feel guilty. This is a way of the ego to satisfy itself. This is not the indication of a man who knows.

A man who knows never makes anybody feel guilty. The man who knows helps people to get out of their wrong patterns, but does not make them feel guilty. It is a great art, the most sublime art there is.

It is very subtle — has to be, because when you are trying to change a person it is very easy to make him feel guilty; it is very easy because the thing is delicate and you are touching his sensitivity. And you are trying to change him, so somehow or other you are saying, "You are wrong as you are." That has to be avoided.

Man is not wrong, never wrong. That should remain the fundamental. Man in his innermost core is always right — even though he may commit a few errors on the surface. But those errors are momentary, of not much value. But his fundamental goodness, his natural goodness, is absolute.

Once a person starts feeling guilty, you have contaminated his natural goodness. You have hurt him deeply; you have created a wound in his soul. So the art is never to create a wound in the soul. The real master is always indirect. He changes people, he transforms people, but his way is always indirect. The person who is being changed and transformed never comes to know of it — or comes to know only when he has already changed, when he is already transformed. Then he feels grateful.

The master's touch is a very subtle touch. It is never offensive, it is never aggressive, it is never violent. There is no condemnation in it. There is compassion. There is love. There is great desire to help, to be of help, but there is in no way any effort, even a slight effort, to make the person feel that he is wrong.

Once you make a person feel he is wrong, you have created a barrier in his transformation process. Because once he thinks, "I am wrong," he loses hope. If he feels guilty he becomes closed up; he is no more open to you. Once he feels guilty, he becomes defensive. Once he feels guilty, he starts fighting back. And if again and again he is made to feel guilty, he starts accepting the idea: "This is how I am. When everybody says, 'You are wrong,' then I must be wrong." Then he starts persisting in his wrongness. Then he says, "Now, everybody says I am wrong so I am wrong, and there is no possibility of my ever being right. So why bother? Then just be as you are. This is my fate! This is how I have been made by God. This is how my parents have brought me up. This is how the society has conditioned me." A thousand and one explanations he finds, and he relaxes...he will forget all possibilities of growing.

Never condemn a man, never make him feel guilty. It is a crime. Rather, when you find a man is doing something wrong, provoke his natural goodness! Remind him of his Tao, of the kingdom that is within, of his divine nature. Remind him of his divine nature first, and with that remembrance he will be able to see what wrong he is committing. You will not even be needed to pinpoint it – he will know himself.

Bring light to him! Don't say to anybody, "You are stumbling and you have broken this and you have fallen on this table and this table is turned upside down" – don't say anything like that. Bring light and give light to the man, and he will know what he has done. But from your side there should be no indication about his being wrong, in the wrong.

The man said, "Sublime Highness, one of your disciples is objecting to the behavior of the people in this quarter."

This is the sign of a stupid disciple. And when I say "stupid" I don't mean that he is not knowledgeable – stupid people can gather much knowledge. Knowledgeable people are always stupid people. To become knowledgeable is their way of hiding their stupidity. They hang certificates and degrees around themselves, and it feels good! Except for a stupid person, who cares about the degrees and the scholarship and the certificates and the examinations that you have passed? It is always the stupid person who becomes interested in these things. These are his ways to prove to the world that "I am not stupid." But in the very effort of proving that "I am not stupid," you are simply declaring that you are stupid.

A man who is wise need not prove that he is wise – his wisdom is enough, a proof unto itself. It is self-evident. It needs no certificates, it needs no degrees, it needs no scholarship.

Jan-Fishan went into the crowd and said to his follower, "Explain yourself."

This is a hot situation. People are there and the disciple was condemning them and, of course, he was clever, logical. He could prove by scriptures; he could quote scriptures and prove to them that they are wrong, that their behavior is wrong. And he was doing that. Suddenly the master appears in the crowd and says, "Explain yourself! What are you doing?"

The disciple said, "These people have been hostile."

Now, if you are wise, it is impossible to say this. Unless you have some ego in you, you cannot feel anybody as hostile. If you have a wound on the foot and somebody touches it, it hurts — but not because of his touch. It is because of the wound. If he touches somewhere else, it will not hurt. It hurts because of the wound, not because of his touch.

Whenever you feel somebody is hostile to you, remember well: you must be having a very very strong ego — he has touched the wound, he has put his finger on your ego. Hence he looks hostile; otherwise, there is no question! He is just himself. How can he be hostile to you? And even if he is hostile, that is his problem; that should not become your problem.

Buddha is insulted by people many times, stones are thrown at him, people abuse him...he smiles. Once he said to a group of people who had come with very great hostility, "I feel sorry for you. You are almost in a rage! You must be burning within. I feel sorry for you. What can I do for you to help? How can I calm you down? You are in a spiritual fever!"

He does not say anything about himself. He is not saying, "You are being hostile to me." He is not saying, "Why are you hostile to me?" He is not saying anything in reference to himself; that is not the point at all.

Somebody asked, "But we are being hostile to you, and you are feeling sorry for us? We are enemies! We want to uproot you and your doctrine completely. And you are feeling sorry for us?"

And Buddha said, "Yes. You may be hostile from your side. For example," Buddha said, "you can throw a burning torch into the river — it remains fire till it touches the river. The moment it touches the river, it cools down. I am cool. You throw fire at me — it remains fire from your side, but the moment it touches me it becomes cool. It disappears! I am not hurt, you cannot hurt me — because the one who used to be hurt is no more. That ego is gone.

"I have searched for it, and it has not been found. There is nobody inside me — how can you be hostile to me? I am not — how can you be hostile to me?"

> The disciple said, "These people have been hostile."
> The people exclaimed, "That is not true: we were, on the contrary, doing him honor for your sake."
> "What did they say?" asked the master.
> "They said, 'Hail, Great Scholar!' I was telling them that it is the ignorance of the scholars which is often responsible for the confusion and desperation of man..."

"And they told me, 'Hail, Great Scholar!' And I was condemning scholars — as Sufis have always been doing — I was condemning scholars and scholarship. And these foolish people, they say, 'Hail, Great Scholar!' This is an insult. This is being hostile towards me.

"I am saying that scholars are the persons who have created the misery in the world, and they called me a scholar! These people have to be put right."

> Jan-Fishan said, "It is the conceit of scholars which is responsible, quite often, for the misery of man. And it is your conceit in claiming to be other than a scholar which is the cause of this tumult. Not to be a scholar, which involves detachment from the petty, is an accomplishment. Scholars are seldom wise, being only unaltered people stuffed with thoughts and books."

The master is saying, "These people are poor people, innocent people. They don't understand great, subtle distinctions between words. They have not been hostile to you! According to themselves, they were praising you. They were saying that you are no ordinary person – you are a great scholar. From their side, nothing is wrong. And from where have you got this conceit that you have gone beyond scholarship? This is an even greater ego, to think that you have gone beyond scholarship.

It is very difficult to go beyond knowledge, beyond the claim of knowledge. It is the last step in the journey. The moment a person goes beyond knowledge, he becomes enlightened. Because the moment knowledge is dropped, he enters back into the Garden of Eden.

Knowledge is not a bridge: it is a barrier. The moment the barrier disappears, you suddenly find that you have always been home. You had never left it. You had not gone anywhere. But remember: to come to that point is a very great accomplishment. Why?

Ordinarily, man is ignorant – ignorance hurts. "I am ignorant, I am inferior."

One of my sannyasins, a beautiful sannyasin, is Shanti. She goes on writing questions again and again that "Osho, I feel very inferior, because I can do only cleaning work or I can prepare food. I cannot be a great group leader. I cannot do something which is important. I cannot be a great editor. I am very inferior."

Now, this poor Shanti is unnecessarily suffering. My whole work consists of cleaning! What else am I doing here? And preparing food – what else am I doing, Shanti? You are just next to me!

But the mind goes on carrying these ideas: "I am just cleaning or cooking food, and I am not a great group leader, therapist, editor, or somebody important in the office. I am nobody." She goes on asking, "What should I do?"

This is the question every child asks in the beginning: "What should I do to become important, to be somebody special in the world?" And there are only a few ways: either have money, more than others have, and you will be special; or have more power, political power, than others have, and you will be special; or have more knowledge than others have and you will be special. Or, if you cannot do anything else then at least renounce everything and become a great mahatma. But do something! Be special!

The inferiority complex inside goes on pulling and manipulating you to do something so that you can stand out, you can be outstanding, so people know who you are.

You can have money. It is not difficult – many stupid people have money. You can become politically powerful, not a problem – only stupid people become politically powerful. You can gather knowledge: so many stupid people have so many degrees and scholarships, names, fame. It is not difficult at all! But deep down you will remain the same: unaltered.

This is not the way to transform your being. You can have as much knowledge as possible, but how is it going to make you more knowing? Maybe others will think you know so much, but you, deep down, will know perfectly well: "This is only in the memory. My being has remained untouched by it."

And then, one day, you can gather another conceit, the greatest there is, that "I renounce all this knowledge too. Now I will be like Socrates – the one who knows only one thing, that he knows nothing."

But deep down you are still hoping that people will think you are a Socrates. You are a plastic Socrates, synthetic, just put together, not a real Socrates. A real Socrates is a great accomplishment.

How does the real Socrates happen? It is not by renouncing knowledge and declaring, "I have renounced knowledge, I am no more a scholar, I don't pay any value to scholarship" – not that way. The real Socrates happens only when, slowly slowly, you understand the unknowability of life and existence – the utter unknowability of existence, the absolute suchness of existence. And there is no way to know it, because we are it! Not that you renounce scholarship, no, but that you fall in love with life itself. Not that you burn your scriptures – that is very easy. Even in burning the scriptures you are paying too much attention to the scriptures; they are still important to you.

There is a famous painting of a Zen monk burning scriptures. If I had been there I would have told him, "Why burn them? Why take so much trouble? Keep them, and if some time you have nothing else to cook your tea with, you can use them. But why take so much trouble in burning a big fire? You can cook your food some day if it is needed — unobserved by anybody, unexhibited. This is an exhibition: taking all your scriptures to the market place and burning them there. It is an exhibition. You are again hoping that "Now people will know here is the real Socrates."

This is not the way to become a real Socrates.

It is not against the scripture that the real happens: it is going deeper into existence and being that the real happens. The scriptures are forgotten! And once in a while, one can look into them, because they are assertions of old masters, beautiful assertions. Of course, you cannot become a knower through them, but they can be great witnesses to your knowing.

Certainly, if you see the sun rising and you enjoy and dance with it, and one day you come across a few immensely beautiful lines of Kalidas about the sunrise, you will be surprised: he has said the thing that you would like to say! but you cannot. You don't have that quality to express. Not everybody is a Kalidas.

Remember: everybody can become a Buddha, but not everybody can become a Kalidas. Everybody can become a Buddha, but not everybody can become a Mozart or Beethoven. Everybody's potential is to become a Buddha, because Buddha is your nature. But these are specific qualities, talents. A Kalidas is a Kalidas! He can sing a song that nobody else may be able to sing again. A Shakespeare is a Shakespeare — the way he can put words together...nobody may be able to put those words together again the same way. He is a magician with words, you may not be.

Scriptures are good! You cannot become wise through them, but the day you become wise you can relish scriptures. You can just go into them — here and there a look — and immense joy arises through them too! Because suddenly an insight that has happened to you is expressed by somebody else five thousand years before. Then you are not only linked with existence through space, you are linked with existence through time too. A new kind of expansion happens. Five thousand years before, somebody sings a song in the Vedas, and one day, reading it, suddenly you see he has stolen your words! Five thousand years have disappeared. Between you and that unknown man, anonymous, there has arisen a bond, a friendship, a love, an intimacy. He has become your contemporary. You are not apart any more! He had seen things the way you see them; he has uttered the things that you would like to utter but you cannot.

These are the two dimensions: one is through space. I am contemporary to you through space. You are sitting in front of me — we are contemporaries. I am contemporary to Buddha, to Jesus, to Krishna, to Rumi, to Hillaj...and to thousands more, through time. They are also sitting exactly in front of me as you are sitting in front of me. You are sitting in front of me in space, they are sitting in front of me in time.

So when I say something about Buddha, Mohammed, Lao Tzu, I am not talking about historical figures — I am talking about my contemporaries. And life is immensely enriched when you can have Buddha on your one side and Lao Tzu sitting on the other side, and sipping a cup of tea. Life is immensely rich.

I am not saying burn the books. They are valuable, but they are valuable only for those who know how to enter into life and existence. Then they can enter even into books, because they are part of life. But if you cannot enter into a tree, into the being of a tree, how can you enter into the being of a book? Impossible. The tree is more alive, contemporary to you in space. You can hug it. The book can become contemporary to you only in time — for that you will have to grow, you will have to expand. You will have to become so huge that time and space both disappear in you. Then not only are the past Buddhas your contemporaries, but future Buddhas too. Then the whole existence exists in this moment, culminates, converges, in this moment. All that has been, all that is, and all that will be, converges into this here now. And then the beauty is tremendous, and the benediction is incalculable, immeasureable.

The master asked, "What did they say? Why did you feel that they are hostile?"

"They said," said the disciple, "'Hail, Great Scholar!' I was telling them that it is the ignorance of the scholars which is often responsible for the confusion and desperation of man."

He was saying it, but he was saying it without knowing it. He had heard it. He was repeating it; it was a mechanical repetition. He was being a parrot.

And that danger is always there for disciples: they can become parrots. That danger has to be avoided. That danger is great! And it comes so slowly and seeps into your blood and bones that you will never become aware of it.

Disciples go on listening, listening, listening, and one day they start repeating. And they have forgotten completely that what they are saying is not their own. Never repeat that which is not your own! because you will be getting into trouble. It will remain formal. And it will be so formal that your whole being will contradict it. You will say one thing and you will do another thing — because your doing will come from you, and your saying will come from all that you have heard. This creates a dichotomy and a very ridiculous situation. And everybody can see it — it is so apparent.

Whenever you repeat something that you don't understand, your whole life will contradict it, will belie it.

I was reading a beautiful anecdote:

Philadelphians have always been noted for their striving towards perfection, as the following story illustrates:

Fenton, visiting the City of Brotherly Love, decided to dine in Philadelphia's most exclusive restaurant.

"Your order?" asked the waiter.

"I'll have the hamburger plate," replied Fenton after examining the menu.

In a few minutes the waiter returned. He uncovered a casserole dish revealing two hamburgers. From a pocket the waiter produced a pair of silver tongs and with them he transferred the meat patties to the diner's plate.

"We never touch anything with our hands," said the waiter, smiling.

"Very nice," said Fenton.

"Cleanliness is our motto," retorted the waiter. "And we never touch anything with our hands."

"That's wonderful!"

"We even have a special rule about visiting the lavatory. See this little piece of string attached to my apron?"

"I noticed all the waiters had them. What's it for?"

"Well," said the waiter, placing a large potato on Fenton's plate with his silver tongs, "if I have to go to the bathroom, I just unzip my pants and take it out with that piece of string. That way everything stays sanitary."

"But how do you put it back?" asked Fenton.

"I don't know about the other men," said the waiter, "but I use these tongs. We never touch anything with our hands."

That is the situation...when you are just repeating, when you have learnt a formality which has not become your being, your whole life will belie it. On the surface you will manage, but life is not lived only on the surface; it has many layers.

The problem for the disciple is that he listens to great truths. The master goes on sharing whatsoever he has experienced. You can become parrots. Remember it. Listen, learn, but talk to people only when it has become your experience, never before.

You can share only your experience, and then it has a beauty. When you start talking about somebody else's experience, it is ugly. And you may be repeating the same words! — that is not the point.

"They said, 'Hail, Great Scholar!' I was telling them that it is the ignorance of the scholars which is often responsible for the confusion and desperation of man."

You can understand only that which you can understand in a certain moment. The master speaks from his vision. You understand from your capacity. The master is like an ocean; you have your small cup — you cannot contain the ocean. To contain the ocean you will have to break your cup; then you will contain the ocean. The ocean cannot be contained in the small cup of the head. The head has to be broken completely. When you are headless, you will contain the ocean.

But that will come when it comes. In the beginning everybody has to listen from the head, and the head goes on playing tricks. You hear one thing, you understand quite another.

Passing a door in the early morning, a drunk noticed a sign which read Ring the bell for the doctor. He did just that and a sleepy-eyed man came to the door.

"What do you want?" asked the man.

"I want to know why you can't ring the damn bell yourself."

It was written on the door Ring the bell for the doctor.... Now the drunk is drunk; he understands in his own drunkenness. He is puzzled why the doctor cannot ring it himself, why somebody else is needed.

People are almost drunk with knowledge, drunk with ego, drunk with blindness. Somehow they manage, just somehow. It is a miracle how people go on managing and living for seventy years. It is really a miracle.

The young couple was going at it hot and heavy on a park bench when the girl was heard to say, "Morris, could you please take off your glasses? They're hurting me." Quickly he whipped them off and went back to work.

After a few moments, the girl could be heard again. "Morris, could you put your glasses back on? You're kissing the bench."

Just thin glasses, just a little consciousness, and it is enough to carry on your day-to-day work. It is not enough to enter into reality. The reality will need eyes all over your being — eyes and eyes. It will need great awareness, it will need awakening.

So this disciple has heard that the master says that scholars have been the cause of the misery in the world. Yes, they have been. Without understanding what they are saying, they have created much misery for humanity. Without understanding what they are saying, they have been advising people. They have poisoned people's minds.

Jan-Fishan said, "It is the conceit of scholars which is responsible, quite often, for the misery of man. It is true. And it is your conceit in claiming to be other than a scholar which is the cause of this tumult."

"Now you are gathering another conceit which is more subtle, subtler than the first. Somebody thinks, 'I am a scholar, a great Scholar.' Now you are thinking that you have renounced all that kind of childishness — you are no more a scholar. You are still a scholar."

"Not to be a scholar, which involves detachment from the petty, is an accomplishment."

Not to be a scholar means one is no more interested in the trivial: one is interested only in the real, in the ultimately real. One is not interested in theories any more: one is interested only in existential experiencing.

"Why are you wasting your time?" the master said to the disciple. "Who are you to teach these people? They may be ignorant, they may not know as much as you know, but they did not mean any offence to you. They were thinking that to call somebody a great scholar is to pay respect. Look at their intention. Their intention was good. They are innocent people. Now you are confusing them. You are not helping them to become more clear. Now you will create a fear in them; now they will be afraid even to use the word 'scholar'. And they will be at a loss as to how to respect somebody.

"And you don't have that accomplishment, because not to be a scholar is the highest kind of consciousness."

The first stage is ignorance, the second stage is knowledge, but both are similar in one way. The first state is unconscious ignorance, and the second stage is unconscious knowledge. And the third state is conscious ignorance. The first comes back, but with a new form. The sage again becomes a child, the circle is complete — but in a totally different way. *Consciously* a child again — this is rebirth.

Jesus says: Unless you are born again you will not be able to enter into the kingdom of God. This is rebirth: Unless you become a child again, unless you become ignorant again, with absolute consciousness that there is no way to know, that there is nothing to know, that there is nobody to know...so all three points of knowledge simply disappear into oblivion, and then the suchness of existence opens up. There is great ecstasy and great benediction.

Yes, love is there and dance is there and celebration is there, but there is no knowledge. That is a great accomplishment. And for that one needs detachment from the petty.

"Why are you bothering about these people and what they have said? Why are you so much interested in words? And can't you see your conceit? — that by trying to teach them that scholars are the cause of misery, you are trying in a subtle way to pronounce, to propound, that you are not a scholar — and you are a scholar, because whatsoever you are saying is not your own experience. You have heard me say it and now you are, parrot like, repeating it. You must have been searching for these people; these people are victims."

Whenever you have some information, you start searching for somebody in whose mind you can pour it; otherwise, it creates a restlessness. Unobserved, you go on searching for somebody unaware. Whenever you have some information, it is very difficult to keep it inside yourself. That's why it is so difficult to keep a secret, almost impossible. It becomes heavy. One wants to say it to be unburdened.

It is very difficult to contain something that you have come to understand and not to say it to others. People search, they move around, they wait for some victim.

*"Scholars are seldom wise," said the master, "being only unaltered
people stuffed with thoughts and books..."*

"And so are you – you are unaltered. You have not yet been
transformed. You have become very much informed, that's true. The
information is so much that you cannot even digest it. And what
you are doing here is just a kind of diarrhoea. You are throwing it
on these poor people. And they have not done anything! You have
just found an excuse: 'You are hostile – you called me a great scholar,
and scholars are the cause of the misery of the world.'"

Unaltered. Knowledge never alters anybody. You remain the same,
knowledge goes on being accumulated on the same Level. And unless
the level changes, unless you have an altered state of consciousness,
nothing is going to help. You can have all the scriptures of the world
by your side, but you will remain as miserable as before.

*"Scholars are seldom wise, being only unaltered people stuffed
with thoughts and books."*

But they become very conceited, they become very egoistic.

A man who had just been promoted to vice-president boasted so
much about it to his wife that she finally retorted, "Vice-presidents
are a dime a dozen. Why, in the supermarket they even have a vice-
president in charge of prunes."

Furious, the husband phoned the supermarket in the expectation
of refuting his wife. He asked to speak to the vice-president in charge
of prunes.

"Which kind?" was the reply. "Packaged or bulk?"

Presidents and vice-presidents and professors and scholars, they
all go on bragging – they are somebody special. On their noses it is
written: "Look who I am. I am not an ordinary mortal." Just puffed
up egos. And just a small prick and the balloon bursts.

Beware of it. The ways of the ego are very cunning. Unless one
is very very aware, it goes on coming back from the back door.

"These people were trying to honor you. If some people think mud is gold, if it is their mud, respect it."

This should be the approach of a really human person. If it is their mud and they think it is gold, why disturb them? It is their mud. They respect it and they think it is gold — let them be happy whatsoever they think. Don't unnecessarily disturb them. And:

"You are not their teacher."

A master is allowed to disturb, nobody else. Why? Because if somebody else disturbs people, he will only disturb, he will not be able to reset. He will not be able to create the harmony again. He will disturb the first thing, and he will not be able to create anything else instead. He will demolish the old building...it may have been a ruin, but still people were living in it. Now they will be under the sky in the rains, and under the hot sun. Don't demolish a building unless you can construct another and better.

Remember it: if you can't give truth to people, don't take their lies away. Otherwise, they will be left in such agony, their lives will become impossible. At least they were living — with their lies they were hoping. Don't destroy people's beliefs if you cannot give them truth. If you cannot give them trust, don't destroy their belief. If you can give them the real coin, it is perfectly okay to take their false coins away. Only masters are allowed, only Buddhas are allowed, to shake, shatter, to destroy, because they can create. Because destruction in itself is not the goal — the goal is creation.

"Do you not realize that, in behaving in such a sensitive and self-willed manner, you are acting just like a scholar, and therefore deserve the name, even if it is an epithet?"

The master has used the situation in a beautiful way. He has made it absolutely clear to the disciple that he has been acting like a scholar — he knows not a single thing. He is a pretender. But he can destroy those innocent people's beliefs, and he can enjoy that he can destroy. He can argue, he can silence those people — although he cannot convince, because no argument ever convinces. Only the presence of a master is a convincing source, not an argument.

> "*Guard yourself my child. Too many slips from the path of supreme attainment — and you may become a scholar.*"

In the world of the Sufis, a scholar is the dirtiest thing. Mm? If you fall too many times from the path you may become a scholar. Just as it is said: When a poet fails he becomes a critic, exactly the same way it can be said: When a sage fails to become a sage, he becomes a scholar.

To you also, I say:

> "*Guard yourself, my child. Too many slips from the Path of Supreme Attainment — and you may become a scholar.*"

Scholarship, to be a pundit, is not an attainment: it is a failure. It is a consolation only. You have missed the real treasure, and now you have just old dirty books — and that is a burden, not a liberation. Books cannot liberate. In fact, books themselves wait for somebody to liberate the truth from them — how can they liberate you?

When a master is there, he liberates truths from the imprisonment of books. That's why I have chosen so many books to speak upon. Many truths are imprisoned there — they have to be liberated. The book cannot liberate you; how can a dead book liberate you? Truth liberates. And if you know the truth, you can liberate truths from books too.

But remember: this is not possible if you only become a scholar. This is possible only when you become a sage. And who is a sage? A child again. A child who has consciously understood the futility of knowledge, and has understood the ultimate beauty of ignorance.

Enough for today.

CHAPTER 10

BUDDHA AND THE BEAST

The first question:

Osho,
What exactly is man?

an is a mere perhaps, a possibility, a potential, a becoming, a longing. Man is not yet. Man has to be. That's the agony of man, and the ecstasy too. The beast is — there is no growth possible. It is a finished product. There is no possibility to seek and search and be. Hence, there is no freedom. The beast is in absolute bondage. The beast lives and dies without knowing that he lives and dies. The beast is, but knows not that he is.

Man is and knows that he is, but knows not who he is.

Man is a constant process. Something is always happening, is always on the verge of happening. Man is an excitement, an adventure, a pilgrimage.

No beast can ever miss its destiny. It is always predetermined. The beast has an absolute fate. Nothing is going to be otherwise.

The beast is pre-programmed. Man has no pre-programme but is just an opening. A thousand and one things are possible. Hence the anxiety: "To be this or to be that? To go to the east or to the west? To live this way or to live that way? And what is right? And what is going to fulfill me?"

Each moment man has to decide. And, obviously, when you decide, there is trembling. You can always go wrong. In fact, the possibilities to go wrong are more. Out of one thousand and one ways, only one will be right. Hence great trepidation, anguish: "Am I going to make it? Am I going to succeed in being myself? Or is it just going to be a long futile effort, and in the end frustration and failure? Will I be able to know life abundant? Will this life become a foundation for a greater life to come? Or is there nothing but death? Is there only the grave in the end, or something more?"

Man is an open being. Everything is possible, but nothing is certain. The beast is absolutely certain. It has a definition. Man has no definition.

So when you ask me: What exactly is man? you ask me a wrong question. Man is nothing exactly. He is just a vague longing, a very vague dream of things to be, of things which may be possible, may not be possible. Man is a hesitation. Each moment man is gripped by hesitation, because any single step gone wrong will destroy your whole life.

Man can lose. No beast can ever lose. But because man can lose, man can gain too. They both come together. Man can grow — man is growth. The mere perhaps can become actual. The potential can be transformed into reality. The seed can become a flowering. That which is just unmanifest can be manifested, and then there will be great splendor, great benediction.

The Buddha is, knows that he is, and also knows who he is. These are the three states of growth: the beast, the man, the Buddha. The beast has only one dimension — he is, he exists, utterly unaware that he exists. Hence he cannot think of death.

Death is not a problem for the beast. Death can only become a problem when you know that you are. With that very knowing the fear arises that some day you may not be — because there was a time when you were not, there will again be a time when you will not be. Your existence is momentary. You can disappear any moment. You will disappear some day. Death is bound to happen. It is only man who knows about death.

That's why man creates religion. Religion is man's response to the possibility of death. It's man's effort to conquer death. No animal is religious, cannot be. Without the awareness of death, religion has no possibility. But before you can become aware of death, you will have to become aware that you are. That's a basic requirement.

So man knows he is — and also becomes aware and apprehensive that any moment he will not be. Time is short. For the beast, time is non-existential, time is not. The beast lives in a timeless world. Each moment. Neither thinking of the past, nor imagining about the future.

Man cannot live in the present. He thinks of the past and all the nostalgia. Days that were golden and are no more. And thinks, imagines, fantasizes about the future — days as they should be.

Man lives in the past and in the future. The beasts live only in the present. But they are not aware that this is the present. They cannot be aware of the present. Only one who is aware of past and future can be aware of the present, because the present is sandwiched between past and future.

The animals have no anxiety. The memory does not disturb them, and imaginations don't stir their hearts. They are simple. Existence has no complexity for them. When they live, they live; when they die, they die. They are innocent. Time has not entered to corrupt their being.

But man lives in time. Is aware that he is, but is not aware who he is. And that becomes a great problem: Who am I? This is the fundamental question that any man can ask. Out of this fundamental question is all philosophy, all religion, all poetry, all art — different ways of raising the question: Who am I? different ways of answering it. But the question is one: Who am I?

If you try to understand man's life, you will see this single question persisting. Yes, the man who is mad after money is also trying to answer the question: Who am I? By having money, he thinks that he will know who he is – he will know he is a rich man. He will have a certain identity. The man who is searching for power is basically trying to answer the question: Who am I? By becoming a prime minister of a country he will know: I am the prime minister.

But these answers are superficial and are not going to satisfy really. They can satisfy only the mediocre. They cannot satisfy the really intelligent person. Even when you have become very rich, your intelligence will go on persisting, asking, "Who are you? Yes, you have money, but who are you? You are not the money – you cannot be that which you possess. Who is this possessor? Yes, you have become the prime minister of a country, but that is just a function, that is not your being. Who are you? Who is this person who was not a prime minister and is now a prime minister, and tomorrow may not be again? This prime-ministership is just an episode – in whose life?"

The question persists. It can't be answered by these superficial efforts and endeavors. But basically man is trying to do that. He becomes a husband, he becomes a mother, father, this and that...but the basic urge is somehow to have a certain identity: "I am the wife, I am the husband, I am the father, I am the mother." Still you have not answered the question. Your being a mother or your being a father is just accidental, on the surface. Your innermost core remains untouched.

This is not real identity. This is a pseudo identity. The child will die – then who are you? Then you are not the mother. The husband may leave – then who are you? Then you are no more a wife.

These identities are very fragile, and man lives constantly in the crisis of identity. He tries hard to fix some definition around himself, but they go on slipping out of his hands.

Only the religious person really asks the question, and asks in the right direction.

The Buddha exists just like the beast. The Buddha knows just like man that he is. But a third dimension has opened: he knows who he is – he has come to see his innermost being. He has not searched for the identity in the outside world, because there can't be any identity. How can it be in the outside world? You are your interiority, you are your inwardness, you are your subjectivity — how can you know it through objects?

You may have a beautiful house, but it is outside. You may have beautiful art, paintings, antique art works, but they are outside! They can't define you. You remain undefined by them. One day the house is on fire and all your identity is burnt, and you are standing on the road, again puzzled: "Who am I?"

That's why people commit suicide. If their money is gone, if they become bankrupt, they commit suicide. Why do they commit suicide? One wonders — why? Money can be earned again.... Look deep into them — that was their identity. They had believed long that "This is me." Now all that bank balance is gone. Again the problem arises: Who am I? And they wasted their whole life in creating that bank balance. Now they are not ready to go into that effort again. It is too much. They have utterly failed.

In fact, by being a bankrupt the suicide has already happened! Their identity is gone. They no longer know now who they are. Their face has disappeared. How can they live without a face? Your woman dies whom you had loved...and you commit suicide, or you start thinking of committing suicide! Because that woman was your identity. Now you are left alone, empty. And to start from the very beginning, from scratch, seems to be too much. It is better to finish this whole thing.

These are the three stages. And when I say the beast, there are many men who are like the beast. They are — they are not even aware that they are. They live mechanically. There are many people who are men — they know they are, but they don't know who they are. And there are only few and far between, those rare people, who know who they are. They become three dimensional.

Man is a bridge between the beast and the Buddha. Remember, man is a bridge. Don't make your house on the bridge; the bridge is not meant for that. The bridge has to be crossed. Don't remain a man, otherwise you will remain in anxiety and anguish — because man is not a place to stay and abide. It is a passage to be passed. It is a ladder! You cannot stay on the ladder. It is only a link from one point to another point.

The beast is, and is in a certain state of contentment. No anxiety, no fear, no death, no ambition, no longing; utterly calm and quiet. But unaware, unconscious. The Buddha is again contented, utterly at peace, at home; has arrived, the journey is finished. There is nowhere to go, he has attained. Between these two is man: half-beast, half-Buddha. Hence the tension: one part moving backwards, one part moving forwards.

Man is torn apart.

Let me repeat: Man is not a being yet. Man has lost one kind of being – the being of a beast. And man has not yet attained another kind of being – the being of a Buddha. And man is constantly moving between these two beings, between these two banks.

You cannot go back, because in existence there is no backward movement. You cannot go back in time; time has only one dimension: it flows forward. You can go only forward. Don't waste your time in thinking that you can also be a beast and can live like a beast: eat, drink and be merry. It is not possible for a human being. He will have to think, he will have to contemplate. He cannot afford non-thinking. And it is very risky to do that, because then you will be stuck and you will become a pool of dirty water. Your freshness, your aliveness is possible only if you go on flowing and flowing till you reach the ocean. That ocean I am calling the Buddha – the Buddha state of consciousness.

Man has to become a Buddha. Create that intense desire, that intense longing, to become a Buddha. Be in a passionate search for it. Put all the energy that you have! Become aflame with that longing...and you can become a Buddha. And the day you become a Buddha, you have become a being again – and a being on a higher level, on the highest Level. There is nothing higher than that.

You ask me: *"What exactly is man?"*

As man, man is nothing exact – just a vague phenomenon, cloudy, foggy. Man is not exact because he is a crowd. Man is many men; hence he is foggy. The unity is missing. You don't have the center

— the center arises only through consciousness. Man simply lives like a driftwood.

That's why I say man is a mere perhaps, a bewildering paradox, an absurd being. He is and he is not. He is an in-between. He is the only animal that can make a fool of himself. No animals can make fools of themselves — only man, because man has the capacity to become wise.

If you don't grow into wisdom, you will behave like a fool. That's what the majority of the people in the world are doing. If you watch from a detached viewpoint, you will be surprised how people are living...in such a mess, in such confusion, in such madness. How are they moving? They are not moving at all — they are jogging on the same place.

And if you watch man, you will be surprised: it is very rare to come across a wise man. Fools and fools...fools abound. But remember: no other animal can behave like a fool. Have you seen a dog behaving like a fool? Never. Because they cannot be wise they cannot be fools. Both the possibilities arise simultaneously.

Watch yourself. Watch your foolishnesses. Be constantly alert about what you are doing with your life. It is a precious life. It is of such value that you cannot measure, you cannot evaluate it. But because it is given to you as a gift, you don't appreciate its value. Because it has been just a blessing from God, you have taken it for granted. This is foolish! Don't take it for granted. This is an opportunity to grow.

And you have to answer to God for what you did with your life. Have you come the same as you had gone? Or even worse? Think of this, that man is answerable. And unless you are a Buddha you will not be able to answer. Because to be a Buddha is to be a God — and that is your intrinsic possibility. And unless you are a God, you will not feel contented.

And only then will you know what exactly you are. Right now, you are nothing, a mere perhaps....

The second question:

Osho,
I have been listening to your words for sometime and I can accept
everything you say on truth and no-truth. Only one question
remains in my mind: If my enlightenment depends on me and
my relationship with totality and nothing else, what is the point
in my surrendering to a human master?

The master is not human, only looks human. The master is a passage to the totality. This is the beauty of being a disciple, because only the disciple is able to see that the master is not human. The curious visitors, or the students, who have come to gather a little bit of knowledge here, will not be able to see that. And then this question will arise.

Kenneth, you are right: you are here, still, unrelated to me. You are here uncommitted to me. You are here uninvolved with me.

You are a spectator, not a participant. And the greater mysteries become available to those who dare to participate. Don't remain a spectator, otherwise I will remain human. Become a participant! and you will see a transforming vision. You will see that something has changed in you. I am the same! But when you become a disciple, you have the eyes which can see that the master is not human.

If the master is human, he is not the master. He is only a teacher. To the student I remain a teacher. To the spectator, how can I be available in my totality? Unless you come close...and what else is discipleship? — courage to come close to somebody where death is possible, courage to come close to a fire where you will be burnt to ashes. And only then is there resurrection.

Jesus was a human being to the Jews who crucified him. But he was not a human being to Luke, to Thomas, to Mark. To the disciples he was Christ, son of God. To the spectators, to the crowd, he was the son of the carpenter Joseph, son of man, and of a very ordinary man. They were not watching the same person, remember; although they were looking at the same person, they were not seeing the same person at all. Their visions made the difference.

To the disciples, Buddha was not human. Hence, they called him Bhagwan. But to the spectators he was just as human as anybody else.

And the problem is that the disciple cannot prove it — these things are beyond proof. They are, but they are not available to proof. And those who were saying that Buddha is just human were more logical — because he feels hunger, becomes thirsty, falls ill. These are the proofs that he is human! What more proof do you need? Became old, and died of food poisoning. What more proof do you need? How can God die? Human beings die; God is eternal. How can God fall ill? And Buddha falls ill. His private physician, Jivaka, has to follow him continuously. Does God need a physician? Only a human being needs a physician.

When it is hot, Buddha perspires. What more proof do you need?! When it is cold, he shivers. A thousand and one proofs can be gathered together that he is just like us. What is the difference?

And the disciple will always be at a loss, although the disciple will laugh about all these proofs, because these are just stupid things that have been collected by the people. They are irrelevant facts, because the disciple has come so close that he has been able to have a contact with the master's soul — the master's body has become irrelevant. The body is just a vehicle.

If I am traveling in a car and the car is broken, I am not broken. If the car is rattling and making all kinds of noises, that is just in the mechanism of the car. So is the body — a vehicle. But something deeper than the body is there, something higher than the body is there — something of the totality. A window has opened into totality.

Who is a master? One who is in tune with totality.

To be in love with a master is to approach totality. To you, totality will be just a word. You can understand it intellectually. And that's what has happened to Kenneth.

He says: *"I have been listening to your words for sometime, and I can accept everything you say on truth and no-truth."*

This is an intellectual understanding. You must be an intelligent person! So what I say, you understand. I am not using very difficult words; my expression is as simple and common as anybody else's. I am not using a special terminology. I am not using any jargon, so you can understand. There is no problem in it.

But to understand that which I say is one thing, and to understand me is quite another. If you only understand that which I am saying, you will gather only the superficial; you will miss the essential, because the essential cannot be said. The Tao that can be said is not the true Tao. And the God that can be uttered is not the real God. Religion in its fundamental richness remains unexpressed.

So what I am saying is not that which I am.

Buddha was passing through a forest. The whole forest was full of dry leaves; leaves were falling. The trees were naked. His disciple, Ananda, asked him, "Bhagwan, a question has been persisting in my mind again and again. And now I cannot resist — I have to ask it. This is my question: you have told us many things — have you told all that you know? or is it only a part?"

Buddha took a few leaves, dry leaves, from the ground in his hand and said, "Ananda, how many leaves have I in my hand?"

Ananda said, "Not more than a dozen, just a few."

And Buddha said, "How many leaves are in this forest?"

And Ananda said, "Millions and millions — cannot be counted."

And Buddha said, "So is the case, Ananda: what I have said is just like the leaves in my hand, and what I have not said is like the leaves in this whole forest. But don't think that I am a miser, that I don't want to say those things — they cannot be said by their very nature. It is impossible to say them."

The student will learn only that which has been said. The disciple learns that which is not said and cannot be said. To the student, words reach, and he will become knowledgeable. To the disciple, the being reaches, and he becomes knowing, not knowledgeable.

That is the function of the relationship between a master and a disciple. It is a love affair! It is intimacy. It is a fan more intense intimacy than happens in any other love. When two persons are in love, it is the intensity of sexual desire, a physical closeness. Soon it will disappear. It is not going to last long. It is momentary, because sexual energy is momentary. The body is momentary.

The relationship between a master and a disciple is the relationship between two souls which are eternal. Once established, it is forever.

> Kenneth, you say: *I have been listening to your words for some time and I can accept everything you say on truth and no-truth.*

And it is not a question of acceptance either. It is a question of being drowned in me! Accepting, you remain yourself. Accepting, you are not coming out of your ego. You say, "Yes, my logic also says this is right — I agree." This is a kind of agreement. You remain you, I remain me, and there is a kind of agreement. But when you dissolve, it is not a kind of agreement. It is not that you accept what I say. There is no question of acceptance or nonacceptance.

Remember: if you accept, any day you can reject — because there is no guarantee that tomorrow also I will be saying the same thing. Today you have accepted something that I have said; tomorrow you may not be able to accept it.

But the disciple is one for whom acceptance, non-acceptance, have become meaningless. He is drowned in me. So if today I am saying one thing, he listens joyously. And there never arises an idea whether to accept it or reject it — there is no question because there is no separation. As if what I am saying, he is saying. Not that he agrees. There is nobody to agree with it. Not that he nods his head in agreement — that head has disappeared; there is nothing to nod. Then tomorrow, even if I say just the opposite of it, there is no problem, because there is nobody to reject.

Yesterday it was like that. Today it is like this. Tomorrow it will be like that. His attunement with my being is so total that he understands. It is not a question of acceptance but of tremendous understanding – which knows no rejection. This is trust. Between the master and the disciple blooms a flower called trust. And it is trust that leads you to God, to totality.

You say: *Only one question remains in my mind...*

And that is not one question – that is thousands of questions. In one question are condensed all the questions possible.

If my enlightenment depends on me and my relationship with totality and nothing...

Yes, I say again and again: Your enlightenment depends on you – but not as you are today, not as you are now. This you has to go. Another kind of you has to come into existence. This you is the barrier; enlightenment doesn't depend on it. Otherwise, it could have happened already. This "I" that you are carrying, this person Kenneth, in you who says "I am" – no, on this enlightenment does not depend. It is the barrier, it is the hindrance.

If this "I" dies, then a different kind of phenomenon arises in you – which is no more "I" but a kind of pure "amness." When you say "I am," I is false, am is true. And you will need a master to destroy your I and to free your am. That amness, undefined, pure existence, being, innocence – that amness is the door to enlightenment.

But where are you going to drop your I? That I is surrounding your am so much that you cannot even conceive what amness will mean without I. In fact, the question will arise: How can there be amness if there is no I? I seems to be more important; am seems to be just shadow to it. The truth is just the opposite.

I is false: amness is the truth.

And when you surrender to a master, you don't surrender your amness – it cannot be surrendered – you only surrender your I. A master takes away things which you believe you have but you don't have. A master takes away your diseases only. And when all the diseases have been taken away, health wells up.

The health cannot be given by the master, that's true — because a given thing will be a given thing. And if it is given, it can be taken away. If it is a given thing, somebody can steal it. If it is a given thing, somewhere you can forget, lose track of it. A given thing is not of much importance. The master never gives you truth: he only takes your lies away. When all the rocks of the lies have been removed, truth flows. That is your innermost spring. Nobody needs to give it to you.

But who will take your I? Who will drink this poison of your I? You will need somebody who has come to a point where his immortality is revealed to him — he can drink all your poison.

You must have seen pictures of Shiva. A beautiful myth is behind those pictures. If you have looked closely into a Shiva picture, you will see that his throat is blue. That is a very very beautiful story. *Devas*, gods, and the anti-gods, *asuras*, were churning the ocean to find elixirs — but you cannot find elixir directly. It is hidden deep.

The first thing that they came across was not elixir but poison. Now who should drink the poison? Shiva drank it. That's why his throat has become blue. Only he could drink it. You can drink death only when you know you are deathless.

When the disciple comes to the master, he brings all kinds of poisons. Unknowingly he has been nourishing those poisons. And the ego is the greatest poison. And before your immortality can be revealed to you, your poison has to be removed. Who is going to drink it?! Only one who knows that he is deathless can drink it.

The master drinks all the poison out of the disciple's system. Slowly slowly, he takes away all the poisons from the disciple. And one day, when all the poison has been taken out, the immortal is there in all its glory.

You say to me: Only one question remains in my mind: if my enlightenment depends on me...

Certainly it depends on you, but not as you are right now. This you is false. This you has to go. This you has to cease, then the real you will arrive.

> *...and my relationship with totality and nothing else, what is the point in my surrendering to a human master?*

It is certainly true that the question is of your relationship with totality and nothing else is needed — but as long as you are, you will resist totality, you will fight totality. You cannot relate with totality. You have to go, only then is the relationship there.

The master is needed only to take away all that is unnecessarily around you — the hindrances, the barriers. The master will give you your real being by taking all that is unreal in you. When you surrender to a master, you surrender only the unreal because you have only the unreal! If you already have the real, there is no point in surrendering to a master. But if you had that, you would not have been here in the first place.

What are you doing here? Why are you even listening to me? For what? It all depends on you and your relationship with totality...why listen to me? This must be somewhere a deep ego which is rationalizing. The ego is very clever. When it listens to such statements, that the enlightenment depends on you, the ego says, "Look, so it depends on me — there is no need to surrender." When it is said that it is only a question of your being with totality, the ego says, "Perfectly true — there is no need to surrender."

I am not interested in your surrender at all — because what have you got to surrender to me? Only diseases, poisons. You have no riches to surrender to me! Only miseries, frustrations, despairs, anxieties. What have you got to surrender to me? But people cling even to their misery. They think it is some kind of treasure.

Watch the cunning ways of the ego.

And when you surrender to a master, you surrender only all that is false. And in that surrendering, the master is just an excuse. If you can surrender directly to the totality, perfectly good — you go and surrender to totality. But where are you going to find the totality?

Where? You don't have the eyes to see the totality. And totality cannot be encountered directly. You will come across it only in indirect ways. You will fall in love with a woman — surrender! because the woman represents a kind of totality. The feminine aspect of it. You may fall in love with a friend — surrender! He represents another kind of totality, another aspect of it. Another window opens. You love music — surrender!

Don't go on using this word "totality". "Why should I surrender to music? I am going to surrender to totality. Why should I surrender to love? I am going to surrender to totality. Why should I surrender to beauty? I am going to surrender to totality."

Where will you find totality? Totality exists in millions of forms...the beauty of the sunrise, and the silence of the night, and the loving eyes of a friend, and the warm hand of a woman. These are all gestures of totality. Totality comes in these ways. These are totality's approaches towards you.

The master is the clearest way of totality reaching towards you, a conscious way of totality reaching to you. The woman is unconscious, the friend is unconscious — they are unconsciously parts of totality. A master is consciously part of totality; hence, there is no substitute for a master.

Jesus is right when he says: I am the way — unless you go through me, you will not reach. He is not talking only about himself — the master is speaking. And whenever a master speaks, he speaks for all the masters, past, present, future.

The third question:

Osho,
Why am I so afraid to ask you a question?

*C*verybody is, because to ask a question means to put your head in front of me. And one never knows what I am going to do with your head. I may hit, I may cut it. I may make a football of it...nobody knows! Fear is natural.

One thing is certain, that I am going to do something drastic. Fear is nothing out of place, but still ask — because that is the purpose of your being here and my being here.

Ask if a question arises; don't be afraid. And if you are very much afraid, you can do one thing a few people do: you can ask in somebody else's name. Then he gets the beating and you enjoy.

But ask. Without asking, it will persist. And it may be important; it may have something of immense importance. It may change...the answer may become a new vision. In spite of the fear, go on asking — till questions disappear and the questioner disappears too.

But fear is natural.

I have heard:

A man came to a doctor complaining that he had an uncontrollable cough. The doctor gave him a bottle of castor oil and said, "Go home and drink down the entire bottle and come back tomorrow."

When the patient came back next day, the doctor asked, "Did you take the castor oil?"

The man answered, "Yes."

The doctor then continued, "Do you still cough?"

The patient said, "Yes, I continue to cough."

The doctor gave him a second bottle of castor oil and said, "Take this, and come back tomorrow."

The next day the man returned. The doctor asked him, "Do you still cough?"

And the patient said, "Yes, I still cough regularly."

The doctor then gave him yet another bottle of castor oil, and said, "Drink this entire bottle tonight and come back tomorrow morning."

The patient returned and the doctor looked at the poor wretch and said, "Do you cough now?"

The patient quiveringly answered, "I don't cough any more – I am afraid to."

You go on asking questions and I will go on giving you castor oil bottles. Sooner or later, one day you will be afraid to cough – afraid to ask a question.

Your system has to be cleansed. Your question should not be just out of curiosity. Remember that. Never ask a question just out of curiosity; that is meaningless. If a question has something important for you, if your life depends on it, if it has something to do with your lifestyle, with your habits – mechanical, robot like – if it has something about it that if it is solved you will become more aware, ask it. Don't ask metaphysical questions, because they are not going to change you. Ask psychological questions – only they are going to transform you.

Bertrand Russell has said: There are three possibilities of man's approach towards life. One is conflict with nature, second is conflict with other human beings, and third is conflict with oneself.

The first has been the way of the Western philosophy, Western science, Western speculation, thinking. A fight with nature. The Western mind became objective: How to transform nature? – that became the root question. They have not been able to transform it, although they have destroyed it. They have destroyed the rhythm of nature. They have destroyed the ecosystem. They have created havoc in nature's harmony. And now there seems to be no going back. The earth is dying.

There seems to be only one possibility, that man should migrate from this planet to another planet. Within a hundred years it will be impossible to live on this earth. It is almost turning into a corpse. This earth has been so much raped by science, so much wounded, crippled, paralyzed, because of that approach: conquer nature! And man became absolutely absorbed and occupied with only one thing: how to conquer nature? – and forgot everything else.

The Chinese mind has moved in a different way. Its sole concern has been: How to live with man? Its concern has been social. Man is a social animal. How to create better moralities? How to create better social systems? How to have a better society? a higher culture? a better civilization? About nature, the Chinese mind has not been in conflict. It appreciates nature, it loves nature. Nature has an aesthetic value for the Chinese. Enjoy it! There is no need to conquer. Celebrate it! There is no need to fight.

The basic problem for the Chinese mind has been: How should we make man more human? The whole struggle is: How to destroy between man and man, — hatred, anger, rage, animality — the beast-like attitudes, the violence? China has created one of most civilized cultures there ever has been.

The Indian mind has taken the third route: How to transform oneself? The West has given birth to science, China has given birth to a higher quality sociology, India has given birth to the supreme science of psychology — the science of the soul. That's exactly what psychology means. In fact, Western psychology should not call itself psychology, because it is not a science of the soul at all. On the contrary, it only observes human behavior — from the outside. It thinks about man also as an object. It reduces man's dignity. It turns man into a mechanism.

It is not important for the Western psychology to think: What is inside man? All that is important is what he does, how he functions — his behavior. But in the Indian consciousness, the only basic problem has been: How to conquer oneself? How to raise one's consciousness to the highest peak possible? How to become a Buddha?

These three approaches have been prevalent.

Never ask a question which is not really of any concern to your spiritual growth. My whole concern here is to help you become more conscious. Don't ask stupid questions. And sometimes even very intelligent people ask stupid questions.

Just the other night I was reading an ancient book written by a great Hindu philosopher, Kumaril. He criticizes Buddha on many accounts, but one thing was so ridiculous that I could not believe that a man of the intelligence of Kumaril should raise such a question!

It is said — by the disciples of Buddha, of course — that he was all-knowing. "All-knowing" does not mean that he was a kind of Encyclopedia Britannica. "All knowing" means that he knew all that is worth knowing. "All-knowing" means that he knew all that is helpful for the consciousness to grow. And what has this Kumaril done? He says, "This is wrong, because he did not know how many insects are in the world." Now this Brahmin, Kumaril, must have been a stupid kind of person. How many insects there are in the world Buddha did not know, so he is not all-knowing.

Sometimes it can happen: you may be an intelligent person on the surface, you may have logical acumen, cleverness, and still, deep down, you are stupid. Now what kind of question is this? It is so absurd just to think of it.

Never ask a question which is not relevant to your spiritual growth. And whenever a question arises about your spiritual growth, put all fear aside — you have to ask it! Even if my answer shatters you, even if I hit hard on your head, I do that, I teach you, by hammering your head...I keep an invisible hammer in my hand always, and whenever I see that some skull is worth breaking, I really break it.

But you will be grateful one day that your skull was broken, that you were killed in your stupidities. So whatsoever the cause of your fear, you have to ask it. That is the only way to come closer to me. Each question asked, answered, brings you closer.

And I am not saying that if there is no question, then too you have to ask — then there is no problem. Don't ask if you don't have any question. That too happens. People are such that they live in extremes. There are people who write to me: "So many people ask questions and I have not asked a single question up to now — am I doing something wrong?" If you don't have a question, there is no need to ask one. But if you have a question, it has to be asked — whatsoever the cost.

The fourth question:

Osho,
What is a mystical experience?

*F*irst: a mystical experience is not an experience at all. It is called "mystical experience" because we have to call it something, but it is not an experience at all.

An experience is always outside you. You see the clouds in the sky, or the lightning in the sky. Or, you can see the same inside too: you can close your eyes and you can see light inside. That too is outside — because the seer remains always outside the seen, the observer remains outside the observed, the experiencer remains outside the experienced. And the mystical experience is not something outside you: it is very special kind of experience, unique.

What is its uniqueness?

The experiencer and the experienced become one, the knower and the known become one. There is no division at all. It is not that you see something, but that you are it. God is never experienced as an object : God is always experienced as your innermost being,. "*Ana'l haq!*" declares Al-Hillaj Mansor — "I am God! " the Sufi says. Or "*Aham Brahmasmi!*" the Upanishads declare — "I am all!" It is not an experience! All experiences have been dissolved. Nothing is left. Only pure consciousness is there, but in that pure consciousness this understanding arises. The knower and the known are no more separate.

The mystical experience is such that you are involved in it with your totality. It is not in the head, it is not in the heart either; it is not in the body, it is not in the mind, it is not in the soul only. It pulsates all over you and beyond you. It pulsates with your totality.

I have heard a very ancient parable:

Once it happened, three saints, very famous saints, well-known saints, were passing through a forest. They all had worked hard, disciplined their lives arduously. They were great seekers. One was a bhakti yogin — a follower on the path of devotion, love, prayer. Another was a gyan yogin — a follower on the path of knowledge, wisdom, intelligence, awareness. And the third was a karma yogin — a follower on the path of action, service, commitment.

They all had done all that a man can do, all that is humanly possible, but yet they had not experienced God. Now they were getting old, and getting a little bit frustrated too. Time was slipping out of their hands, and the goal was as far away as ever, and sadness was settling. But that day a miracle happened.

Suddenly, it started raining,. They all had to rush into a small temple. The temple was very small; just four pillars and a roof, open from all sides, and the rain was really strong, and the wind was strong, and the wind was bringing rainwater inside the temple. It was getting wet almost over the place. So they all had to stand just in the middle, surrounding the Shivalinga — it must have been a Shiva temple. And as the water started coming more and more inwards, they had to come closer and closer.

They were coming so close that they were touching coach other. Suddenly, when they touched each other, they felt that they were not three there but four. Surprised, startled...and the fourth, and the presence of the fourth, was so strong that they asked each other, "What are you feeling?" And they all said, "Something strange is present here."

Slowly slowly, the presence became very clear and radiant. It was such ecstasy to see that presence. They all fell on their knees, and they asked the presence — because it was so clear that it was God and nobody else — they asked, "Why? We have worked our whole life and we could not even see a glimpse of you, and today what has happened? Why have you suddenly come?"

And God laughed and said, "Because you all are together here. Touching each other, you have become total. And I can only be available to you when you are total. Now, you are not fragments. Up to now you have been fragments: one was working through the heart, another was working through the head, and the third was working through the body. You were fragmentary. And I am not available to the fragments: I am available only when somebody becomes total. In this moment, your energies met and mingled with each other.

"I have always followed you, but have remained invisible because the I can only see me when it is total. Now you can touch me! Now you can have me! You have been missing me for only one reason: you were adamant, stubborn; you were clinging to one fragment — and God is a totality."

This is my message to you: A mystical experience is a total experience — of the body, of the mind, of the soul. All is involved in it. Nothing is outside it. So don't reject anything in your life; let everything be absorbed. That's why I say "from sex to super consciousness" — everything has to be absorbed in it, nothing has to be rejected. The person who rejects anything has rejected God himself — because God is totality.

Accept all, appreciate all. Rejoice in all! And let your life become a total organic unity. When you are organically one, you will have that orgasmic, oceanic experience called the mystic experience. It is not an experience...you are it. The experiencer is not separate from it.

God is not seen: one becomes God.

Liberation does not happen to you: you become liberation. Nirvana is not something in your hands: you are Nirvana.

Enlightenment is not something that happens in you: you are it!

Hence, though we call it, "spiritual experience," it really cannot be called spiritual experience. There are sexual experiences, but no spiritual experiences. There are aesthetic experiences, but no spiritual experiences. There are many kinds of experiences, but spiritual, mystical experience is not one of them: it is absolutely a separate reality. It is all alone. It is a category in itself.

The basic thing to remember: in all our experiences, the knower remains separate from the known; in spiritual, mystical experience, the knower and the known dissolve into each other. And that is the beauty of it, and its benediction, and its freedom.

Enough for today.

Information About
The Original Audio Series

Books by Osho are transcriptions from discourses given before a live audience. All Osho discourses have been published in full as books and are also available as original audio recordings. Information about the audio recordings and the complete text archive can be found at the OSHO Library at www.osho.com.

About Osho

Osho defies categorization, reflecting everything from the individual quest for meaning to the most urgent social and political issues facing society today. His books are not written but are transcribed from recordings of extemporaneous talks given over a period of thirty-five years. Osho has been described by The Sunday Times in London as one of the "1000 Makers of the 20th Century" and by Sunday Mid-Day in India as one of the ten people – along with Gandhi, Nehru and Buddha – who have changed the destiny of India.

Osho has a stated aim of helping to create the conditions for the birth of a new kind of human being, characterized as "Zorba the Buddha" – one whose feet are firmly on the ground, yet whose hands can touch the stars. Running like a thread through all aspects of Osho's talks and meditations is a vision that encompasses both the timeless wisdom of the East and the highest potential of Western science and technology.

He is synonymous with a revolutionary contribution to the science of inner transformation and an approach to meditation which specifically addresses the accelerated pace of contemporary life. The unique OSHO® Active Meditations™ are designed to allow the release of accumulated stress in the body and mind so that it is easier to be still and experience the thought-free state of meditation.

OSHO® International Meditation Resort™

Every year the OSHO® International Meditation Resort™ welcomes thousands of people from over 100 countries who come to enjoy and participate in its unique atmosphere of meditation and celebration. The 28-acre meditation resort is located about 100 miles southeast of Mumbai (Bombay), in Pune, India, in a tree-lined residential area, set against a backdrop of bamboo groves and wild jasmine, peacocks and waterfalls. The basic approach of the meditation resort is that of Zorba the Buddha: living in awareness, with a capacity to celebrate everything in life. Many visitors come to just be, to allow themselves the luxury of doing nothing. Others choose to participate in a wide variety of courses and sessions that support moving toward a more joyous and less stressful life, by combining methods of self-understanding with awareness techniques. These courses are offered through OSHO® Multiversity™ and take place in a pyramid complex next to the famous OSHO® Teerth Park™

People can choose to practice various meditation methods, both active and passive, from a daily schedule that begins at six o'clock in the morning. Early each evening there is a meditation event that moves from dance to silent sitting, using Osho's recorded talks as an opportunity to experience inner silence without effort.

Facilities include tennis courts, a gym, sauna, Jacuzzi, a nature-shaped Olympic-sized swimming pool, classes in Zen archery, Tai chi, Chi gong, Yoga and a multitude of bodywork sessions.

The kitchen serves international gourmet vegetarian meals, made with organically grown produce. The nightlife is alive with friends dining under the stars, and with music and dancing.

Online bookings for accommodation at the OSHO® Guesthouse which is inside the meditation resort can be made through the website below or by sending an email to:

guesthouse@osho.com

Online tours of the meditation resort, how to get there, and program information can be found at: www.osho.com/resort

For More Information
www.OSHO.com
a comprehensive multi-language website including OSHO books, talks (audio and video), a magazine, the OSHO Library text archive in English and Hindi with a searchable facility, and extensive information about OSHO Meditation techniques.

You will also find the program schedule of the OSHO Multiversity and information about the OSHO International Meditation Resort.

To contact **OSHO International Foundation** go to www.osho.com/oshointernational

OSHO International Meditation Resort
17 Koregaon Park
Pune 411001 MS, India
resortinfo@osho.net

FULL CIRCLE

FULL CIRCLE publishes books on inspirational subjects, religion, philosophy, and natural health. The objective is to help make an attitudinal shift towards a more peaceful, loving, non-combative, non-threatening, compassionate and healing world.

FULL CIRCLE continues its commitment towards creating a peaceful and harmonious world and towards rekindling the joyous, divine nature of the human spirit.

Our fine books are available at all leading bookstores across the country.

FULL CIRCLE *PUBLISHING*

Editorial Office

J-40, Jorbagh Lane, New Delhi-110003
Tel: 24620063, 24621011 • Fax: 24645795
E-mail: contact@fullcirclebooks.in
website: www.fullcirclebooks.in

Bookstores

23, Khan Market, 1st & 2nd Floor
New Delhi-110003 Tel: 24655641/2/3

N-16, Greater Kailash Part I Market
New Delhi-110048 Tel: 29245641/3/4

Number 8, Nizamuddin East Market
New Delhi-110013 Tel: 41826124/5

FullCircle@Chamiers, New # 106, Chamiers Road
R A Puram, Chennai-600028 Tel: 044-42030733 / 42036833
www.chamiersshop.com